MY GOP

It is time for Republicans to get back to the principles of Ronald Reagan

Perry Books

Representative Jeffrey Davis Perry

My GOP

It is time for Republicans to get back to the principles of Ronald Reagan

www.MyGopBook.com

Political Commentary

Copyright © 2009 by Jeffrey Davis Perry

ISBN 978-0-615-27561-1

Library of Congress Control # 2009900815

Published in the United States of America by:

Perry Books
7 Burning Tree Lane
East Sandwich, MA 02537
www.PerryBooks.com

Dedication

To my wife Lisa:

 For more than twenty years we have shared a journey of life and love which so many are only able to dream of. Whether writing this book, seeking political office or becoming an attorney, none would have been possible without your unquestioning love and support. You make me want to be the best person I can possibly be. You inspire me to stay on course.

 You make my life complete.

J.D.

Acknowledgements

I used a variety of resources to put together My GOP. Much of the Republican history was derived from Republican National Committee sources. I made a strong effort to provide references to sources I was quoting, including news media accounts or governmental agencies.

To be clear, My GOP is intended to be a book of political commentary and not a non-biased history or political science book. My GOP is a one-sided story of political commentary from the author.

I do not speak as an official of the Republican Party nor do I expect to always agree with its platform or the positions of its leaders. The political commentary which follows is my own.

Prior to publishing, I asked several people to proof read my manuscript. For their efforts to make me look good, I express my heartfelt gratitude.

Contents

About the Author

Jeffrey Davis Perry was born in 1964, in Attleboro, Massachusetts. Jeff is happily married to his wife Lisa and has one son, Christopher, who along with his lovely wife Tiffany have two granddaughters, Paige (who will forever live in our hearts) and Faith.

Currently serving his fourth term as the State Representative for the 5th Barnstable District, Jeff is the Ranking Member of the Committees on Ethics, Education and Public Safety & Homeland Security. He also serves as a member on the House Ways and Means Committee and the Committee on State Administration. In addition, Jeff serves as the Governor's Appointee to the Juvenile Advisory Committee and holds a Legislative Appointment to the Corrections Advisory Committee.

Jeff is a partner in the Law Firm of Flannigan and Perry P.C. The firm has offices in Hanover and Hyannis and offers a wide variety of legal services and counsel, including the areas of Civil Litigation, Constitutional Law, Juvenile Law, Personal Injury, and Real Estate.

Jeff is an Adjunct Professor at Cape Cod Community College in West Barnstable teaching courses in Criminal Evidence and American Government. He has also taught Constitutional Law at Bridgewater State College.

Jeff graduated with a Juris Doctorate Degree from New England School of Law where he was presented the Dean Timothy J. Cronin, Jr. Award, which recognizes the student who has shown the greatest promise of outstanding contributions to public service. Jeff also has a Bachelor of Arts Degree in Sociology from Curry College and an Associates Degree from Bristol Community College. He successfully completed an executive management program at the Law Enforcement Executive Center at Babson College. In addition, Jeff is a graduate of the Plymouth Police Academy and served as a Wareham Police Officer/Sergeant for eight years.

Chapter 1 - Setting the Stage

When Ronald Reagan took the stage in 1984 to accept his party's second nomination for President, wholly consistent with his second to none ability to communicate directly with the American people, Reagan addressed the Republican faithful who were energetically gathered on the convention floor at the Reunion Arena in downtown Dallas. Reagan, in his grandfatherly-like style, clearly set forth the choice which was before the American voters and the vast differences between the Republican and Democrat Parties:

> "The choices this year are not just between two different personalities or between two political parties. They're between two different visions of the future, two fundamentally different ways of governing, their government of pessimism, fear, and limits, or ours of hope, confidence, and growth. Their government sees people only as members of groups; ours serves all the people of America as individuals. Theirs lives in the past, seeking to apply the old and failed policies to an era that has passed them by. Ours learns from the past and strives to change by boldly charting a new course for the future. Theirs lives by promises, the bigger, the better. We offer proven, workable answers."

Ronald Reagan was right in 1984 and despite the passage of some twenty-five years and four subsequent Presidents, his statements and views are just as accurate today as they were back in 1984. There are indeed two visions for the future of America. The Republican vision of personal freedom along with personal responsibility and the Democrat vision of more government dependence and reliance from cradle-to-grave styled programs.

So, to make things clear from page one of this book, I admit it, I am a red blooded conservative Republican. I share the same basic ideology of Ronald Reagan and generally believe in the core principles of the

Republican Party. The title of this book "My GOP" reflects its own truth. The words, beliefs, opinions and issue positions that follow are my own and not from any pre-approved GOP party boss or platform. I offer them to you the reader, whether you are a right- wing nut, or a left-wing moonbat. My first goal is to encourage my GOP to return to the party of the principles of Abraham Lincoln and Ronald Reagan.

Based on the failures of the last two elections, it is clear the American people have lost an understanding of what the Republican Party stands for. By reconnecting with our core principles and standing firm, I believe it will not be a difficult road to win back the hearts and minds of the voters.

From the start of our time together on these pages and chapters which follow, let us not get confused by the contemporary actions of some of the elected officials who label themselves as Republicans or some who choose to register as a "R' but act a lot more like a "D." I will be talking about what I believe are real Republican values and beliefs, at least as far as I see them, and not simply some politically correct modern version of a Republican platform. From supporting billion dollar bailouts, ignoring illegal immigration to engaging in unethical behavior, too many Republicans have let us down. Sure, we are down at the moment, but my GOP is far from being done.

I guess that is really the overall purpose of this book; to talk about my GOP, where it came from, where it is today and where it should be in the future. Since I already fully disclosed my political bias, let me also stake out from the beginning that I am a frustrated member of the political party which I firmly believe is the best chance we have to keep America great and provide a better life for the future generations. If we are going to achieve this as Republicans, my GOP can only do so if we get back on course, meaning back to the fundamental principles of the great people who established the Republican Party and have fostered its principles, people such as Abraham Lincoln, Teddy Roosevelt, Dwight Eisenhower and Ronald Reagan. Now, please do not think I wish to take America backwards, I do not. Our great nation always needs to be looking forward, but while doing so, we must have the lessons of our past and our core principles in our hearts and minds.

To assist you in understanding my personal perspective, let me set the political and personal stage from where I write this book. I am a Republican State Legislator from Cape Cod, Massachusetts. Despite what some might believe, being from the home state of Ted Kennedy, John Kerry, and serving in a state legislature where ninety percent of the seats are held by Democrats, it really is still possible to embrace conservative values and fight for them as an elected representative. In reality, I often find that the voters of Massachusetts are a lot more conservative than the elected leaders who purportedly represent them. More about this later, but there is a tremendous disconnection from the values the people of Massachusetts hold and the actions of the very elected officials they vote for to represent them. I guess the same could be said for those who represent us in Washington, D.C. as well.

While most national Republicans likely consider the Bay State to be a lost cause in the sea of blue states which is the Northeast (as of the 2008 election, there are now zero Republican members of Congress from New England), I have been blessed to find myself in a legislative district that consistently supports Republican candidates and even voted for George W. Bush both in 2000 and in 2004. While my district did vote from President Obama in 2008, I was reelected by a 69% - 28% margin. I don't suggest that the majority of voters in my District are registered Republicans. At last count it was about 18% Republican, 21% Democrat, and most other folks labeling themselves as "unenrolled" or commonly referred to as independents. I guess the primary reason I am able to win elections while touting a conservative Republican agenda is that the people of my district are open-minded patriotic Americans first and then a member of a political party second. If only all of Massachusetts citizens were so open minded.

Depending on who is reading this and where they live will greatly influence what their first impression of what being a conservative Republican in Massachusetts actually means to them. The words "conservative" and "Republican" certainly do not denote the same meanings in Massachusetts political circles as they would in Texas or Wyoming. Being a Republican legislator in the bluest of blue states is a bit like living in a foreign nation at times. It is an all too common occurrence that I am among a very small group of loyal souls fighting against an overwhelming tide of liberalism. These battles most often occur on Beacon Hill in Boston where the State House sits. This land was once owned by John Hancock, the first Governor of Massachusetts, and the first person to sign the United States Declaration of Independence. I often wonder what our Founding Fathers would think of the condition of the Massachusetts political system.

In fact, it is not uncommon for people to express shock and surprise when meeting me and learning that I serve in the Massachusetts House of Representatives as a Republican. If I have heard "I didn't know there were any Republicans left in Massachusetts," once, I have heard it a thousand times. While tough to deny that such a perception does exist, it almost becomes a self-fulfilling prophecy in some ways. I suspect that there are many Republican minded people in Massachusetts who would make great legislators and political leaders, but will never step forward and seek elective office simply because they fear that it is not possible for a Republican to win an election in Massachusetts. While the odds are certainly not favorable, it has and can be done with the right candidate, effort and message. As I will discuss in detail, part of the problem with my GOP, is that we sometimes seem fearful of standing up for Republican principles in some type of fear of being politically incorrect. Too many Republican politicians seem to ebb and flow with the political and media driven winds, rather than being men and women of principle first and politics later.

To put things in further perspective on the political climate of Massachusetts, the Republican Caucus makes up only sixteen of the one hundred and sixty House of Representative members. Also, being the home state of Ted Kennedy, John Kerry, and a cast of liberal members of Congress (including Barney Frank and Bill Delahunt) firmly places me in the minority no matter how one would define the Massachusetts political environment. I am not even sure if the term "Minority Party" is appropriate as we are such a small percentage of the Legislature that we literally meet in the private office of our Minority Leader to discuss the issues of the day!

Let me say from the outset, despite our small numbers the Republican Caucus in the Massachusetts House of Representatives has an important role, especially on procedural matters and exposing abuses of power which are inherent with one party rule. At each informal session of the House, members of the Republican Caucus are present to monitor the activities. Basically we are there as a safeguard or watch dog against potential abuses of the process or the passage of legislation that we object to. On practically every critical issue, the members of our Caucus will rise and request a roll call be taken as compared to a voice vote.

While this might seem insignificant in the grand scheme of things, it truly is not. Many times in recent memory, simply by being ready to stand and demand a recorded vote on the House record, the Republican Caucus was able to keep liberal causes from moving forward in the first place. In reality, as we are such a minority on Beacon Hill, our Caucus spends about eighty percent of our efforts trying to stop the liberals from wasting your tax dollars and making government even more powerful. Without question, any effort is worth every ounce of energy we can muster.

While many Democrats are fine with allowing certain things to pass "off the record," due to the potential backlash from voters for a recorded vote, they are often unwilling to push the button in favor of a given left-wing piece of legislation. They also clearly understand that such an issue could come back to haunt them in the next election. Among the other roles that we as a minority have is to do our very best to keep the process fair, honest and open to the public. We do this by forcing critical issues to formal recorded votes at each and every possible opportunity. Many times such efforts go unnoticed, but believe me, without such an effort, more of the liberals' agenda would become law.

The best example of this scenario was when a piece of legislation allowing illegal immigrants to receive taxpayer subsidized college tuition came to the House floor. The proposal was offered by Representative Marie St. Fleur, a Democrat from Boston who seems dedicated and sincere to her causes, but is someone I rarely agree with. The bill was moving along the legislative process in informal sessions (no recorded votes are required).

During the session, myself, Republican Representatives Donald Humason of Westfield and Daniel Webster of Pembroke were in the House Chamber and noticed an attempt to approve the benefit package for illegal immigrants on only a voice vote. We quickly objected and requested a formal recorded vote. This in effect, killed the legislation. Most Democrat members who might have no underlying philosophical objection to providing benefits to illegal immigrants understand politically that the people of their districts do. Simply by being present and forcing a recorded vote, we were able to stop the bill from passing. By delaying the vote to formal session, we also gained additional time to take this issue to the press.

Even among the sixteen House Republicans, we are a diverse group of people all along the ideological spectrum. Not to cast aspersions onto any of my fellow Republican Caucus members, as we obviously need to stick together when we can, but we are not made from the same ideological mold. This is due to the nature of Massachusetts politics. In practice we rarely are able to stand together in unison. This of course is one of the reasons why Massachusetts citizens have such a problem recognizing what my GOP stands for or is willing to fight against.

It is disappointing that we are not able to take a unified stand on most of the social issues. Many of the fiscal and tax matters result in disagreement and a splitting of our votes. Not only do we lose any political clout we may have as a Caucus, but equally important is that the voting public is unable to define what we stand for as a political party. When Election Day comes around, unless the voter has a solid understanding of how a Republican challenger will vote on any given issue, often times the old saying of "the devil you know is better than the devil you don't know" results in the incumbent Democrat being reelected. While I don't have a specific solution to this longstanding problem, in subsequent chapters I will outline a number of issues which I believe embrace GOP principles and would connect with the voters. It remains my contention that only when Republicans become firmer and clearer in our convictions, will the voters of

Massachusetts embrace our candidates and the numbers of elected Republicans increase.

This is not going to be an easy task. If I were to introduce some of my fellow Republicans from Massachusetts to Republicans from the mid-west or southern parts of this great nation, I would suspect they would wonder what kind of joke I was trying to pull on them. By way of example, there are more than a few folks who run under the Republicans banner who are pro-choice, pro-gay marriage, pro-universal health care and who would regularly get in line to get as much "pork" from a budget bill as they can. Now I am not suggesting that all Massachusetts Republicans are the same or unique in their moderation on many of today's political issues. In fact, from my experiences and observations, the liberalization of the party of Lincoln and Reagan is not unique to Massachusetts at all. It is a systemic problem across many parts of America and ultimately is also one of my primary motivations for writing this book.

From supporting benefits to illegal immigrants; to getting in line for the annual political pork fest during the budget process; to voting in favor of same-sex marriage, to embracing universal health care; the positions of some of my fellow Republicans constantly shock me and leave me wondering if the days of Republicans fighting for limited government and traditional family values are over. Obviously, I don't think they are over, or why would I waste my time with this book or fighting on the Massachusetts House floor where we are outnumbered ten to one? But to be clear, my GOP needs to take account of itself and make a determined effort to look to principles and values of our Party and step away from the "politics" of the modern American system of governance. When this is done consistently and passionately, I believe the American people will follow us. They have done so before when we have stayed committed to our core values and there is no reason to think they would not in the future.

Unfortunately, with growing frequency, Republicans seem to be losing their way along the path of conservatism. This is not due to the lack of a worthy national party platform, or because of a seismic shift by the country to the left. From my view and experiences, it emanates from a lack of political leaders who are willing to stand on principle and a growing number of American people who more and more want government to take care of their every need or desire. The good news, at least for now, is that these people are still in the minority (yes, I really do believe this). We still have time for my GOP to get America back on track towards smaller government and other conservative values.

Along with conservative beliefs and fighting to keep government at all levels as small and as close to the people as possible, I believe the voters correctly expect Republicans to be scandal free, both politically and in our personal lives. While no one has a closet without skeletons, voters hold Republican candidates and elected officials to a substantially higher standard than our Democrat opponents. When my GOP recognizes this as an advantage and stops complaining about some liberal media bias, the difference of personal character and integrity can be used as a political plus for Republicans.

I should stop and note that while the Massachusetts Republican House Caucus encompasses the entire ideological and political Republican spectrum, it has been refreshing that our Caucus has been scandal free. The same cannot be said by the majority party. I have seen and heard a lot during my time on Beacon Hill. While there are many times I sincerely disagree with some of my fellow Republicans on conservative issues, I am proud that I have never seen a position taken to be based upon a dishonest motive or improper influence.

There is absolutely a double standard when it comes to personal and ethical scandals and how the media reports them. Democrats are often given a pass or promptly forgiven (need I mentioned Bill Clinton?) while Republicans either resign out of respect to the office or are driven from office from an unforgiving conservative political base. While unfair, such a double standard can give the GOP a real advantage, but only when we live up to the expectations of the voters and avoid personal and professional scandal.

Much of my frustration with government in general and my GOP specifically is related to the growth of the power and scope of government at all levels. You will likely notice a number of Ronald Reagan references and quotations throughout this book. The "Great Communicator" as he is fondly remembered, had an ability to put things in simple but tremendously powerful terms. Reagan's words of, "I hope we have once again reminded people that man is not free unless government is limited. There's a clear cause and effect here that is as neat and predictable as a law of physics: as government expands, liberty contracts." clearly explains my own views on the recent expansion of the power of government. In too many instances, my GOP has failed to live up to the warning offered by Reagan. Until we get back on track and again fight to reduce the size, scope and expense of government, we are missing our true calling as Republicans.

We are also neglecting what the American people expect and deserve from the elected officials of the Republican Party. My GOP is the only political party that has any interest in controlling (I wish I was saying reducing) the size, scope and costs of government. If we don't become more proactive in this mission, we lose yet another critical reason people pull the lever for Republicans. Simply put, my GOP has failed in the last two election cycles because we have failed at upholding the values the American people expect from us.

Shortly after winning my first election in 2002, where I defeated a three term liberal Democrat while embracing a very conservative and common sense based message, I developed a simple three part test to determine whether or not I could support any given piece of legislation brought before the House. While it certainly is not a perfect test, it has proven extremely helpful to remain consistent with my core values. The test helps to not become distracted by the multitude of distractions of politics and the endless special interests which permeate the political system. It has helped guide me and stay firm on what the proper role of government is.

I am not trying to overly simplify the legislative process, but before casting a vote, I ask myself these three questions, 1) <u>Is this bill a proper role of government?</u> Many times, a legislative proposal will not overcome this first hurdle as it is clearly outside the scope of government's power. I often reflect and discuss how our Founding Fathers would view a given proposal to expand government's power. For example, when the state mandated universal style health care bill came before us, it was clear to me that it is not the role of government to force, under the power of the state, to compel citizens to purchase a given insurance policy. Thus, despite the fact that only Representative Daniel Webster (R-Pembroke) and myself (yes, only two out of two-hundred House and Senate legislators) were willing to push the "no" button, it was clearly the "right" thing to do. In a later chapter I will discuss this bill in detail and offer why it is an example of a dangerous step for our nation. I wanted to touch upon it here as it serves as a great example of a bill clearly outside the appropriate role of government. Can you imagine what John Adams, Thomas Jefferson and George Washington would think about the state forcing people to buy a certain insurance product or face a sanction from government? I believe I can say without hesitation; our Founding Fathers would not be pleased at how government has expanded its reach, power and influence over all of us.

When a given legislative bill does pass my Question 1, next I will ask Question 2) <u>Is this proposal good for my District or the Commonwealth in general?</u> Simply because a proposal is a proper role of government does not equate to my approval. To garner a "yes" vote, the bill must have an overall benefit to the state as a whole, or perhaps meet a specifically articulated need to a given area. In other words, I am more than willing to vote against bills and budgets that do not measure up to a standard of appropriate spending.

In fact, despite a tremendous amount of pressure as a freshmen legislator in 2003, I decided that the proposed state budget up for a vote in my first term was packed with too much wasteful spending and I voted against it. I did the same in the most recent budget passed in 2008. While it is difficult to avoid feeding at the pork barrel trough, I do my very best to stay consistent and protect the taxpayers' money. If we had more Republicans (or Democrats who were willing to stand up to their party leaders) in office who refused to go along with wasteful spending proposals, we as a Commonwealth would likely have the financial resources to address the appropriate roles of government, such as our educational, public safety and transportation needs.

The final test is perhaps the easiest to understand. Question 3) asks, <u>Can we afford it?</u> Lots of times a legislative proposal will be for a valid purpose of government (Question 1), have a proven benefit to the Commonwealth (Question 2), but does not result in my pushing the green "yes" button on my desk due to the fact that we simply cannot afford it.

A recent example is Governor Deval Patrick's twelve billion dollar, five-year plan for new college classrooms, laboratories, roads, bridges and other construction projects that he says were pushed aside as the state grappled to cover the ballooning cost of the Big Dig project. The plan would begin to fulfill a host of ambitious promises Governor Patrick made during his campaign and the early days of his administration by making the first investments in a commuter rail line extension to New Bedford and Fall River, and the construction of a stem cell bank at the University of Massachusetts Medical School.

While reading the above proposals, each seems reasonable and would probably pass the requirements of Questions 1 & 2, but we must also consider that the overall price tag is simply too expensive. In my view, passing such a mammoth broad bond authorization would surely result in future generations of the citizens of Massachusetts paying higher taxes. This would leave the state without the ability to respond to any unforeseen capital and infrastructure needs. Passing along debt to our children and grandchildren is simply an unacceptable burden. I believe there is a better and more appropriate way to meet our current infrastructure needs.

The way I look at the role of an elected official may be different than the majority of the folks I have the honor of serving with in the Legislature, but I believe we are actual stewards of your tax dollars. It is after all, your money! While it might seem easier to simply throw money at any given problem, such as Governor Patrick proposing the twelve billion dollar bond bill, we have a moral and fiduciary responsibility to the citizens of the Commonwealth to consider possible reforms to government BEFORE suggesting more revenue is needed. Unfortunately, since so many of the reform ideas that float around the State House from time to time involve the elimination of someone's job (possibly involving someone's uncle or cousin), the choices in government are usually to tax and spend, tax and spend, and if that doesn't work, tax and spend a little more. Ensuring fiscal responsibility is a primary area where my GOP needs to always firmly stand up for the taxpayers. By consistently doing so, we are demonstrating a compelling difference between us and the Democrats.

On a wholly personal level, while I am honored to have the self-attached label of Republican since I cast my first vote for Ronald Reagan as President, I should disclose in this opening chapter that I was not raised to be a loyal soldier of the Grand Old Party. I officially grew up in a house full of proud Democrats. My childhood home included my grandfather, George W. Davis, a World War I Veteran who served as my defacto father. "Pop" as I called him, was hard as nails, but as good and honest a man as I have ever known. Along with my loving and devoted mother, Mildred Perry, and the sweetest grandmother any child could have wanted, Annie Davis, there was my wild-eyed, but ever compassionate sister Kendra. The adults were all solidly "D's" and true worshipers of Franklin Delano Roosevelt's political party.

With each passing election, the local Democrat running for office had their campaign sign on our front lawn and there were more than a few campaign meetings at our kitchen table. The Democrat Party of my grandparents and my mother is not the Democrat party of today. More about this in later chapters. It is clear and not debatable that the "Greatest Generation" as described brilliantly in Tom Brokaw's best selling book, many of whom embraced the principles of F.D.R and J.F.K, would not today embrace the beliefs of Barack Obama, Nancy Pelosi, Deval Patrick and Ted Kennedy. These same folks seem to pull the "D" lever at each passing election with expectations that the modern day Democrats embrace the same values and character of F.D.R. and J.F.K. If only this were true…

Coming of political age during the late 1970s and early 80's and seeing the clear difference between the leadership of Jimmy Carter versus that of Ronald Reagan made it perfectly clear to me which direction I believe America should head. I think the major difference I perceived between the two major political parties during my impressionable years was how each party viewed the future of America. The Democrats vision was dark and negative, while Republicans talked with pride, respect, a positive future for this Country, believing in the people themselves. Despite the fact that Ronald Reagan was older than any prior President, he projected a positive youthful spirit and determined sense of optimism. This positive patriotic spirit was the same as was taught in my home.

At the end of Jimmy Carter's tenure in office, public cynicism about the government was at an all-time high across America, including inside the home I was raised in Attleboro. According to a study conducted by the Miller Center at the University of Virginia, half of the American people were pessimistic about the future of America during Carter's final period in office. This was compared with only 30 percent in 1975. Those optimistic had also declined from 47 to 21 percent. America was certainly not feeling very good about herself.

Ronald Reagan recognized that Americans needed a boost in our spirit. His words of: "morning again in America," "springtime of hope," "a promised land," "the last best hope of man on earth" clearly set forth his hopeful vision for this nation. While the imagery varied each time Reagan spoke, there remained a single overarching principle, and it was Reagan's pledge to return America to its essential role as "a shining city on a hill," a place of goodness, promise and hope. This sense of a positive and patriotic vision of America made a direct connection with me, my family and millions of others across America.

I knew that my family expected very little from government and firmly believed in personal freedom and personal responsibility. I recall the many hardship stories my grandparents and mother would share with me and my sister, Kendra. Believe me that none of the tales of heartache and struggle contained any request for assistance from Uncle Sam. I recall one particular story my mother told us. During the scarlet fever outbreak, which she and her sister were inflicted with, the entire family was under quarantine and required to remain prisoners in their home to avoid infecting anyone else.

Obviously not able to work, shop, or even make a trip to the pharmacy, the family was in a real desperate position. They, like most folks from her generation did not look to government for assistance. Neighbors and members of the church stepped forward, brought food by the house, ran errands and helped out as needed. While my mother and her parents did survive, sadly her sister, Shirley, succumbed to the scarlet fever. Whenever there was a challenge, people in need turned to family, friends and their community and not to Uncle Sam. When did America change from helping our fellow man to depending on government for all of our needs and desires? I was taught by those who raised me that government existed to provide for national security, roadways, schools, police and fire services. All other needs came from family, friends, neighbors, church or other private charity.

I recall one evening as my family was gathered around the television set in the late 1970's watching the evening news. There was a report regarding the long gas lines and how Jimmy Carter had issued some directive via his Secretary of Energy. My grandfather was taken back that Carter was injecting government influences into a free market. Pop, was equally shocked that we even had a Department of Energy. I recall his words and tone to this day: "What the hell is a paper-pushing bureaucrat in Washington, D.C. going to do to get more gas at the pump across the street from us? They will only make matters worse. If government gets out of the way, things will take care of themselves." Now there was a true believer in the free market! Obviously, we know my grandfather was correct as Carter's energy plan failed miserably and ultimately it was the free market and the old supply and demand theory that would ultimately solve the energy shortages.

As I saw then and continue to view it today, Jimmy Carter in the late 1970's and Deval Patrick and Barack Obama today seem to sincerely believe that the American people need government programs and interference to protect us from ourselves. They believe the future is bleak and that unless government provides benefits and services to the masses, the majority of people will be forced into the streets. Without the help of the elitist liberals, Americans would probably even fail to get out of bed every morning.

Democrat leaders in Washington, D.C. and in state capitals across the nation are consistently pushing for universal health care, amnesty of illegal aliens, higher taxes for business and entrepreneurs and an overall greater reliance on government in general. Some political experts attribute the Democrat's policy goals to be purely electoral based, meaning that the more voters who become dependent on government handouts and programs, the more voters will see a need to vote for politicians who support such programs and will continue to increase their benefits. From a political strategy or business plan point of view, such efforts by liberals make a lot of sense. The more people (voters) who rely on government to meet their needs, the more people will vote for those candidates who promise to deliver more government services and benefits.

In other words, each time Teddy Kennedy is successful at his efforts to grant citizenship status to another million illegal immigrants, he is securing another group of voters who will likely pull the lever for a "D." After all, it was the Democrat Party who gave them the ability to vote, so it is entirely reasonable to expect those dependent on government to vote accordingly. Looking at this solely as a political tactic, Senator Kennedy and company have a pretty solid game plan, if successful, to ensure another generation of Democrat voters. It is indeed a vicious, but politically successful circle.

Traditionally, it would be assumed that the Republican Party would be standing firmly against any and all such attempts to expand government and to be the party of law and order. Unfortunately, as much as I wish this was our stance one-hundred percent of the time, it is not. Once again, it is not that the principles I speak of are no longer shared by the majority of Americans. The problem as of late has been a lack of true conservative leadership within my GOP.

Whether it is because of the fear of being labeled as not being politically correct or intimidated by the numerous and powerful special interest groups that permeate our political system really matters not. The underlying point is that Republicans need to always base our votes and political efforts on principle and never allow the noise of the liberals or the lobbyists to get us off track.

Now, while it is relatively easy for Republican elected officials to agree in theory, in practice things are often not that simple and straightforward. From my observations serving in the House of Representatives, at times people of principle sometimes do get sidetracked and forget about their core values and beliefs. The reasons are many, but not the least of which is culturally based. That's right, cultural. I am referring to a political culture that exists within the walls of the Massachusetts State House and I would suspect in the halls of Congress as well. The longer one is in office and the more time you physically spend in the building, increases the potential you may suffer from what many call "drinking the Kool Aid." If you spend enough time "in the building" it can become rather easy to forget the very reason you ran for political office in the first place.

This is not a Republican or Democrat phenomenon, even Deval Patrick when he was running for Governor spoke to the way things are on Beacon Hill. During a debate on September 7, 2006, he made the pitch to the voters that he could change the political culture if elected:

"I have no obligations, no debts to the political establishment on Beacon Hill. If you want the same old same old, the politics of money and connections, I'm not your guy. But if what you want is the politics of hope and a change of culture on Beacon Hill, I am your guy, and I want your vote."

From my observations, whether or not the Governor is fulfilling this promise, along with many other campaign promises is doubtful, but it cannot be denied that what occurs inside the State House is quite different than what the good citizens of Massachusetts would like to see from their government.

Unfortunately, Republicans serving in state capitols and in Washington, D.C. sometimes also get swept away by the pomp and circumstance of elected office and in an effort to get along with the current power structure in government, they become an engrained piece of the existing culture. In most jobs it is totally normal when you start off in a new position that you want to be viewed as a team player and someone who is cooperative with the leadership. However, if you entered the political arena, especially in Massachusetts, with the sincere desire to change the culture of Beacon Hill, you have to be willing to stand up against it and believe me, this can be a lonely and uncomfortable place to be at times.

While I acknowledge that Beacon Hill or Washington, D.C. are not going to change overnight, my GOP needs to remember that when Republicans forget the very reason they entered office they end up getting in line for their share of pork barrel spending. They become agreeable to increased taxation, allow procedural abuses of the political process or support the efforts for government's power to expand. This causes the voters to lose their ability to appreciate the need for more Republican elected office holders.

During Ronald Reagan's 1966 campaign for Governor of California, Republicans established the so-called Eleventh Commandment: "Thou shalt not speak ill of any fellow Republican" and believe me it is not my intent or desire to do so on these pages. My goal is to simply lay things out on the table in as honest fashion as I can in hopes of encouraging a reconnection to the principles which make my GOP the best choice to take Massachusetts and this country to even greater prosperity and freedoms.

I surely do share Ronald Reagan's view of not relying on the institution of government to solve our problems. Ronald Reagan said it better that I ever could, when he stated:

> "Government is not the solution to our problem; government is the problem...We've been tempted to believe that society has become too complex to be managed by self-rule, that government by an elite group is superior to government for, by, and of the people."

So, what has happened to Republicans uniformly standing together for smaller government and for personal freedoms? Why did Republican Senator and GOP nominee for President John McCain stand with Ted Kennedy pushing for amnesty for millions of illegal immigrants who have invaded our nation and threatened our economic prosperity and national security?

What motivated former Republican Senator Lincoln Chafee of Rhode Island who appeared to be the best friend of Democratic Leader Harry Reid? Senator Chafee has long supported liberal policies with his support of abortion measures, gay rights, federally funded expansion of health care, overreaching and unnecessary environmental protections, including strongly opposing drilling in the Artic National Wildlife Refuge (ANWR). To put the icing on the cake, Chafee was the only Republican in Congress not to endorse President Bush's reelection in 2004 and one of three who tried to defeat President Bush's tax cuts.

It is no wonder that Chafee lost his reelection bid in 2006. Since he stopped acting like a Republican, GOP loyalists did not support him. The liberals will never support any Republican, even if they are one in name only. In February of 2008, the now former Senator Chafee went all the way and even endorsed Barack Obama for President. Well, at least my GOP can finally say good bye and good riddance to Lincoln Chafee and hopefully all those like him.

One wonders why such politicians choose to self-label themselves as Republicans in the first place. It certainly is not because they subscribe to the GOP's national platform or wish to promote the principles of Abraham Lincoln, Teddy Roosevelt or Ronald Reagan. While certainly disappointing to see such elected Republicans "get into bed" politically speaking with the liberals who are working to increase government's size and scope, it is also a significant reason why my GOP is losing its identity and desirability with many Americans. For any organization to be successful it must have a solid and clear identity. This is especially true in politics. Based on the election results of 2006 and 2008, the American people no longer identify with the Republican Party.

Americans are very busy and do not have the time or in many cases, the interest to thoroughly research every candidate and their issue position for the office they seek. Voters want and deserve to know that if a person calls themselves a Republican, that certain basic core beliefs can be assumed. When this is not the case, the voters become unclear about the difference between the parties and disengage themselves from the political process entirely. They may simply keep the current office holder there until they retire or become embroiled in a juicy personal scandal. In a state such as Massachusetts, this is especially disturbing as the practice of automatically reelecting the current office holder has resulted in one party dominance for far too long.

When I was first elected to the Massachusetts House of Representatives in 2002, I was sure of my convictions and beliefs. I sincerely believe this has not changed. Despite the constant pressure on elected officials from the endless special interest groups, lobbyists, and the generally liberal media, I hope my constituents would agree that I am basically the same person, with the same values as I was when I first entered into the political life. The process of spending countless hours at my home computer putting my thoughts on these pages together has been a gratifying and reaffirming experience. By putting ones principles down on paper for the world to see, one certainly does get a strong sense of their own convictions.

In addition to the influences of my mother and grandparents, without question others have molded my political beliefs and vision of the future. The birth of my son Christopher would probably also qualify as a political awakening. While certainly not viewed as a Republican or conservative epiphany, becoming a parent provides one with a totally different focus on life. No longer is the world about you as an individual. Now the problems of society and our political system grow larger and more pressing as you start to consider how they will affect your child's future.

Becoming a grandfather in recent years has once again reaffirmed this focus on future generations and instilled a motivation to do all that I can to ensure my child and his children live in an America where freedom rings for all citizens. One where the government is limited and personal responsibility and opportunity are available to those who work to achieve the American Dream.

Although some may take it this way, I am writing this book not for the purpose of criticizing certain people or my GOP in general. I offer my thoughts because I firmly believe Republicans need to refocus on who we are and what we are all about. This can only be done by "coming back home" to our history and the leadership of those great Republicans who came before us. While times do change, and at times particular political positions can and in some cases should evolve, core fundamental beliefs and values really should not.

In order to reconnect with the American people and guide America in the right direction, Republicans from local town boards to Washington, D.C. need to get back to the basics and stand solid on our principles of smaller government, individual rights, personal responsibility and free enterprise. If not, we face a future where the American people will remain confused and unclear about what each of the major political parties stands for. Such a lack of a clear political identity will likely lead to a further disengagement by the American people and an increased sense of distrust towards elected officials.

In concluding this opening chapter, I want to be completely clear that I do not claim to speak for the Republican Party in any formal way at all. However, I firmly contend that unless the followers of leaders like Ronald Reagan start to stand up and demand that my GOP gets back to what the American people expect us to be, my GOP might just lose its ability to guide this great nation into the future.

Chapter Two - Lessons from the Train Wrecks of 2006 & 2008

As the polls were closing at 8:00 P.M. on Tuesday, November 7, 2006, I found myself at my usual election night spot, the Sandwich Hollows Golf Course. My loyal and faithful group of Republican supporters gathered around the television set at the far end of the room. There was a sense of anxiety that we were in for a difficult night both on the State and national levels. Fortunately, for my own political future, I was unopposed for reelection to my third term to the Massachusetts House of Representatives.

Prior to election day, the media polls of just about every television, print and internet news outlet indicated the GOP would likely lose control of the House of Representatives and Senate in Washington, D.C. In Massachusetts, Kerry Healey who was attempting to hold the Governor's office for the Republican Party was also trailing badly behind the ultra-liberal Democrat candidate Deval Patrick. While we had few reasons to be optimistic, my usual group was cheerful and hopeful that things would turn out better than the polls indicated.

Well, just as the political experts had predicted, the Republican Party got its political clock cleaned and suffered widespread losses across Massachusetts and the nation. There were no surprises or miracles to be had on this election night. As the results continued to come in from across this great country of ours, the spirits of my conservative friends lost any sense of optimism they might have had going into the evening.

On November 4, 2008, the setting was the same for me as we gathered at the Sandwich Hollows again. Now seeking my fourth term, I faced a liberal challenger by the name of Glenn Paré. Mr. Paré seemed well positioned with a wave of pro-Obama energy rallying around the country. His positions were indeed liberal and he had the support of the Governor and the local Congressman.

Early on in the campaign, I decided to stay on my strong conservative message and continue my mantra of talking about the core GOP principles of law and order, fiscal accountability and the need to clean up the corruption that permeates Massachusetts state politics. This message and the indescribable energy of my supporters rewarded me with an overwhelming victory of 68% to 28%.

While my victories were certainly rewarding, politically speaking for my GOP as a whole, the 2006 and 2008 elections were equivalent to horrific train wrecks with very few survivors emerging from the crash scene. So, why did the Republicans lose the 2006 and 2008 election so badly?

Many Republican insiders and many of the talking heads on our televisions have their own opinions and most share the currently politically correct line of thinking that is was the fault of President Bush. After all, it had become politically correct to bash and blame President Bush for everything that was wrong with America. From the war in Iraq, to the sub-prime mortgage crisis, to the wild fires in California, the liberals who control most of America's media outlets are quick to somehow find a way to lay fault at the feet of President Bush.

In my opinion, this hatred for Bush stems from the 2000 election and all of the hanging chads and subsequent court battles that followed. The liberals have never been able to accept the fact the George W. Bush was their President for eight years. I bet some of them who are reading this book are actually saying "He was not my President" while reading this. To his very last day in office, they retained that sense of resentment and believed that George W. Bush was an illegitimate President, thus everything that is wrong with America is his fault!

"W" certainly is not exempt from his share of blame for the dismal election nights results for the Republicans. Now, I do not say this lightly, but from my point of view the primary reason the GOP did so poorly is that too many GOP elected officials either forgot their conservative principles (I will presume that they must once had some) on which they ran for office in the first place or they somehow thought that the American people no longer shared them. Either way, they made the fatal personal and political mistake of forgetting who they were and why they chose to attach the Republican label to themselves to begin with.

There are certain traits and beliefs that voters attach to every political party and by association to its candidates. While these can certainly change over time, there are basic assumptions that the voting public makes when you call yourself a Republican. Such things as ensuring fiscal responsibility, fighting to make government smaller and closer to the people, protecting family values and reducing taxes are beliefs that if you choose to label yourself as a member of the Republican Party, you had better be prepared to conduct yourself in accordance with such principles. When a member of the GOP fails to embrace the Party's core value system, they face the significant risk that the voters, who typically support Republican candidates, might just choose to stay home on election day or, as we have seen with an interesting frequency, cast their vote for some third party candidate as some form of a protest statement. Additionally, when a fresh and inspiring new face appears on the political scene, one like Barack Obama, many middle of the road voters become so captivated by charm and personality that the political party without a clear message has virtually no chance to compete.

Furthermore, from my experiences as both an elected official and a student of politics in general, voters need to know two basic things about any candidate, whether they are a person running for the first time for a local town office or a multiple term incumbent running statewide. First and foremost, voters want a basic understanding of who you are as a person. I am not talking about your views on the current political issues. What I am speaking of is who you are outside of politics. Voters do not need to know every intimate detail of your time here on earth, but at the very least they need to know enough to have an overall sense or impression of what type of person you are.

More or less, voters want to be able to describe you in a simple paragraph or two. Voters are busy folks and while the political junkies (like you apparently, since you are reading this book) watch all the debates, read position papers and have a solid understanding of where each candidate stands on the major issues, most people do not have the time or the interest to fully educate themselves on where a candidate stands on the important issues of the day. Voters want a sense whether a candidate is a decent and honest person. Someone that they would like to have as a neighbor, co-worker or friend is the same person they would like to cast their ballot for on election day.

For example, Mitt Romney can easily be described as the former Governor of Massachusetts, a highly successful businessman, a Mormon, and the man who also is credited with saving the Olympic Games in Utah. They would also probably think of him as a family oriented person with a whole bunch of children who all look like they belong on a slick fashion magazine cover. Romney is someone most people consider to be intelligent, well spoken and attractive to look at. For those who have been watching closely, they will know his father was the Governor of Michigan and he also ran for President. To most voters that is probably good enough to meet the first half of the equation.

Speaking of the public perception of a candidate, let's take a look at the Presidential ambitions of Senator John McCain. Without question John

McCain has enjoyed a long career of public service and made significant sacrifices for his country. In case you are unaware of his story, it is surely worth knowing. After graduating from the Naval Academy in 1958, McCain began his career as a Navy aviator. While serving in Vietnam, McCain's A-4 Skyhawk plane was shot down by an enemy anti-aircraft missile, which forced him to crash land in enemy territory of North Vietnam.

The young McCain shattered both of his arms and one leg after ejecting from his soon to be destroyed airplane. He was captured by enemy forces and tortured without any mercy by soldiers from the North Vietnamese military. His enemy interrogators crushed his shoulder with the butt of a rifle and bayoneted him in his left foot and stomach causing serious internal injuries. McCain was then transported to the infamous Hoa Lo Prison, also known as the "Hanoi Hilton" where he suffered unspeakable mistreatment at the hands of the North Vietnamese. Young John McCain was held as a prisoner of war for over five years refusing an early release due to the fact his men would not be set free. Without question, this country owes John McCain a debt for his service which cannot be repaid.

In 1982, John McCain was elected to Congress representing what was then the First Congressional District of Arizona. In 1986, he was elected to the United States Senate to take the place of Arizona's great conservative Senator and former GOP Presidential hopeful Barry Goldwater. McCain is currently the senior Senator from Arizona and is generally well respected by his peers in the Senate. As you will remember, in 2000 Senator McCain ran unsuccessfully for the Republican nomination for President of the United States and has continued to serve in the Senate without significant personal scandal for over twenty years.

On paper, John McCain was an obvious choice for the GOP to rally around for the Republican nomination in 2008. Certainly John McCain's service to this nation is second to none and his experience in the House of Representatives and United States Senate provides a solid political foundation to become President. I believe the voters all across America know of the sacrifices and service of John McCain and most likely have a positive impression of him as a person, his character and integrity.

Whether all of the above traits of Mitt Romney and John McCain are positive or negative to a particular voter is not significant for this first point to be satisfied. The critical factor is that the voters understand who the candidate is as a person. From there, the issues and the candidate's vision for the future will decide if a particular voter is supportive.

The second critical fact that a voter needs to know before they will be comfortable casting their ballot for someone; why is this person running for office and what does he or she stand for? This is where the Republican Party got into trouble in 2006 and 2008. Traditionally, Republican elected officials and candidates have firmly stood for smaller and more efficient government, support of the military and veterans, traditional family values, moral and ethical behavior and honoring the rights of the voters when they speak at the ballot box. These are just a few of the principles people associate with the Grand Old Party of Lincoln, Eisenhower and Reagan.

Unless the Republican Party as a whole embraces these core values and principles, and successfully executes them in office, we are likely to face more elections similar to 2006 and 2008. I am not suggesting every Republican does or should agree with the platform position of my GOP, but there are certain principles that as a whole my GOP must always be talking about to the American people. In the last two elections, this did not occur and my party suffered the consequences on election night.

It is my contention that all of those principles, and more that I discuss in this book, remain at the core of the Republican Party. In 2006 and 2008, it appears that some members of the GOP got off track and failed to speak loudly enough about who we are and what we believe. In some cases it almost seemed as if Republicans were overly hesitant to stand up for the principles of their Party. This unfortunately occurred in the local, state and national elections.

Perhaps it was the fear of being labeled by the liberal media as a cold- hearted conservative that ultimately dissuaded some GOP candidates and elected officials from shouting our beliefs from the roof tops. The reason or motivation is relatively unimportant. The fact is that when Republicans become politically weak-kneed and fail to stand for what is "right," we lose elections and do long-term and serious damage to our Party.

Now, I am not suggesting that every Republican who lost his or her seat did so because they abandoned the Party's platform or failed to be firm enough on conservative issues. Such an analysis would be overly simplistic and also downright untrue in some cases. What I am stating is that even when the voters have a solid understanding of who a candidate is as a person, when the candidate or especially a GOP incumbent no longer stands for what the voters expect, there is very little reason for the voter to cast their ballot for such a candidate. The predictability of any elected officials, of any political party, is almost always a recipe for failure on election day.

Others may suggest that the Iraq War or the economy was the primary reasons Republicans lost control of Congress and the White House. In Massachusetts, many have argued that the anti-Bush sentiment doomed GOP candidates these last two election cycles. In many ways it is difficult to dispute that this was as a significant factor. I believe that it is not because Americans do not support conservative beliefs, which I firmly believe they do, but more likely was due to Republicans failing to stand on their principles and were too easily shifted enough to the left. Too many members of my GOP were influenced by the noise of the liberal media. The voters were left unsure whether the Republicans were the party who would ensure the success in the war against terrorism or restrain the overspending of government budgets. After all, when Republican members of Congress are not standing tall on such traditional GOP issues, what are the American people supposed to think? Regarding the War in Iraq, it is surely logical for the general public to lose faith in President Bush and his efforts if even Republicans are not defending him.

When our brave men and women are in harm's way, more than ever Republicans need to stand up for their honor and for their mission. I am not suggesting that we close a blind eye to things that may be going wrong on the battlefield. When the Republican Party's faithful fail to stand with the Commander in Chief, it is only logical for our soldiers on the battle frontlines and the American people at the ballot box to wonder if the sacrifices of the battle are worth the cost associated with any military conflict. If Republicans stop promoting freedom and national security, it is no wonder why the American voters kicked so many "R's" out of office. So often elected officials get lost in the short-term politics of any given issue and lose focus on principle. In 2008, despite John McCain's unparalleled military service record and a solid plan for victory, the American people never really embraced his candidacy.

To be clear, I am not suggesting that the base conservative vote abandoned the Republican Party in 2006 and 2008. They did not. Just as the liberal vote will never swing over to a Republican candidate no matter how much they are courted (or should I say pandered to?). Neither the left nor the right wings of the political spectrum ultimately decides elections in

America. It is the middle, the "Silent Majority" who votes their conscience and what they believe is in the best interest of the nation as well as their own.

When Republicans fail to act like Republicans, enough of these middle voters are willing to vote for the Democrat which results in a GOP defeat. Republicans should not pander to any group of voters. They should not do so on grounds of principle and in fact, they do not need to. Time and time again when Republican leaders of character and integrity step forward and tout the core beliefs of the GOP, they are most often celebrating a victory on election night. The examples are practically endless and are discussed in Chapter Ten. For now, just remember that Ronald Reagan won Massachusetts twice!

On a more local level, in 2002 I unseated a three term liberal Democrat. It was not because more Republicans had moved into my District or that the incumbent was inherently flawed in some way. I believe it was because I was willing to stand on certain conservative principles and firmly articulate them to the voters. People understand that government is too intrusive and expensive. Americans want their votes honored at the ballot box. Voters want fair and equitable spending on education. People want to believe in their military and honor our veterans. These are Republican values and my GOP must stand tall and firmly state our beliefs. When we do, we win elections and our party, community, state and nation are better for it.

It certainly was not just illegal immigration or the War in Iraq that caused enough voters to cast their ballot for the "D" choice. Another issue which resulted in GOP defeats in 2006 and 2008 was our inability to get control over the federal budget and spending in Washington, D.C. Despite the fact that we had a majority in both the United States House of

Representatives and Senate up until the 2006 election, along with the White House, disappointingly the budget earmarks, pork-barrel spending, and special interest spending continued without a pause.

At the end of 2008, when AIG, CitiBank and the auto makers were lining up for their bailout checks, where was the Republican Party? Even during the race for President, John McCain had a crystal clear opportunity to demonstrate the fiscal differences between himself and Barack Obama when the $700 billion dollar bailout bill came to the Senate floor. Rather than standing tall against the corporate giveaway and the $100 billion plus of earmarks contained in the bill, McCain went along and quietly voted "yes." One does not have to wonder why the voters never did understand the difference between the would-be policies of McCain versus Obama.

In fact, The Club for Growth, a national network of thousands of Americans from all walks of life who deeply believe that prosperity and opportunity come through economic freedom, did a survey concerning a variety of issues impacting the decisions of voters and their own political supporters. The Club for Growth found that a major issue for their followers was that Republicans who typically are the champions of the middle class failed to deliver on the promise of fiscal conservatism. History unmistakably tells us that when my GOP stands firm on issues such as family values, lower taxation and government reform we connect with the voters across the country. This message gets directly to the people through the actions of our current elected officials and via the campaign message of our candidates. When John McCain votes for the bailout, Republicans across the county suffer.

Republicans also failed to be the party of reform, particularly on ethical matters, which is an expectation that voters have of the GOP. The liberals in general and the media specifically successfully portrayed

Republicans as the party of big corporations and big corporation welfare. If this is how the folks who would normally support a Republican candidate view the Republican elected office holders, it is no wonder that the casual voters were a bit unclear as to what we stand for as a political party. Remember, I am not suggesting that this happened in all cases, but because many Republicans were too timid to stand up and fight for our core beliefs, the average voter had no other choice than to believe the slander emitting from the mouths of those noisy liberals. Just like the issue of supporting the President on the War on Terrorism, Republicans shied away from this issue and the American people lost another reason to vote for my GOP in 2006 and 2008. This can be a short-term electoral mistake or a long-term problem depending on whether Republicans recognize the need for principle based stands over the temporary political posturing of any given issue.

In Massachusetts, for the 2006 election cycle our most disappointing defeat was the loss by Kerry Healey. Healey lost her bid for the Governor's Office to the political newcomer, Deval Patrick. Despite the Commonwealth being one the bluest of the blue states, the GOP had previously held the Governor's post for the prior sixteen years. While it may seem hard to believe to an outsider to Bay State politics, the corner office of the Commonwealth was taken over in 1990 by Republican Bill Weld soon after the so-called "Massachusetts Miracle" of alleged prosperity went sour, and Michael Dukakis lost his Presidential election bid to George H.W. Bush in 1988.

Dukakis left Massachusetts deeply in debt facing a budget shortfall of more than $1.5 billion. The voters of the Commonwealth sent a very clear message to the Democrats that they had had enough of higher taxes and wasteful spending. Following Bill Weld were Republicans Paul Celluci, Jane Swift and Mitt Romney, who all held the Governorship for the

Republican Party despite the state being an overwhelming stronghold for Democrats in practically every other elective office of significance.

After four successful and reasonably well-liked Republican Governors, one has to ask some obvious questions. Why did the voters of Massachusetts select an ultra-liberal candidate like Deval Patrick? Was Kerry Healey qualified to be Governor? Did the voters choose style over substance and simply buy the optimistic tone of Deval Patrick? Was there some national factor or trend that doomed Kerry Healey's campaign before it was able to get off the ground?

Having worked directly with Kerry Healey for four years, without question, Healey's political experience of serving as the former Chair of the Massachusetts Republican Party and then being the Lieutenant Governor for the four years under Mitt Romney provided her with plenty of experience to step into the job at full speed.

Kerry Healey's political resume and educational accomplishments were far above the field of other candidates and she had without a doubt the deepest grasp of the issues facing the Commonwealth. Financially, Kerry Healey was well positioned to have the resources to keep the string of Republican Governors going. Her husband, Sean Healey, a now semi-retired successful businessman is said to be worth over $100 million and reportedly invested several million dollars into his wife's campaign war chest. At the start of the campaign season, it appeared that Kerry Healey was extremely well position to retain the Governor's office for my GOP. So, what happened to cause her defeat and what can be learned from it?

Kerry Healey insiders will offer the explanation that she lost her race because of the national momentum sweeping across all fifty states that benefited Democrats from local offices to the United States Congress. While perhaps overly simplistic, I cannot argue that the negative Republican bias that occurred was a significant factor in Healey's and many other GOP defeats. Certainly, alone it was not enough to account for a nineteen percentage point loss, which was the margin of victory that Deval Patrick enjoyed when all the votes were counted. Some other GOP loyalists also cite the presence of a third-party candidate, Christy Mihos, in the race. While Mihos did capture the hearts of many reform-minded voters, with only slightly over six percent of the total vote, the blame for Healey's loss cannot be solely attributed to Mihos.

Looking back on this election, it is my opinion that we lost the Governor's race in 2006 for four primary reasons, which if corrected, will serve us well in the future. First, I concede the national anti-Republican trend accounted for a certain percentage of votes. While much has been written as to how large a percentage this national anti-Republican bias was actually responsible for, the median consensus seems to be approximately five to seven percent. By looking at several nonpartisan national election analyses, there seems to be general agreement indicating that the Democrat leaning vote was approximately 54% to 55% Democratic and 45% to 46% leaning the Republican's way.

Accepting this to be true would result in an approximate 5% decrease in the GOP's share of independent voters as compared to the election just two years earlier. As Massachusetts is already a more heavily Democrat state, the range could be slightly higher than the national averages indicated. Either way, the anti-Republican tone at the ballot box was a determining factor in many state legislative races, but it certainty did not rise to a level that would have resulted in a Kerry Healey victory, even under the best of circumstances. Even if one were to eliminate the pro-Democrat sentiment and give Healey the votes Christy Mihos earned, she still would fall short of making it a close race.

Secondly, like many voters in Massachusetts, I was disappointed that the Healey campaign depended so heavily on negative political advertisements, especially during the critical months of the fall campaign when many voters are making their most important, first and often final decision who they are going to cast their vote for. While some of Healey's television advertisements attempted to draw distinctions between herself and Deval Patrick, they seemed to go too far. For example, a television commercial by Healey criticizing Patrick for serving as the lawyer for the killer of a Florida highway patrol officer gunned down on a rural road. The facts were that in 1985 (twenty-one years is a long time ago to bring up) Deval Patrick who was at the time a lawyer for the NAACP Legal Defense Fund, argued to reverse the death sentence imposed on Carl Ray Songer.

Critics of Healey's advertisement argued that it confused the proper role of criminal defense lawyers in the judicial system and that everyone has the right to a lawyer and a legal defense. The guilt by association tactic by the Healey campaign was not embraced by the average Massachusetts voter and seemed to unfairly paint Kerry Healey as a negatively styled campaigner. Once labeled as running a negative campaign, it is next to impossible to change the public's sentiment.

Soon after the Songer advertisement, Deval Patrick next successfully criticized the Healey campaign for leaking details of the 1993 rape of Patrick's sister by her husband. The Healey campaign firmly denied any involvement in the leaks to the press. To this day, I sincerely doubt Kerry Healey would release such information, but by the time this was developing, the Patrick campaign had assumed the role of the victim and his liberal friends in the Boston media went right along with the story. By this point in time, too many voters had a negative impression of Kerry Healey. From my experiences, the exact opposite is true. But as we know too well, perception often trumps reality in the world of politics. It needs to be recognized that without question, there is a clear double standard in the area of political advertisements in Massachusetts. When a Democrat goes "negative," it is called a comparison ad or a discussion of the record of their opponent. But when a Republican chooses to use such tactics, they are quickly labeled as a partisan politician who is on the attack. We saw the same result on the national level when John McCain's ads were widely criticized as negative. The bottom line is that negative advertisements do not work and should almost always be avoided by my GOP. We need to give people a positive reason to vote for us, not a reason to vote against someone else. This is especially true with local municipal races where the electorate actually knows the candidates involved and will often rally around a candidate under attack.

Once Kerry Healey made the correct decision to spend the final two weeks of the campaign highlighting her own accomplishments, which were numerous, and sharing her own vision for the future of the Bay State, more and more voters were able to imagine her as a leader and someone who would be a good governor. Unfortunately, it appears that by the time Healey's campaign message changed, too many voters had made up their mind to embrace the positive and optimistic tone of the "Together We Can" message of Deval Patrick. As usual the Democrat was bombarding the airways with the seemingly endless financial support of labor unions and other liberal special interest groups.

Thirdly, from my vantage point in the election, Kerry Healey either neglected or failed to appreciate that voters needed to have a sense of the candidate as a person. As discussed earlier in this chapter, voters are busy folks and probably do not watch all the debates or have an in-depth understanding of where each candidate stands on the issues. A successful candidate must directly and personally connect with the voters somehow and identify themselves, or their opponent will likely do it for them.

For example, on a personal basis, when I first ran for office in 2002, I branded myself as an outsider to politics, someone who was angry as a voter and taxpayer. As a former local business owner, youth sport coach and police officer, the voters of my district had a sense I was just like many of them. I was doing my best to operate a small business, raise a family and serve my community. Many people knew my wife Lisa and my mother, as good honest, hardworking neighbors and friends. Once again, a candidate does not need to open the front door to the entirety of their personal life, but the bottom line is that if you are seeking their votes, the public deserves to understand what kind of person you are. When you fail to personally connect with the voters, rarely do they provide you an opportunity to earn their votes on the issues. Connecting with the voters can easily be done in many ways, but it requires "letting people in" your personal and private life. If you are not willing to do so, politics is probably not the correct career path for you.

Kerry Healey failed to get personal with the voters. She seemed to be hesitant to share personal stories or get her family intimately involved with the campaign. While it is certainly understandable why one would shield their loved ones from the harshness of a statewide political campaign, the voters never connected to Kerry Healey as a person. Healey has a great American personal story of family struggles and achievements, but it was never successfully communicated. I believe this was a shame, as knowing Kerry Healey personally provided me with a level of confidence in her ability to serve as Governor without any reservations whatsoever.

Fourthly and perhaps most importantly was that as intelligent, educated, experienced and attractive as Kerry Healey is, she never delivered the conservative Republican message to the voters. Some may suggest that she should not have, as after all, Massachusetts is not a conservative State, but I would wholly disagree. It has been proven time and time again that when conservative candidates are firm in their convictions and principles and articulate them clearly to the voters of Massachusetts, then the people of this blue state will embrace them. Let us again not forget that Massachusetts voters cast their ballots for Ronald Reagan twice and as just mentioned, elected a sixteen year string of Republican Governors. We have elected many Republican congressmen to represent us. Bay Staters are also even willing to send a Republican to the United States Senate when the right candidate comes along.

While is was some time ago, Republican Edward William Brooke III does not only have the claim of being the last GOP Senator from Massachusetts, but he was also the first African American to be elected by popular vote to serve in the United States Senate. Senator Brooke was reelected by the people to serve a second term in 1972, but failed in his efforts for a third term as he lost much of his popularity after a contentious and widely-publicized divorce. Democratic Representative Paul Tsongas defeated Brooke in 1978 by a 55%-41% margin. The point is that Republicans can and do win elections even in this blue state, but only when we act like real Republicans! It appears as Senator Brooke had moved toward the left during his tenure in the Senate and after allegations of personal misconduct, the voters were no longer comfortable with his representation. Yet another telling example of a lesson my GOP needs to take to heart!

Despite the election results of 2006 and 2008, to simply write off GOP future victories in Massachusetts is a mistake. What is needed the most is a change in our message and issues. I am not speaking of a new message or platform, but a reconnection with the core fundamental tenets of the GOP. In recent years, some Republicans have started to focus on and respond to the issues the liberals are talking about. While every elected official and candidate should have a broad spectrum of interest and knowledge on the issues of public and media concern, if someone decides to run as Republican, they need to include in their campaigns the issues of decreasing government spending and taxation, family values, ethics and being strong on law and order matters.

For example, when a GOP candidate neglects to present their ideas and follow with plans on how to make government smaller and more efficient, the voters lose one of the primary reasons to support a Republican candidate. Voters rightfully expect Republicans to stand for certain things and when we don't, why would anyone listen to us at all, never mind support our candidates?

Specifically lacking in the 2006 Healey campaign was the tough talk on law and order and fiscal issues. These issues played right into Healey's experiences with the Department of Justice and serving as the Romney Administration's point person with municipal officials would have been a perfect message. The conservative issues which often consume political campaigns were seemingly left off the Healey campaign agenda, which of course did more to alienate the Republican base than convince a liberal to cast a ballot for a Republican. A good example of avoiding the issues that conservative voters (Republican, Unenrolled or Democrats) cared most about (discussed later in Chapter Seven) was just prior to the 2006 election season. Massachusetts was mired in the debate over same-sex marriage, but surprising to most conservatives, Healey seemed to avoid the pending marriage ballot question almost completely.

Along with these issues, Kerry Healey is pro-choice and while attempting to use the illegal immigration issue to her advantage, her message was too late and too weak. On election day, I believe the voters made the wrong choice, but then again, I know Kerry Healey personally and have faith in her political credentials. From my involvement and observations of her campaign, she never did explain to the voters just who she was as a person. Her failure to embrace the principles of her party left voters feeling unsure what type of governor she would be. Just like so many other elections, when one candidate fails to deliver the expected message of their party, the voters cast their ballots for the optimistic alternative message, even when the message is delivered by someone who they probably disagree with on the underlying issues of the campaign.

In 2008, with John McCain at the top of the GOP ticket, we had a tremendous opportunity to focus the campaign on national security and government waste. After all, McCain's own military record and legislative history against budget earmarks in the Senate provided him with the credibility to demonstrate the drastic differences between himself and Barack Obama. Disappointingly, McCain failed on both accounts. When Americans were concerned about border security and illegal immigration, McCain stood with Teddy Kennedy and favored amnesty. When the financial services $700 billion bailout bill was before the Senate, again McCain failed to take a principled conservative stand and voted the same as his then opponent Barack Obama. It was no wonder that McCain never connected with the conservative-leaning voters.

If the Republican Party learns the lessons of 2006 and 2008, moves back to our history by returning to the principles of Abraham Lincoln, Teddy Roosevelt and Ronald Reagan, then I am confident we can get back on track and rightly convince the voters that America's best days are yet to come ahead and that the Republican Party is our best hope for this state and this nation.

The question remains as to what are those principles that Republicans need to embrace to stay true to the cause and reconnect with voters across this state and this nation. From my point of view, the issues and principles are not something new or different from our past. Republicans need to be fighting for a smaller and more efficient government, one that is as close to the people as possible. Republicans need to respect and honor the will of the voters. The GOP must be the party of law and order. Republicans must also embrace family values and Republicans must always be stewards of the taxpayers' dollars and only spend in appropriate ways.

While perhaps easy to articulate as broad value statements on a party's official platform, often times members of my GOP assume the voting public knows that we stand for such things; however, this is not always the reality. It appears lately that in an effort to reach new voters or rebut the noise from the liberals on the left, with an increasing frequency, Republicans are forgetting to stay on the conservative message and are getting distracted into debating their opponent's or the media's liberally based agenda. For example, many times the liberals will run for political office on such issues as increasing affordable housing, expanding social service programs, universal health care and raising new revenue sources. (Republicans must always call those taxes). When the conservative candidate makes the decision to also make those very same issues the core of their campaign message, the voters and media assume that those issues are the most important ones of the race.

In the campaign that follows and in the subsequent debates, mailings, and media stories, the focus is only on the issues the candidates are speaking of and lost is any discussion of the Republican issues. On election day, if the only issues before the electorate are liberal styled issues, who do you think the voters will choose to represent them? Why would any independent voter elect a Republican to work on matters that are typically thought of as being Democratic?

Republicans need to drive the debate and issue discussions toward the issues we care most about. The American people in the middle care about our conservative issues as much as those on the left. We need to force the opposing side to talk about family values, illegal immigration and lower taxes. When we do, not only do voters have a clear understanding of why we wish to serve in elected office, but equally important, we get to expose the Democrats for their liberal agenda, which I can assure you does not reflect the same views of a majority of the people.

No matter what level of political office one is seeking, it is hardly ever a winning message to simply be against something or opposed to your opponent. A successful candidate will need to offer a positive message and vision about the issues that are most important to them and their constituency. Independent voters will elect the candidate and political party to address the issues which are most important to them. Very likely if those issues are presented as liberal ones, the Democrat will be a more attractive choice. However, when my GOP drives the discussion towards conservative-based issues, those middle voters are more than willing to entrust in us the responsibility to represent them.

<u>Chapter Three - Parties change, why don't people?</u>

The transformation of political parties has been well documented and discussed in countless books on the subject. We know from a study of political history that political parties come and go. Have you seen any members of the Whig or Bull Moose Party around lately? What is worth discussing is the apparently unanswered question: Why don't the members of a political party change their political affiliation when their own values and beliefs are no longer consistent with their own political party?

Take for example the common Massachusetts conflict of why would a Catholic, pro-life, pro-traditional marriage, anti-tax candidate for office in Massachusetts make the confirmatory choice to call themselves a Democrat today? After all, the Democrat establishment here in the Commonwealth holds the opposite point of view on all of these issues.

Could it be as simple as since a person's parents were Democrats, thus they feel that tradition and loyalty demand that they remain a member of the Party of F.D.R. and J.F.K.? While each person would probably have a slightly different reason and answer as to why they choose the label of their political party, I remain baffled as to why when political parties change, people don't.

The primary reason to associate with any political party is to join with other people who hold similar values and points of view about the government's role. While many people choose to be associated with a certain party, they are not expected to share exactly the same beliefs, but the core beliefs and values should be fundamentally consistent. For me, no matter how proud I am to call myself a Republican, I can state with complete confidence, if my GOP abandoned the fight for smaller government, disregarded the will of the voters, and became soft on law and order issues, I would leave my political party and find another more in line with my own personal core values. The alternative is illogical and counterproductive to the very purpose we have political parties in the first place.

It is not just elected officials who face the question whether to change their political affiliations when the core beliefs of their party change and no longer are in line with their own core value system. For example, Supreme Court Associate Justice Clarence Thomas spoke to this very issue in his recent bestselling book, "My Grandfather's Son." While discussing his nomination to the Supreme Court by President George H.W. Bush and the subsequent downright ugly and divisive confirmation process, Justice Thomas wrote, "Daddy (his grandfather) had once asked me why I'd become a Republican, to which I replied that the Democrats no longer represented the things he'd taught me."

The political transformation of Justice Clarence Thomas was not a fundamental change in his own political ideology, nor was it a change from the values he was raised with, but was more of a change in the core values of the Democrat Party itself. While Justice Thomas recognized that the lessons of his grandfather were more in line with Republican values, his grandfather refused to detach the Democrat label despite they no longer shared the same underlying principles.

Like so many other people of Justice Thomas' generation, the time in history of my parents and grandparents, who were young in the years following the Great Depression and stock market collapse of 1929, the Democrat Party of that time represented beliefs that are not consistent with the modern era Democrat Party. Without question, many proud Americans of the 1930's needed a helping hand from government and Franklin Delano Roosevelt, a true blue Democrat, was there to guide this nation through those difficult times and a World War.

While some partisan political observers on my side of the aisle are quick to criticize F.D.R. for the tremendous expansion of government programs during his terms in office, I take a slightly different approach. An honest review of history shows that most of the programs started during the Depression era were intended to be temporary relief measures and were designed to provide a day's pay for a day's work. F.D.R. put Americans back to work unlike most of the Democrats who followed him. Modern Democrats appear not to understand that the work component is the most important element of any social benefit program.

Unfortunately, the mindset that Roosevelt started in the 1930's of the government being the distributor of funds has gone far a field in both time and scope from F.D.R.'s intentions of a day's pay for a day's work. For those who lived and suffered through the years following the Great Depression, it is no wonder why so many have such a strong affection for Roosevelt and his Democrat Party. He not only led the nation out from under the Depression, but served as an outstanding Commander in Chief during the darkest days of World War II.

It is completely understandable why people living under a F.D.R. presidency would label themselves as a member of his party. Now, over sixty years since the passing of F.D.R., why so many people still adopt the Democrat Party as their own, when so many of their own beliefs are in direct opposition with the platform of the Democratic Party, is difficult to reconcile. Of course, the transformation of political parties is not unique to the Democrats. As discussed in a later chapter of this book, the Republican Party has undergone many changes as well throughout history. The unanswered question remains: If parties change, why don't the people abandon their political party or join the current political party which best represents their own beliefs? Or perhaps even start a new political party that is more consistent with their own value system.

As will be discussed in detail in the chapter "We have a Proud History," members of the Whig Party did just that. When the leaders of the Whig Party refused to adequately address the growing problems and constitutional conflicts of slavery, many former Whigs abandoned their political party and ultimately formed the Republican Party. A totally logical response by people who felt their political party no longer served their interests.

One of the most notable people to change their political affiliation due to the party's change away from his own value system was Ronald Reagan. Reagan was not always a Republican Party member. In fact, Reagan was a self-admitted Democrat and proud of it during his younger years. Like so many other Americans of his time, Reagan was born into a family of Democrats and thus he defaulted into that party. At the 1984 GOP convention, Reagan shared the story of his own personal journey to the Republican Party:

> "I began political life as a Democrat, casting my first vote in 1932 for Franklin Delano Roosevelt. That year, the Democrats called for a twenty-percent reduction in the cost of government by abolishing useless commissions and offices and consolidating departments and bureaus, and giving more authority to state governments. As the years went by and those promises were forgotten, did I leave the Democratic Party, or did the leadership of that party leave not just me but millions of patriotic Democrats who believed in the principles and philosophy of that platform? One of the first to declare this was a former Democratic nominee for President Al Smith, the Happy Warrior, who went before the nation

in 1936 to say, on television or on radio that he could no longer follow his party's leadership and that he was "taking a walk." As Democratic leaders have taken their party further and further away from its first principles, it's no surprise that so many responsible Democrats feel that our platform is closer to their views, and we welcome them to our side."

The political transformation of Ronald Reagan is logical and well reasoned. In fact, it somewhat parallels my own family's personal experience. As I have previously stated, I was born into a house of three staunch Democrats. All true followers and believers of F.D.R. As their party began the shift towards socialism with the never ending promotion of social welfare programs, my grandfather, grandmother and mother all began to question the direction of their political party. While only my mother made the complete switch to actually registering Republican, my grandfather (my grandmother had passed away) would finally have to admit in 1980 that he could not support Jimmy Carter for President and cast his first vote for a Republican of his lifetime when he voted for Ronald Reagan for President. Surely, a logical decision considering where the two men stood on the issues, but change came hard to my Pop and those of his generation.

Often described as a "political pendulum," both the Democrat and the Republican parties have had their highs and lows over the course of history. Just as individuals can and do change, so do the political parties themselves and their platform issues. I do not question the fact that political parties change; however, when a political party alters its core values, either over a period of years, or overnight by the election of the new leader, I continue to be surprised how many individuals remain faithful to it. If the essential purpose of any political organization is to promote the values of its members and support the candidates who share those very same positions, why do so many people remain loyal, faithful soldiers when they no longer have the same political goals? I am not referring to a difference on any single issue but wholesale shifts in political beliefs and idealology.

Taking a brief look at the official platform of the Massachusetts Democrat party (www.massdems.org/about/platform.htm), we see the Democrats from the Bay State support rights and benefits for illegal immigrants; oppose the Patriot Act, which provides law enforcement tools on the war on terror; support gay-marriage; oppose the death penalty under any circumstances; embrace universal/single payer health care; support abortion; support English as a Second Language programs; oppose additional Charter schools; and even condemn reducing the state's income tax despite what the voters said at the ballot box. So, if by chance you happen to be a registered Democrat (a special thank you for buying this book), do you share the same views as your Party's official platform? If so, good for you. If not, why are you a Democrat?

While it might appear to be just my own perspective and the legislative district that I represent, the people I speak to and who contact me regarding issues before the Legislature do not share most of the views of the Democrats' platform, yet the plurality of them continue to be registered "D's." You don't have to take my word that the people of Massachusetts share more the beliefs of the Republican Party over those of the Democrat Party. The fact is, when the voters of Massachusetts have the opportunity to vote on ballot questions, they often vote as a Republican would. For example, in the past, voters in the Commonwealth have approved an income tax reduction, expressed their support for the death penalty, and requested the legislature to allow donations to charities to be deductible from their state income taxes. It is certain that the majority of Democrat elected leaders do not share these views as they have refused to enact the expressed will of the voters on numerous occasions.

In just the last few years, the Republican legislators I have the privilege of working with brought forward two such issues to the floor of the House of Representatives. Regarding the income tax rollback, each and every legislative session, the GOP Caucus members have sponsored a bill to honor the will of the voters and reduced the state's income tax back to 5% as the voters clearly mandated. We also made an effort and offer a budget amendment to roll back the income taxes during each annual budget debate. Time and time again, the Democrats either use a procedural tactic and disallow a vote on the issue, or on several occasions have voted against the income tax reduction despite the people of their respective districts voting otherwise.

The opponents to the income tax roll back state that if we roll back the taxes there will be less revenue to send back to local towns for education and public safety. This position is overly simplistic and ignores two important facts. First of all, we have seen time and time again that lower tax rates often lead to higher government tax collections and thus likely more revenue would be later available for the state's budget needs, as well as aid to cities and towns.

It is Economics 101, which should be a mandatory course for everyone who works in government, that when government collects fewer taxes from the citizens, the additional money is put into the stream of commerce. This will stimulate economic activity, which leads to higher sales and employment tax collections and less people dependent on government programs and services. This is exactly the logic of the federal government lowering interest rates or sending everyone a rebate check when the economy slows down.

The second incorrect and shortsighted position which some opponents to the state income tax roll back take is that we should use the excess funds to create new social service programs. While this is certainly an option, I continue to be shocked how many elected officials easily disregard the results of the ballot question mandating the tax roll back. Putting the economic arguments aside, is there not a moral and ethical obligation to honor the will of the voters when they clearly speak at the ballot box?

The bottom line is that voters statewide approved a ballot law calling for the rate to be rolled back to 5 percent. In Barnstable County, the vote was 81,254 in favor of the tax reduction and 36,558 against. If this vote is not a clear mandate from the voters, I would suggest the citizen referendum process is just about dead in Massachusetts. I am extremely concerned that the citizens' right to speak at the ballot appears to be in serious jeopardy in our Commonwealth. Whether it is the issue of charitable deductions or the state's income tax rate, the Legislature has a disappointing record of ignoring the vote of the citizens. Perhaps these are not issues that you personally care that much about, but just wait, sooner or later you will. As Republicans, we must stand on principle and always fight for a fair and open political process where the rights of the voters are paramount. Even when the proposal being discussed is a liberal one, Republicans should never partake in employing procedural manipulation of the rules. During my time in serving in the Massachusetts House, I am most proud of our Caucus's efforts on procedural matters. This small, but feisty group has remained true to honoring the rules and process, even when it would have been politically easier not to.

So, the people of Massachusetts (many of whom are Democrats) vote a certain way on a ballot question, which is consistent with that of the

Republican Party, the elected Democrats ignore their will and legislatively frustrate their votes. These same people reelect the same Democrats back into office. Not to be overly repetitive with the ongoing question, but if the principles and beliefs of the current Democrat Party have changed to be so inconsistent with those of the electorate, why don't the people change their political party designation? Even if long standing Democrats don't wish to change their political affiliation, they could at the very least stop casting their votes for those who continuously fail to promote their own interests and beliefs.

I can say with great confidence that I never automatically vote to elect every Republican on the ballot. For the long term good of my GOP, while no one should be dissuaded from running for office, Republican activists should only support those candidates who embrace the core beliefs of the Party. When Republicans in name only (RINO) gain the support of GOP leaders we discredit our Party. The general public becomes uncertain about what we stand for. While I am not suggesting any single issue litmus test, caution is advised of who we nominate and select to be the leaders of my GOP.

Another telling example of the disconnection between the people and their elected officials can be found on the issue of the death penalty. In November of 2007, Republican House Leader Brad Jones was able to get the GOP death penalty bill (of which I am a cosponsor) to the floor for a formal debate and roll call. The final vote was 46 in favor of creating a limited death penalty bill and 112 opposed. Previously, the closest House vote on the issue came in 1997, when a bill to reinstate the death penalty ended with a tie vote, which is a defeat under the rules. It is clear that the majority of Democrat legislators oppose the death penalty, but according to a University of Massachusetts poll taken after the death penalty bill was originally filed, the majority of Massachusetts residents supported the death penalty by a 54-to-45 percent margin. While the death penalty is just one issue, when you start to count up all the issues where the people of Massachusetts feel one way and the Democrat Party acts in another, it is difficult to explain.

In Massachusetts, one of the most telling issues which has caused life-long Democrats to question if their party has indeed wholly abandoned their values, is that of gay marriage. The public opinion polls on this issue indicate a very close call on whether the people of Massachusetts would clearly define our state constitution as requiring that marriage be between one man and one woman. On the question of voting on the question, the polls are not close. The citizens of Massachusetts want to be heard on this issue.

It is clear and not honestly debatable that the people of Massachusetts and the United States have strong feelings and views on gay marriage and want their voices to be heard at the ballot box. Now, I am not predicting what the results of the vote would or should be, but without question, the issue deserves to be put before the people to decide and not left to politicians who are impacted by the endless pressures from political leaders and special interest groups.

However, in case you have been living under a rock and had not noticed, both in Massachusetts and on a national level, the Democrat Party is now the party of the liberal left-wing activists. I am not suggesting that this is not a proper role for a political party to take, but my overriding point is, does it really reflect the views of a majority of those who register themselves as Democrats? And if not, why do the traditional and conservative leaning Democrats continue to associate themselves with such a liberal political party? From my vantage point, it seems as if they have no real influence on the positions or actions their political leaders are taking.

On Beacon Hill, Governor Deval Patrick, former House Speaker Sal Dimasi, and Senate President Therese Murray, all of whom are Democrats, worked tirelessly to defeat a citizen's petition to allow the voters of Massachusetts to voice their feelings on the issue of same-sex marriage at the 2008 ballot box. Having well established that a majority of voters in Massachusetts are Democrats, or at least vote that way when they select their elected officials at the ballot box, why would the legislative leaders from their very own political party be so fearful to allow the people to vote?

Could it be that they are actually afraid that members of their own political party do not share their views on this issue and would have approved a constitutional amendment defining marriage as only between one man and one woman? Just like dozens of other states, including California in 2008, where the question has been put forth for the voters (more about this in Chapter Seven), my liberal friends know full well what the voters of Massachusetts would have likely said at the ballot box. After all, as discussed previously, the people of Massachusetts have voted in a conservative Republican leaning manner regarding their income tax rate, charitable deductions and on the death penalty. Why would the issue of same-sex marriage be any different?

If you are a member of the majority party in Massachusetts and support gay marriage, one would think it would make common sense to put the measure on the ballot and allow your fellow Democrats from all across this great Commonwealth to vote and validate the right of same-sex couples to marry. After all, there is no better method of changing social policy than to have the electorate support it. The issue would have ended there at the ballot box. The people of Massachusetts would have spoken. As a conservative Republican, I believe these type of questions fall under the category of states' rights and thus the issue would have been resolved once and for all. But as we know, that was not what the political leaders chose to do.

It is evident that we will likely never know the answer to this question of what the voters of Massachusetts actually want the definition of marriage to be, because those wishing to bring this issue to the ballot are fighting against an overwhelmingly entrenched liberal political establishment. At the very least it should serve as a wake up call to those who registered themselves as Democrats based on the principles of former great men, such as F.D.R. and J.F.K. Today's Democrat Party has been infiltrated by far left-wing liberals and it no longer stands for the values it once did. Perhaps I may be overboard with my generalizations, but when you take an honest and objective look at public policy being promoted by Governor Patrick and many Democratic leaders who share his beliefs, there really is no other conclusion.

There is absolutely nothing wrong with liberals promoting a liberal agenda. In fact, I guess that is exactly what they should be doing; however, all too often these same individuals are successfully convincing (I would suggest "fooling") the voting public that they are moderates. Come on people, wake up and judge your elected officials on their actions and votes and not on their political rhetoric! Where are that property tax relief and 1,000 new police officers Governor Patrick promised? Most politicians count on the likelihood that you will forget about their campaign promises.

Granted, I am a member of the opposing political party, so I am not asking Democrats to take my comments at face value. My comments and questions are designed to challenge conservative and moderate Democrats to make an honest appraisal of whether their party is truly representing their own moral values and political positions. From denying the rights of the voters to speak at the ballot box, to promoting benefits for illegal immigrants, to universal health care, the modern Democrat Party looks pretty liberal and out of touch to me.

This is certainly not a Massachusetts-only phenomenon. Liberal Democrats and advocates of gay and lesbian rights have influenced the debate for the White House hopefuls as well. In August of 2007, all the candidates for President in the Democratic primary got together for a forum on gay rights. According to an ABC news report, "They came, they saw, they pandered."

The first message from all of the candidates speaking to the lesbian, gay, bisexual and transgender crowd was to share their understanding of their concerns and problems. "I come to these issues…as a friend of a lot of members of the lesbian, gay, bisexual and transgender community," said New York Senator Hillary Clinton. Illinois Senator Barack Obama said, "When you're a black guy named Barack Obama, you know what it's like to be on the outside." Not to be left out in the effort to win their support, New Mexico Governor Bill Richardson noted, "I'm Hispanic. I felt the sting as a kid of being stereotyped." The candidates spent a couple of hours attempting to persuade the crowd that they would best represent the interests of the gay community if elected. This is the perfect example of the liberal pandering that goes on to the countless special interest groups. The same type of thing goes on with immigrant groups, labor unions and pro-abortion supporters.

All the time the blue collar conservative Democrat probably believes that his party is looking out for them, as they really once did. So, what about the interests of those who oppose gay marriage or those who believe that one's sexuality is not relevant to politics? While Republicans certainly do not speak in one uniform voice on all issues, including the rights of same-sex couples, I hope we never stoop to the level of such pandering to any special interest group.

There is absolutely no way to reconcile the Democrat Party's efforts to reward illegal immigrants which in turn hurts union members. Supporting gay rights shuns conservative Democrats and promoting pro-choice only candidates snubs Catholic Democrats. One can only imagine what special interest group the Dems will be pandering to next. Stay tuned, I am sure we will not have to wait too long to find out.

On gay marriage and the associated issues, the real difference between the two political parties is that most Republicans (including myself) believe this is a matter best left for the voters to decide for themselves. Basically, the Democrats believe they know better than the voters. I admit such a statement is not one-hundred percent accurate. There does remain a handful of conservative Democrats in office who do stand up for principle. Also, there are some Republican office holders who disappoint me on almost a daily basis, but the significant majority of Republicans stand for the rights of the voters, while a growing number of Democrats have not done so.

On the specific issue of getting the marriage question on the ballot in Massachusetts, supporters of the proposed amendment to define marriage as being between one man and one woman (many of whom were Catholic Democrats) collected more than 170,000 signatures from registered voters in an effort to place this measure on the ballot in 2008. To get a spot on the ballot, the measure needed the backing of fifty legislators, but at the end of the day (more about this story in chapter seven), of course the Democrats pulled together and denied the voters of the Commonwealth an opportunity to be heard.

Wherever you stand on this particular issue, you should be extremely concerned that the initiative petition process is being ignored by the majority of your elected officials. This is a dangerous precedent being set by your government, and I am fearful of what abuse of the democratic process may be next. The Democrat Party has a growing history of either ignoring the voters when they speak at the ballot box or with the case of the marriage issue, not even allowing the matter to get to the voting booth. Perhaps one day the citizens of this great state will begin to see that many of the people they choose to elect, while talking a convincing game during political campaigns, do not actually represent them or their values. Only by holding accountable the elected officials who are not in line with your own beliefs will government meaningfully change for the better.

Our Founding Fathers understood that for our system of government to endure and not be perverted by special interest groups, there needed to be separations of powers and a system of checks and balances. By distributing the functions of our government among three separate but equal branches, and allowing the people to redress their government when necessary, our Founders have laid out a system that has allowed America to be the most free and prosperous nation in the history of the world.

Our system of government and distribution of power is genius in its design and function; however, it relies on the basic assumption that the citizens will remove elected officials from office who no longer represent their best interest or share their value system. When elected leaders are returned to office time and time again, despite voting against the will of their own constituents, I guess they people get the government they deserve.

Today, it has become apparent that the Democrats have abandoned those Americans who still embrace traditional family values. Before I go on, I must share with you that once when I used the words "family values" in a public speech, I actually had constituents (yes, Democrat ones) tell me that they were offended by my usage of such "hate speech." I wish I was exaggerating, but I am not. To think that political correctness has gone to the point where speaking of the positive value of a home with caring parents is now termed hate speech is not only outrageous, I believe it is dangerous to what so many of us believe America is. For my part, I shall continue to use such terminology to describe what is the most important part of our great nation's success, the American family and the values which have been traditionally attached to it.

Being from Massachusetts where a significant number of our politicians are either of Irish or Italian decent, and also predominantly members of the Catholic religion, it leaves one wondering how to reconcile how so many Catholic voters continue to be members of the Democrat Party when their elected officials have wholly rejected so many long standing teachings and beliefs of the Catholic Church they attend each week.

Obviously, in Massachusetts the biggest disconnect between the formal doctrine of the Catholic Church and the Democrat Party leaders is the issue of same-sex marriage. In fact, the Pope and the Administrative Committee of the United States Conference of Catholic Bishops have called for a constitutional amendment to protect the unique social and legal status of marriage. According to Catholic Church's own words, "marriage is a faithful, exclusive and lifelong union between one man and one woman...we offer general support for a federal marriage amendment to the United States Constitution as we continue to work to protect marriage in state legislatures, the courts, the Congress and other appropriate forums."

By way of full disclosure, I am not Catholic. I was raised a Methodist and do not claim to have anything more than a superficial understanding of the values of the Catholic Faith. Having admitted my limited knowledge of the religion, it is an undisputed truth that the Catholic Church leaders and believers feel that marriage is to be between one man and one woman. During the same-sex marriage debate, a significant portion of the 170,000 signatures collected to bring the constitutional amendment before the people where obtained from efforts related to Catholic churches.

Compare this against the official platform of the Democratic Party, which clearly is in favor of marriage for gay and lesbian couples. I am not suggesting that simply because leaders of a given political party do not share the same views of a particular religion on a single issue that this should result in a universal rejection of said political party. But when you add other political conflicts, such as the differences in abortion and providing sex education in school to young children, just to name a few of the obvious contemporary examples, it does seem difficult to fathom why such folks would continue to be a member of a political party that is the complete opposite of so many core beliefs. The overriding question remains: Why do so many Catholics continue to vote and support candidates who reject their values?

Speaking to the issue of abortion, it now appears to be wholly unacceptable for a member of the Democrat Party to be pro-life, or anti-abortion. In fact, Boston's Catholic Cardinal Sean P. O'Malley recently said that the Democrat Party has been persistently hostile to opponents of abortion rights.

In his sharpest comments about the political landscape since he was installed as Archbishop of Boston in 2004, Cardinal O'Malley made clear that he views abortion as the most important moral issue facing policymakers. "I think the Democratic Party, which has been in many parts of the country traditionally the party which Catholics have supported, has been extremely insensitive to the church's position, on the gospel of life in particular, and on other moral issues." Acknowledging that Catholic voters in Massachusetts generally support Democrat candidates who are in favor of abortion rights, O'Malley said, "I think that, at times, it borders on scandal as far as I'm concerned."

On the Republican side of the aisle, it is acceptable to be pro-life or pro-choice and while most conservative members of the GOP are anti-abortion, Republican candidates on either side of this controversial issue are welcomed and embraced. In our House Legislative Caucus, I would say the split is about even and no one is ever pressured to be either pro-life or pro-choice. The same cannot be said for pro-life Democrats. With the influences of Emily's List, who's "members are dedicated to building a progressive America by electing pro-choice Democratic women to office" and Planned Parenthood who in many ways are not much more than political wings of the Democrat Party, pro-life Democrat candidates are often left out in the cold. To test my hypothesis, can you name a pro-life Democrat who holds a major political position? If you can, that person would certainly be the exception to the general rule of my observations and impressions.

I do not suggest that there is a simple or a single answer as to why so many registered Democrats remain faithful to a political party which no longer shares their values. It is at least partially out of a sense of loyalty. We all want our "team" to win, whether it is a sporting event or a political contest. Just as most people who were born in Massachusetts are fans of the Red Sox and remain loyal fans during championship seasons and disappointing ones, perhaps so goes the loyalty to the political party in which you were raised.

Just as we continue to cheer for the Red Sox no matter what, those who were born into Democrat families during the time when F.D.R.'s or J.F.K.'s well deserved popularity was at it height, many Democrats have a continuing sense of loyalty to their political party. In my experience of running for office, after being confronted with the formal positions of their party, more people than I could keep track of have stated to me, "I have no idea why I am still a Democrat."

For someone to admit that their political party no longer represents their values is indeed a difficult process of self-reflection. It is one which many people do not wish to put in the necessary time and effort. After all, it is much easier to remain a Democrat, if you have always been a Democrat and your parents were Democrats.

My mother is a perfect example of an "old school" Democrat who feels her former party has left her, but the transformation to the GOP did not come quickly or easily. Born in 1926, and growing up during the Great Depression, her parents were faithful followers of F.D.R. Roosevelt who was elected President in November 1932, to the first of four terms, knew that America needed quick and prompt government action. It was a time where there were more than 13,000,000 unemployed. Almost every bank in the nation was closed, or at least on the verge of closing. In Roosevelt's first "hundred days" in office he proposed and successfully ushered through sweeping programs to bring recovery to businesses, farms and the millions of unemployed. Highly ambitious job programs, such as the Tennessee Valley Authority put Americans back to work. Locally, these job programs included the construction of the three bridges which still span the Cape Cod Canal today.

People like my mother and grandparents believed in F.D.R.'s policies not because it was a government handout, but because it provided

Americans with an opportunity to earn an honest days wage for an honest days work. A lot has changed over the past seven decades within the Democrat Party. Instead of looking to promote a society that expects its citizens to provide services in exchange for government assistance as F.D.R.'s programs called for, the Democrat Party of today has developed into the party of entitlements and free handouts.

The party of F.D.R. and J.F.K. is not the party of Barack Obama, Ted Kennedy or Deval Patrick. No longer do they represent the traditional family values or the plight of the common hard working taxpaying American. From what I have seen, many of today's Democrat Party and most of those elected under it, represent the far left liberal point of view. Don't get me wrong, as I have said before I know a good many conservative Democrats in the Massachusetts Legislature who I am happy to call friends. I would be more than happy to share their stories with you, but to be honest, I need all the conservative friends I can get. "Outing" them would serve little purpose and could result in painting a target on their backs for the liberal wing of their party to attack.

Regarding the change of the Democrat Party from the working man's party to the socially liberal party, Ronald Reagan said it best in 1984, when seeking reelection to the Presidency. In his usual style of making political points by expressing them via a personal reflection to his own life and experiences, Reagan stated:

> "I began my political life as a Democrat, casting my first vote in 1932 for Franklin Delano Roosevelt." Specifically addressing a group of mostly Democrats, Reagan continued, "I was a Democrat most of my adult life. I didn't leave my party and we're not suggesting you leave yours. I am telling you that what I felt was that the leadership of the Democratic Party had left me and

millions of patriotic Democrats in the country who believed in freedom."

Whether the traditional or conservative Democrats will ever figure out that their political party has abandoned their core values, or care enough if they do see the truth is certainly yet to be determined.   If such voters actually want a government to represent their own beliefs and values, many Democrat voters need to wake up and realize that political parties change and people should too.

Otherwise, the conservative members of the Democratic Party will continue to be left without a voice in their own political party.

Chapter Four - Size does matter…especially in government!

"I hope we have once again reminded people that man is not free unless government is limited. There's a clear cause and effect here that is as neat and predictable as a law of physics: as government expands, liberty contracts." In case you did not guess it on your own, the above are the words of President Ronald Reagan and as with most things he said while serving as President, they are just as true today as they were when he said them. Perhaps with the passage of time and the ever increasing size of government, Ronald Reagan's quote should be taken to heart even more today and certainly be at the forefront of every Republican's campaign platform.

Although happening in small and seemingly innocuous increments, the growing size and scope of government at all levels is one of the greatest threats to the freedoms we enjoy as Americans. Often, politicians and the public in general are willing to allow small increases in government's power in hopes that government will be able to solve some perceived problem we as a society are currently experiencing. However, this slow and steady erosion of our personal freedoms and personal responsibility is mounting a cumulative negative effect on the founding principles of the United States. Rather than going along for the ride, my GOP must take principle based stands to ensure freedom prevails over government expansion and intrusion.

Of course the concerns of a large and all powerful central government have been with us since our founding period. During these years, many long and heated debates occurred over the proper size and appropriate functions of the new federal government. Some of the Founding Fathers were most concerned about creating a system of government which would grow into the one they had just won their independence from. Even the discussions of creating Article II in the Constitution, the office of the

President, drew fear that a single executive would ultimately lead to yet another King George, III.

During the Constitutional Convention in Philadelphia and subsequent ratification debates, James Madison who is often credited as being the Father of the Constitution, developed a growing fear of a strong central government. It was Madison who started the work toward a Bill of Rights in an effort to protect the rights of individuals and restrain the power of the new federal government. Madison's foresight of the need to both protect individual rights and limit the power of the central government has without question been one of the keys to our Constitution's long standing success, despite the tremendous increase in the size and influence of the federal government.

Soon after George Washington completed his two terms as President, two distinct political parties began to emerge. A battle began on the issue of what the proper size and scope of the federal government should be as the nation was starting to expand its borders and influence westward. During Washington's Presidency it became obvious that the central government was practically impotent when it came to raising taxation or addressing many of the young nation's issues, including the pressing need for national defense. Two groups started to form with greatly opposing points of view.

John Adams, a son of Massachusetts, aligned himself with the Federalists who would be led by Alexander Hamilton. The Federalists, as the name implies, favored a stronger central government. The opposing point of view came from the Democratic-Republicans led by Thomas Jefferson, who was much more egalitarian and favored a sharply limited federal authority with more power retained at the state and local level. To replace George Washington, John Adam's view (under Hamilton's influence) ultimately was victorious over Thomas Jefferson in the election of 1786 by a 51% - 49% margin of victory.

Four years later with the election of 1800, once again it was Adams's big government views and Thomas Jefferson's opposing the Federalist policies. In an election that would make the election of George W. Bush in 2000 appear calm and orderly, and after much political wrangling and deal making, Thomas Jefferson defeated John Adams, along with Aaron Burr, Charles Pickney and John Jay. After this point in history, the Federalists' power had been diminished greatly. In fact, their party would never again elect a President. Quite ironically, despite the demise of the Federalist Party, the federal government has continued to grow and grow.

At the point of the founding of the United States, a credible case could be made for either view of the proper size and scope of the central federal government. Today, however, I am confident in stating that whether it be Alexander Hamilton, John Adams or Thomas Jefferson, all would be deeply concerned on how much power and influence the central, state and even local governments have over the lives of Americans.

To be clear, I do not believe that even the Massachusetts big-government liberals are ill intended as they promote their policies to save us from ourselves. From my political experiences inside the halls and backrooms of state government, I have observed many well intentioned people with seemingly reasonable ideas successfully convince others to pass yet another law, create another new government agency, or fund another new position in a shortsighted attempt to solve a perceived problem that society is currently having.

What is often lost in the debate of the underlying question or issue of the day is the long term impact on our individual freedoms and the erosion of America's principle of personal responsibility and independence. Politicians, and unfortunately often times I am including members of my GOP in this category, are so focused on the headlines and sound bites of whatever the hot current issues might be, they neglect to consider what the long term impacts are to making government just a little bit bigger, just a little more expensive, and just a tiny amount more powerful. Socialism does not happen overnight. It is a slow and seemingly painless journey, until one day a nation wakes up and realizes the government is now in control of practically every aspect of their lives. America is not at that point today, but unless we are willing to take a stand and fight now against the growth and power of government, the personal freedoms and opportunities we all enjoy and take for granted might not be there for our future generations.

The most perfect and contemporary example of a significant and what I believe shortsighted expansion of government occurred on April 4, 2006, when the Massachusetts House of Representatives and State Senate passed a bill to mandate that every citizen in the Commonwealth be required to purchase a private health insurance product. The new law also mandates that all businesses with ten or more employees provide health insurance coverage or face a new assessment. Businesses who fail to pony up and provide health insurance will likely face significant fines, loss of their business licenses and although only speculated at this time, one has to wonder if criminal sanctions might also be considered.

While I fully understand and agree with the underlying goal of expanding health care for all citizens (yep, I meant to use the word citizens), in my opinion, state government should not mandate, under the power of the state, that each and every citizen of the Commonwealth, regardless of their personal financial situation, be required to purchase a specific type of private health insurance product. It does make one wonder when we face future problems, will government's response be to mandate that everyone in our state pay for yet another product or create yet another tax?

Republicans need to take principled stands against the expansion of government, even on those issues that may "feel good" to go along with the crowd. The American people expect and deserve the GOP to be their guard at the door fighting against increased regulation of business and more intrusion into our personal rights and freedoms. When we fail to do so, we lose elections and do long term damage to the perception that voters have of future Republican candidates.

I believe health insurance is a tool and benefit that employers use to attract the employees they wish to employ. When did our society change from a free market economy where employers decide the compensation package to their employees, to this new form of government mandated socialism? When did we reach the point where government can now require all businesses to provide certain fringe benefits to all employees or be subjected to a new tax and penalty?

Do we really want to have a government that has the power to dictate, under the threat of oppressive sanctions that each and every person must purchase a certain product? If this can be done with health insurance, it is entirely reasonable to believe that in the near future the same logic will be applied to long term care insurance, disability insurance and why not life insurance. And don't think for a minute that the liberals are not thinking about these and other areas of our lives to better protect us from our own stupidity.

From a public policy point of view, I believe these types of government expansions serve as a disincentive for small companies seeking to locate or expand their business in Massachusetts. It is also likely that some business owners will choose not to treat employees as such and will attempt to classify them as "independent contractors" in an effort to avoid the new health insurance tax. This will likely result in lower state payroll tax collections as well as no longer providing these "independent contractors" with unemployment and workers' compensation benefits. This will lead to a significant number of unintended consequences which may result in a loss of revenue to the Commonwealth. It will create less worker protection with no real increase in health insurance coverage. Once again, these are just two of the many negative consequences when government expands its power and influence without careful consideration of the long term impacts on our personal freedoms and responsibilities.

While this general discussion is mostly about the threats of a growing government, it should also be about being financially honest with people. For example, as you may be aware, our hospitals are required by a Supreme Court decision to provide medical services to everyone who walks through their doors, including illegal immigrants or those who simply lie about their identity. The cost to the Commonwealth to reimburse health care providers for these services is approximately $470 million annually.

While one of the bill's stated goals is to get these individuals off of this "free care pool," the funding of this program has not seen the decrease as proponents originally suggested. As taxpayers, we will still continue to pay for the health care of illegal immigrants and non-residents. It is unclear what the state will do with those individuals who refuse to purchase this mandated health insurance product, and who seek coverage in our emergency rooms. It is my prediction that my liberal colleagues will later use this financial loophole to push harder for true universal health care, a la Hillary Clinton style, where the government operates the entire health care system.

Some political figures label the new mandated health insurance, "health care reform." While perhaps technically correct as "reforming" the health care laws in Massachusetts, at the end of the day all we really did was make government stronger and the people weaker. We did nothing to reform tort liability, mandated coverage requirement or the numerous administrative burdens on doctors and hospitals. What we did do is take away your personal decisions and responsibility to provide for yourself and your family and shifted that to a law, which tells you what you must do or face the wrath of the power of the state. In the end, personal responsibility is gone, personal freedom does not exist and the role of government in your life is greatly expanded.

Webster's Dictionary defines Socialism as, "any of various economic and political theories advocating collective or governmental ownership and administration of the means of production and distribution of goods." Government mandated and regulated health insurance sure seems to fit the definition to me and defies the principles which have made the United States the greatest nation on earth.

In reality, one reason why our health care costs are so high is that the Commonwealth already mandates that certain types of coverage are included in every policy. This new law does nothing to reduce or eliminate these mandates and furthermore it does not allow for real customer choice of insurance products as Governor Romney suggested in his original proposal. We also failed to reform the various administrative burdens on health care providers. Sadly, what we did was to mandate that everyone in the Commonwealth must purchase a health insurance policy and impose a new tax on the business community.

While some have made estimates that the cost of this program will be in the billions of dollars, a real long term projection is not possible as

Massachusetts is the first in the nation to take this approach. My fiscal fear, along with my biggest fear of becoming a socialist state, is that we have grossly underestimated the cost of this program and there will be many unintended consequences.

It should also be expected that if the new tax on businesses is not enough to fund the subsidized health care benefits for low income individuals, the Legislature will be forced to raise taxes again to make up the difference. My suspicion is that the deficit for subsidized health care benefits will be long lasting and ultimately run into the billions of dollars.

What seemed like just a bad joke a few years ago may have turned into the latest big government idea to save us from ourselves. Take for example the recent new laws to ban certain types of fat in our foods. Just a few short years ago in the context of the debate on primary enforcement of seat belt use in automobiles, opponents of the increased police power questioned in jest, "What is next after mandatory seat belt laws; laws that dictate what we can eat?" Well, be careful of the questions you ask around certain folks as you just might give the liberals another brilliant idea how they can protect the rest of us unenlightened folks from ourselves.

In December 2006, New York City became yet another governmental body to do our thinking for us. Following the passage of the new law to ban trans fats at the city's restaurants, the New York Times front-page story "New York Bans Most Trans Fats in Restaurants" the article also had the sub-headline: "A Model for Other Cities." Well, it did not take Massachusetts long to follow suit. In March of 2008, Boston public health officials unanimously approved the elimination of trans fats in restaurants and grocery stores. Boston joined the City of Brookline in banning this ingredient found in french fries, donuts and many other fried foods. As I write this chapter in 2009, there is currently another legislative proposal is the House to ban trans fats statewide (I held the bill up in Committee last session). While I cannot state with certainty whether the bill will ultimately pass, my suspicion is that sooner or later our nanny state of Massachusetts will enact yet another law protecting us from ourselves.

If the New York Times liberal writers and those who subscribe to such a big government ideologically have their way, government will ultimately assume the role of watching our personal choices and decisions as we are much too stupid to make important life decisions without their guidance.

Whether it is the banning of transaturated fats from our foods, restricting the places where cigarette smokers can inhale, banning cell phones in cars or requiring seat belt use, all such laws are enacted under the title of "public safety." What is often swept under the rug during the discussions about such issues and feel good pieces of legislation are the consequences of a larger and more powerful system of government. What the liberals consistently fail to appreciate is that our individual liberties and responsibilities are diminished with each and every expansion of government. My GOP must stand firm against each and every attempt by government to take away our personal responsibility for our own decisions. When we take such positions based upon the principles of limited government, our message effectively resonates with the voters. When my GOP remains silent or even worse, joins the liberal band wagon, even those true conservatives start to question why they support Republican candidates and the Party as a whole.

Sure, trans fats are bad, seat belts are good, and no one should smoke, but is it really government's role to make laws with penalties attached to tell us all of these things? Are Americans really that stupid? Perhaps liberals sincerely believe in their hearts that we are…

On the Massachusetts state government level, I am often in the minority of legislators who are fighting against the ever increasing power of the state and its influence in just about every aspect of your lives. Ask yourself what part of your life is totally without some governmental interference. While I am sure someone can come up with some sort of answer that will debunk my question, I remain confident in my proposition that whatever list you might be able to offer, it is substantially shorter than it was one-hundred, fifty, ten, or even five years ago.

I would suspect that most people have heard of the Family and Medical Leave Act (FMLA). This federal law passed in 1993 allows people the right to take up to twelve weeks of unpaid time off to care for a child, spouse, or parent with serious health conditions, or for women, twelve weeks unpaid leave if they are sick and unable to work during pregnancy. Seems like a fine idea to protect workers while they are caring for their loved ones. The federal law does not require an employer to pay the employee for their time off, it simply ensures the employee will have their job when they are ready to return. The law promotes taking personal responsibility for the care of your family and does not unduly burden businesses.

But that is not good enough for some folks who want to mandate a new program into yet another Massachusetts "feel good" giveaway. While the ink is still drying on the mandatory health insurance law, some liberals on Beacon Hill are now trying to push a new state law change which would allow an employee to take up to twelve weeks of PAID leave to care for newborns, adopted children or sick family members. The paid benefit would also be available to care for elderly family members, or even if the worker gets sick down the line, they could have their employer pay up.

Remember this is not sick time or vacation time (which would have to be used first), this is additional paid time off after other benefits.

There are already many reasons why Massachusetts is not an attractive place to do business. In many of our major urban areas, we have significant challenges with transportation, housing and industries that are no longer viable in our global economy. Already labeled "Taxachusetts" by some, new government regulations concerning government mandated fringe benefits are serving as a deterrent to expand or relocate businesses in Massachusetts. Think about it, if you were a CEO desiring to move to the northeast to expand your operations, would you really consider Massachusetts?

While my GOP is often accused of being the protector of big corporations, I take a much different view on such a mischaracterization. Republicans favor promoting the free market and working towards reducing government regulations which hinder positive economic activity. At the core of the GOP philosophy are lower taxes, less regulation, sound fiscal policies and decreased wasteful spending.

Not only is government generally getting bigger and more intrusive, but bigger government is getting bigger. By this I mean that the federal government is more and more in the states' business and states are increasingly involved with the affairs of local city and town government's traditional roles. One such recent example of this occurred during the summer of 2007, when the state ripped the power from local pension boards to make their own investment decisions.

During this debate the big government types took the position that because the state pension system had outperformed some of the local systems during an arbitrary period chosen by the Legislature, thus the state was justified to end the longstanding tradition of local control over the pension investments of town and county employees. To be clear, there were no votes of the local pension holders or local towns, nor were there any union bargaining units asking the state to take over their pension systems. It was just the power of the state being exercised over the power of the locals. Under the logic of "the state can do it better," the local decision making ability for where local government employees' pension dollars should be invested was shifted to Beacon Hill.

Of course, the proponents of this big government power grab neglected to mention that the state does not guarantee the level of return and the bill as passed does not contain any provision for the state to supplement any shortfalls in the local pension fund it may experience in the future. Furthermore, it did not seem to matter that the relative risk taking tolerance of the State versus the local pension boards might be different.

Yes, the state board's return had been slightly higher than several of the local boards in the period of time reviewed, but this fact alone is not a fair assessment of total performance. Many local pension boards have made deliberate decisions of reducing the risk in their equity/stock investments, which during a strong market results in a lower return when compared to the state board that has a history of being more aggressive in their investment choices. With the significant downturn in the stock market at the end of 2008, such a conservative approach by many of the local pension boards proved to be incredibly prudent.

When we experience a stock market decline, such as in 2008, it is likely that retirement boards such as Barnstable County (who purposely had decided to take a more conservative risk tolerance position) will experience a better rate of return than the more heavily invested boards, such as the state. The bill which passed, and that I voted against, still requires the local communities to make up any deficiency in the funding schedule. Also, the bill does not allow a local pension board that is taken over by the state to opt-out of the state system even if the state board's rate of return is far below projections. In other words, the state takes control of the local employee's pension dollars and the investment decisions, but provides no assurance of future returns or dollars to make up for unfunded pension liabilities. The risk stays locally and the power grows in the state.

Along with my desire to limit the State's power over local governments and the risks inherent in the bill, I also voted against the proposal because the elected Barnstable County Commissioners clearly expressed their desire for the Cape Cod Legislative Delegation to oppose the legislation and retain local decision making. As a Representative, I believe one of my primary responsibilities is to help town and county governments with their missions. My "no" vote was representing the interests of Barnstable County and not the special interest of the Beacon Hill investment community.

The Cape Cod Times newspaper took a shot at me on their editorial pages for my opposition to this bill. They were correct with their comment that I "prefer local control over big government." Whether or not our Cape Cod Times has noticed, the state and federal governments are getting bigger and more powerful with each passing year. Just in the recent past, state government has refused to listen to the people's clear vote to roll back the income tax level to 5%; mandated that everyone purchase health insurance or face a penalty; refused to allow people to vote on the definition of marriage; increased education mandates on local school districts and now has taken over local control of pension boards. And let us not forget, the state and federal budgets are at an all time high level of spending.

Under the logic of the supporters of this bill and news media outlets like the Cape Cod Times who support it, if the state can do something at lower cost than the local government, the state should do so. Does this mean we should end local control of police, fire, libraries and public works? After all, the same logic applies to the takeover of the pension systems. The bottom line is that if we do not draw a line in the sand and stop the growth of government, can we really predict what may be next to be ripped from local control?

My political philosophy is certainly one that distrusts big government in general. Thus, I believe that decisions should be made at the most local level possible. The smaller the governmental body is, the more likely it is to have the best interest of the taxpayers at hand. I, and hopefully my GOP, will continue the fight to restrain government's power. While I fully acknowledge and agree that one of government's primary roles is to care for and provide services to those in our society who are not able to care for themselves, government is not the only answer. I am continuously amazed at the increasing frequency with which Americans are looking to government as their best answer to solve whatever problem they are having. In the words of Ronald Reagan:

> "Government is not the solution to our problem; government is the problem.... We've been tempted to believe that society has become too complex to be managed by self-rule, that government by an elite group is superior to government for, by, and of the people."

Speaking of government becoming part of the problem rather than the solution, the string of big corporate bailouts by Congress at the end of 2008 and into 2009 is indeed worrisome. From government handouts to banks, insurance companies, auto manufactures and any others who could configure a way to get in line for the hundreds of billions of your money, the Democrats and sadly to say, more than a few Republicans somehow believed it was acceptable to use the taxpayers' money to interfere with our free market economic system. For those of us who share the view that it is appropriate for poorly run businesses to fail (and thus not get bailed out by the taxpayer), we also believe that a true free market restricts direct government intervention in economic matters in almost all instances. Of course government does need to regulate against manipulation of consumers and fraud among market participants.

Despite the liberal Congress and President Bush going along with most of the bailout requests, many Republican conservatives did stand up against the giveaways. For voters to understand the differences between Republicans and Democrats, Republicans needed to explain that the bailout was little more than an expensive gift to big corporations as well as an irresponsible government intrusion into the private sector. A few members of my GOP attempted to do just that.

"This massive bailout is not the solution. It is financial socialism and it is un-American" said Senator Jim Bunning of Kentucky during a committee hearing. Before the debate even got started, Republican Representative Louie Gohmert of Texas requested that the House adjourn without taking up the bailout package "so we don't do this terrible thing to America." Overall, my GOP failed their duty during the bailouts. We had a tremendous opportunity to stand up for the taxpayers and for the free market system. Unfortunately, the people across this great nation were let down by the political party which is suppose to speak for them on such issues of fiscal restraint. Hopefully, my GOP will learn this lesson and once again become the protector of the free market system.

Another great example on the federal level of how media headlines and pure politics can persuade some elected officials, including unfortunately some weak-kneed Republicans, occurred in October of 2007, when President Bush appropriately vetoed the original version of the "State Children's Health Insurance Program" bill (SCHIP).

Headlines in most every major American newspaper made it appear that the President was opposed to providing health insurance and services to children from poor families. If the critics had actually bothered to read the legislation that was first proposed and had actually studied the history of this entitlement program, they would have soon discovered that the original purpose of the State Children's Health Insurance Program was to help children whose families could not afford private health insurance, but otherwise did not qualify for Medicaid. The original legislative intent was not for the government and thus the taxpayers to pick up the tab for all childrens' health care costs. By desiring to manage all health care for children, the liberals would be moving towards their ultimate goal of the federal government operating our entire health care system. Can you smell another attempt to take a small step towards socialism and universal health care? I surely can!

The bill President Bush appropriately affixed his veto stamp to would shift SCHIP away from its original proper purpose and turn it into a program that would cover children from families of four earning almost $83,000 a year, whether they had a private health care policy or not. Under the cover of some great headlines, the liberals made their best efforts to paint President Bush as an uncaring evil man who was withholding health care to poor kids. In fact the original version of the bill was simply designed to be yet another step towards a "Hillary" type universal single-payer health care system.

In addition, under this bill government coverage would actually displace private health insurance for many children. If this proposal was enacted, one out of every three children moving onto government coverage would be moving from private coverage into the government plan. The bill also did not fully fund all of its new spending which results in hiding the true future cost. It ultimately would have resulted in likely raising taxes on all working Americans. Let us not allow the facts to get in the way of a good headline now and spoil all the fun for the liberals!

At the end of the day, I am pleased that the conservative point of view won out this time and Congress passed and the President signed a revised version of the legislation to extend SCHIP. The approved legislation comes without the unnecessary significant expansion of having the government pick up the tab for already privately insured children.

Helping poor children with their health care is a proper role for government and this revised bill ensures that this important program for America's low-income children will remain in place. Ultimately, our goal should be to move children who have no health insurance to private coverage; not to move children who already have private insurance to government coverage. Because the Republicans (most of them anyway) stood firm on this principle, we are all better off.

While most of the expansion of government's power comes from legislative and executive branches, with increasing frequency, conservatives need to be concerned about the judicial branch of government as well. In what can only be described as one of the most significant reductions to property rights in America, on June 23, 2005, the United States Supreme Court issued a controversial five to four opinion taking away certain Constitutional rights protecting private property owners.

In the case <u>Kelo v. New London</u>, the court ruled for the first time that taking private property by right of eminent domain for the purpose of economic development satisfies the "public use" requirement of the Fifth Amendment to the Federal Constitution. As a refresher for those who have not read the Bill of Rights recently, the 5th Amendment Takings Clause states, "…nor shall private property be taken for public use, without just compensation." Respect for private property rights is a founding principle of our nation and serves an important role in our modern political economy. This principle is also one that is at the core of the Republican Party.

It is my strong belief that the policy set forth in the Court's majority opinion goes against the intent of our Founding Fathers and our constitutional history. Up until this decision, private property rights have been held to the highest esteem and we as a society have made sure eminent domain takings are limited to situations where there is clear necessity to seize property in the name of the public good, such as new public hospitals, schools and transportation improvements. This decision is a direct assault on the rights of all Americans and a significant step against our freedoms.

As Justice O'Connor pointed out in her strong dissenting opinion, the court abandoned the long-held, basic limitation on government power. Under the banner of economic development, all private property is now vulnerable to being taken and transferred to another private owner, as long as it might be upgraded. This decision and general mindset of the liberals of the Supreme Court should greatly disturb every American, especially my GOP who should always attempt to restrain the seemingly never ending growing power of government.

In an effort to protect our citizens from abusive governmental takings and to make sure the Supreme Court's ruling does not adversely impact our laws here in Massachusetts, it is necessary for Republicans to expand the existing protections offered by our laws at the state level. To do this, Republicans from across Massachusetts should support a three-pronged approach that Republican legislators are attempting to move forward on Beacon Hill.

First, my GOP supported a resolution offered by Republican Leader Brad Jones titled, "Supporting Private Property Rights in Massachusetts and Protecting them from Abuse of the Right of Taking by Eminent Domain." Hopefully this will send a clear expression of the opinion of the House of Representatives that the Supreme Court's opinion is wrong and that its policy should not be applied to Massachusetts cases. While the resolution offers a strong statement of legislative intent to oppose the sort of takings sanctioned by the court, more must be done. Republicans must lead the charge to ensure the citizens of Massachusetts are not subject to an overactive Court with a liberal agenda, which increasingly seems to have a desire to be in the legislative business. All courts owe the principal of separation of powers deference to a legislature's judgment concerning the public policy of whether the government owns, or the public has a legal right to use, the taken property. It is my hope that this Resolution sends a clear and convincing message to our state courts, but this is not enough.

Secondly, Republicans must support proactive changes to the statutory components and amend Chapters 121A, 121B, and 121C of the Massachusetts General Laws. This would clearly state that the taking of property for the sole purpose of economic development, except under a few very limited circumstances, shall not be permitted in the Commonwealth.

The third line of protection for property owners and tax payers requires a state constitutional amendment to the first paragraph of Article X to the Massachusetts Constitution. Republican leaders have drafted language for such an amendment, which would mirror the statutory changes and make permanently enshrined in our state constitution the protections Americans already thought were provided by the Bill of Rights. Each and every Republican in office or seeking an elective position on the state or federal level should be talking about our efforts to protect private property rights. This is not solely a Republican or a conservative issue. This decision strikes at the core of American founding freedoms as we know them. The potential abuses of ever growing governmental power must be trimmed back as they continue to over step into our freedoms.

Back in Massachusetts, especially in the executive branch with an unfortunately increasing frequency, I am disappointed by the continuous expansion and influence of government. For another example, take the recent idea of Governor Patrick who issued an Executive Order to allow (some suggest require) state employees to volunteer their time to certain agencies and charitable organizations. Sounds pretty good at first blush, doesn't it? As a society, we should all attempt to assist those less fortunate. Spending a few of our free hours helping at a school or homeless shelter surely wouldn't hurt any of us and would likely make a positive impact on society. So what's the problem? Simply put, Governor Patrick has changed the definition of "volunteering." Under the Governor's liberal leaning logic, state employees collect their full paycheck and associated benefit while they "donate" their time. Yes, that's correct, based on the provisions of Executive Order # 479, "Establishing a Policy for State Employees to Provide Voluntary Services" issued in January 2007, state employees get paid time off to "volunteer."

While I think all organizations should promote community service and volunteering, the definition of work is where the Governor and I part company. According to the Oxford English Dictionary, a "volunteer" is defined as "a person who freely offers to do something; or a person who works for an organization without being paid." The state employees who volunteer under Governor Patrick's Executive Order are in no sense of the word volunteering as they are paid by the state for 100% of their time.

Thus, a state worker earning $40,000 a year would be "paid" almost $2000 for 12 days of volunteer work allowed by the program. Of course, assuming that very same state employee actually has work that must be done by someone else while they are absent "volunteering", additional compensation is required to hire people to back-fill shifts of those in essential positions (police, health care workers, etc.) who are off volunteering. In many cases, overtime pay will be needed for employees who have to work additional hours to complete official state work they could not perform while volunteering. But hey, it is not real money, it is just the taxpayer's dollars.

Volunteering is a great way to be involved with your local community and organizations and should be highly encouraged by elected officials and public figures. Giving freely of your time offers the opportunity to build various skills, friendships and new experiences. The concept of community service in politics seems to have changed from one of public service to one of self service. This modern liberal approach is one of a selfish volunteerism, or volunteerism for the sake of some personal or political gain. Paying any volunteer contradicts the definition of the word and defeats the patriotic contribution of volunteering. Even worse is the idea of using your tax dollars to benefit programs and services of private charities that perhaps you do not support and certainly the legislature has not approved.

It is a form of defacto government appropriation without the checks and balances of the legislative process. The public policy message of paying volunteers sets the wrong tone in our society. It is also very dangerous government action, as it might set a precedent for our government to next require the private sector employees to participate in this practice. This would be truly outrageous but certainly not beyond the reach of many far left-wing liberals who hold elective office today.

The bottom line is that whether it is mandating citizens purchase a certain insurance product, banning certain foods from our diets, providing taxpayer money for corporate bailouts or paying state employees to "volunteer," government is growing more intrusive and powerful with each passing generation. While socialism does not occur overnight, unless those who believe in the core principles of my GOP stand up and fight against each and every unnecessary expansion of government, one morning in America we might just wake up and realize we have lost our personal freedoms that we hold so precious.

Chapter Five - What part of "illegal" don't they understand?

Simply stated, "A nation without borders is not a nation." These eight simple words were spoken by Ronald Reagan and really say all that is needed to say regarding the problems of illegal immigration in America. From issues of national security, economic protectionism and even our nation's own sovereignty, I believe the most important issue our country is currently facing is the ongoing and increasing threat of illegal immigration.

Generally speaking, Republicans are rightly viewed as the party of law and order, and thus fighting against the invasion of our nation by law breakers seems to be a no-brainer for my Party to rally around and speak with a unified voice. Unfortunately, this has not always been the case in recent history.

The national illegal immigration debate is not something new, nor are the concerns of the Republican Party on the impact it has on our entire nation. During the late 1800's and early 1900's, Republicans firmly expressed their support for a systematic, fair and organized plan permitting legal immigrants to enter the United States and become a part of the American dream, but only when done so under our system of laws. For example, Republican Theodore Roosevelt stated in 1907:

> "In the first place, we should insist that if the immigrant who comes here in good faith becomes an American and assimilates himself to us, he shall be treated on an exact equality with everyone else, for it is an outrage to discriminate against any such man because of creed, or birthplace, or origin. But this is predicated upon the person's becoming in every facet an American, and nothing but an American...There can be no divided allegiance here. Any man who says he is an American, but something else also, isn't an American at all. We have room for but one flag, the American flag...We have room for but one language here, and that is the

English language... and we have room for but one sole loyalty and that is a loyalty to the American people."

Theodore Roosevelt's concern about illegal immigration continued long after he was out of the White House. It remained consistent with the general GOP tone then, as well as what it should be now, of a necessary predictable and legal process for those wishing to come to our nation and live the American dream. In a letter he wrote to the President of the American Defense Society on January 3, 1919, which by the way was just three days before Roosevelt died, the now former Republican President wrote, "Every immigrant who comes here should be required within five years to learn English or to leave the country...English should be the only language taught or used in the public schools."

Demanding the learning of English and the assimilation into our American culture and our way of life has been labeled "Americanization" and from my point of view is the just and proper approach that we must encourage all new residents to embrace. Call me old fashioned if you like, but if our great nation is going to endure long into the future, America must be based on certain principles. Many of my liberal colleagues would call this "hate speech" or label me as suffering from a cold and uncaring heart for saying as much. But I am more concerned about protecting America for future generations, than being called names by those who believe we should weaken our system of law over feelings.

To demonstrate what I am specifically talking about, during a legislative debate in the Massachusetts House of Representatives on whether or not we should provide taxpayer funded college tuition breaks for illegals, the Cape Cod Times (CCT) labeled me a Xenophobe. I must admit that I needed to pick up the dictionary to find out what those unnamed editorial writers were calling me as this was a new term for me. Well, in case you are like me and do not know the definition of a Xenophobe, here it is according to Webster's Dictionary: "A fear and hatred of strangers or foreigners or of anything that is strange or foreign."

This Cape Cod Times lead editorial appeared on Sunday, January 8th, 2006, where they once again took the position that your tax dollars should be used to subsidize the college education of illegal immigrants. While it may "feel good" for the CCT to take such a liberal point of view, from my own perspective, such a policy violates the rule of law, promotes illegal behavior, is unfair to taxpayers and puts law breakers ahead of those who follow the immigration rules. All of which are contrary to the principles of my GOP as well as the lessons I was taught by my own family.

By encouraging illegal behavior, what greater message does this send to immigrants who enter this country legally? In fact, the people who are the most upset about government subsidies to illegal immigrants are legal immigrants who followed our laws to come to America. Being a nation built on immigration and supposedly also a nation of laws, promoting a public policy of providing the same government benefits to those who break our laws as to those who obey them is nothing more than a slap across the face of every immigrant who followed the rules and procedures to come to the United States.

The issue of immigration must be looked at from two different points of view. The first dealing with those people who are in the United States legally and the second deals with those here illegally. While I believe it is the role of government to provide people with a helping hand, I do not support taxpayer dollars going to provide assistance to people of illegal status. Any Republican office holder who does, in my view, should not be supported by my GOP, as such a position undermines a core reason why so many Americans support Republican candidates.

The CCT's editorial cited that since Massachusetts is losing population, we should embrace "feel good" programs such as taxpayer funding for college for illegal immigrants in an effort to keep or encourage illegal immigrants to come to Massachusetts. This position is ridiculous and outrageous for so many reasons that a response is almost not worthy, but I have learned that when liberals say something often enough and it goes unchallenged, that the people in the middle of the political spectrum actually start to believe it if not refuted.

Did the editorial writers and those who share their left-leaning beliefs ever stop to think that Massachusetts is losing population because of our political polices such as this, or perhaps our high cost of living, growing government mandates and taxation that might be causing people to leave the Commonwealth? Unfortunately, many conservatives are leaving Massachusetts and other states in the northeast seeking a better climate, both weather and politically related! Remember that Massachusetts is one of the few states in America that is actually losing population. Our current population is approximately 6.39 million, which dropped by nearly 19,000 between 2003 and 2005 and will continue to suffer from slow growth until we ease the many burdens of living here.

While many factors account for long time residents choosing to flee the Bay State, based upon a significant number of people I speak with, the political climate is certainly one of the motivations for seeking to vacate Massachusetts. No one has ever suggested to me that if we only had more illegal immigrants that everything in Massachusetts would somehow be better.

So, back to one of those issues which frustrate the average Massachusetts citizen, tax dollars being sucked away from needed services to assist those who are trespassing in our country. Specifically on the issue of college tuition, the fact as I see it is that it is grossly unfair to force taxpayers to subsidize the college education of illegal immigrants when the Commonwealth has many and more pressing priorities. For example, some time ago, I had a disabled man who served in the Army National Guard in my office who was in desperate need of dental work, which is no longer provided to low income individuals by the Commonwealth.

This proud and modest veteran was extremely upset that the state was considering providing benefits to illegal immigrants while telling him they could not afford to repair his painful teeth. How can we as a Commonwealth tell this man who has served his country "no", but say "yes" to creating entitlements to illegal immigrants?

The proposal being constantly pushed by the liberal Democrats around the Massachusetts State House and other state capitols across the nation would actually put illegal immigrants ahead of citizens from other states. As an extreme example, but a very true one, if a solider just returning from Iraq who previously lived in Florida moved to Massachusetts to attend one of our public colleges, he would pay substantially more than an illegal immigrant who came to our country criminally. The soldier would be considered an out-of-state resident and not benefit from the in-state subsidy, but an illegal immigrant who happens to be living in Massachusetts would get a tax payer subsidized college education...whether or not they would ever be able to work in the United States.

It does seem that many times the media is looking for a specific headline and fills in the facts that can support the effect they are seeking. If the CCT's had read the actual text of the legislation, they would have discovered that the measure as worded did not limit the taxpayer subsidy to those who have already applied for citizenship. The language created a huge loophole for each and every illegal immigrant. Additionally, the bill did not limit the benefit to illegal immigrants from Massachusetts.

If passed, this measure would have created a wide open door for illegal immigrants from all over to compete with Massachusetts students. As it is unclear if citizenship will be granted to many of these students in the future, it is likely that many will never be able to pay income taxes. Thus we are paying for their education without the likelihood of gaining taxes later. But hey, why worry about the details or the actual language of the proposal when it simply feels so good to support it?

I believe that a core Republican principle is to offer legal citizens and residents with a temporary helping hand in an attempt to encourage them to become productive and taxpaying contributors to our society. The logic which my GOP traditionally supports provides that it is appropriate to make an investment in someone thus allowing them to become better educated or trained. They will then be able to secure employment and pay into the system via increased income taxes.

The real key to a sustainable system of government support is that it is both beneficial to the recipient and fair to the taxpayer. All social entitlement programs should require any government assistance to be temporary in nature and only provided to those who will be able to later contribute. The obvious problem of providing entitlements to illegals is that they likely won't ever be able to pay income taxes due to their illegal status. As we have limited resources available in our state and federal budgets, shouldn't our investments be made in folks who are in the United States legally?

Again, I just shake my head and wonder about our priorities in government. Take our foster children as a perfect example. The state has the responsibility for thousands of children who find themselves in the Department of Social Services "DSS" system. The DSS foster care programs attempt to provide a safe home and compassionate foster parents for children who are removed from their homes due to abuse or neglect, unsafe or dangerous conditions. Many times, these children remain in a foster parent's home for long periods of time and thankfully some are ultimately adopted by countless caring and loving people. Wouldn't it make good common sense from both a public policy and economic point of view to encourage and provide complete educational assistance for these children to attend college? I doubt many folks from the left or right side of the political aisle would disagree.

This is a no-brainer and should be done immediately in Massachusetts. In fact there is already a legislative proposal (Senate Bill 127 in 2008) which would waive college tuition and fees at public colleges or universities for foster children who have either aged out of foster care, been adopted from foster care or are in a legalized guardianship placement. These children are in the state's care and custody and the Commonwealth must support these young people so they can have a chance to succeed at becoming productive taxpaying citizens. Well, like so many other good ideas floating around the halls of government, the most common excuse for government failing to act is that there simply is not enough money to fund such a program for our foster kids. At the close of the last session, this bill remained stuck in committee.

This is the type of disconnection that I often speak about that pervades Beacon Hill. While many of my Democrat friends are pushing for state subsidized college tuition breaks for illegal immigrants, our foster children have virtually little chance of attending college because so many of our foster families are also struggling financially. This is not a complicated decision or choice. Government budgets and related legislation are really nothing more than decisions about our society's priorities. What I completely fail to understand is how some elected officials can put the interest of law breakers before those of our kids in foster care. It is beyond me. Members of my GOP need to boldly stand up and publicly discuss these issues during political campaigns. I am completely confident that the hard working people of Massachusetts, as well as those across America, share our same beliefs. They will support candidates who have the courage to challenge the ill-conceived policies of providing benefits to those who have broken into our nation.

Another point related to the short sighted goals of liberals conveniently neglects to mention that there is currently a law suit filed in the federal courts which could hold that programs that benefit illegal immigrants over citizens from other states is unconstitutional under the 14th Amendment to the United States Constitution. If this lawsuit is ultimately successful, any state offering discounted tuition to illegal immigrants would also have to offer it to citizens from other states. This could result in Massachusetts citizens losing the ability to have a discounted tuition all together. But hey, let's not get all wrapped up in the facts, they could mess up a good headline!

The bottom line is that it is wrong to reward illegal immigrants who have violated our laws. It sends the wrong message to those immigrants who have spent many months and even years waiting in line to enter this country legally and is grossly unfair to the taxpayers to be forced to subsidize law breakers. It is my view that the government should be allocating our resources to improving education and ensuring public safety and not for any benefits to illegal immigrants! Judging by the hundreds of calls and e-mails I received following my appearance on the Howie Carr radio show following the defeat of this proposal on the House of Representative's floor last session, I'd say that my constituents agree with me…and these are the people I have been elected to represent and the ones my GOP should be focusing on.

This issue is far from over, as the liberals keep bringing this subject up time and time again. Now they have Governor Patrick who shares their desire for giveaways for illegals. I am confident that the House Republicans I serve with will continue to do battle on this issue, but I must admit it would be a whole lot easier if the electorate would send a few more Republicans to the State House!

Teddy Roosevelt was indeed correct some one-hundred plus years ago and the modern Republican Party must take this up as one of our key platform issues if our nation and our political party are expected to survive. Only when an immigrant comes to America legally and in good faith with the specific intent to assimilate themselves to our way of life should Republicans support programs designed to lend a helping hand to live the American dream.

We can never accept a divided allegiance to America. To be clear, and before the liberal media starts calling me names again, I am not suggesting in any way that immigrants, or anyone for that matter should shed their ancestry or heritage. We should all know where we came from and show pride for who we are. But if any nation is to prosper and continue to exist, we have room for only one flag, the American flag; one language; the English language, and one rule of law, the Constitution. If we are willing to let any of these principles be marginalized because of our "feelings" for individuals, we do so at our own peril. Like so many other great nations in world history, ours will someday come to an end.

Along with the many threats to America and the rule of law and order, the problem of illegal immigration comes with a heavy financial price that all citizens and taxpayers have picked up the tab for. According to the Center for Immigration Studies, low-skilled American workers lose an average of $1,800 a year because of competition for their jobs from illegal immigrants. We know this too well in many regions of Massachusetts, including Cape Cod where countless illegal immigrant contractors are competing on landscaping, roofing and painting jobs. For each job that goes to an illegal immigrant, it is likely that a legal citizen has lost the opportunity to earn those very same wages. This problem has been magnified by the recent increases in unemployment.

While consensus estimates are difficult to ascertain, somewhere between $11 billion to $25 billion is spent by the federal government on welfare to illegal aliens each year. In addition, approximately $2 to $3 billion a year is spent on food assistance programs such as food stamps, and about $4 to $6 billion a year is spent on Medicaid for illegal aliens. Of course we need to add in the $12 to $15 billion a year spent on primary and secondary school education for children here illegally. We should also add in the costs of subsidized college tuition, transportation expenses and costs to your criminal justice system.

Some supporters of illegal immigration attempt to suggest that the taxes illegal immigrants pay, such as sales and gasoline taxes offset the costs of providing them with education, health care and other benefits. But even when illegals do find their way onto a payroll (usually via document and identity fraud), due to their usual low wages, most illegal immigrants don't even pay any income taxes. Of course, the liberal argument about illegals paying taxes assumes their income is recorded "above the table." While statistics such as these are difficult to determine with any real accuracy, each and every time an illegal immigrants is paid off the books, the state and federal taxes which are not being collected hinders government ability to provide services.

While not politically correct to speak about in some circles, illegal immigration brings public health risks that are real and serious. For example, unlike those who are legally admitted for permanent residence or who are visiting America as a tourist, illegals undergo no medical screening to assure that they are not infected with any contagious diseases or that they possess the required vaccinations to enter the United States.

Again demonstrating the wrong mindset that so many of my Democratic liberally-minded colleagues have, while they are trying to force all teenage American girls to receive a new three-shot vaccine which has been reported as a breakthrough in cancer prevention for its ability to prevent infections from some strains of the human papilloma virus (which can cause cervical cancer), these same liberals are totally ignoring the threat of illegal immigrants who often have zero vaccinations. In the name of political correctness, we are exposing ourselves to risks the liberals are ignoring and the conservatives seem to be too afraid to talk about. Republicans should be willing to discuss such matters without the fear of being labeled as something we are not.

While serious enough on its own, the public health problem related to illegal immigrants is deeper than the threat of infectious diseases. There are significant financial costs associated with illegals using our health care system. Most of the time they are doing so without paying for it. Illegal immigrants are more often than not uninsured and are using our hospital emergency rooms (who are not allowed to refuse to treat anyone) as their one-stop location for all of their medical needs. The costs of the medical care of these uninsured illegal immigrants are passed directly on to the taxpayer via higher health care costs and premiums for health insurance.

In addition to the direct costs, providing such free care is putting a tremendous strain on the financial stability of the entire health care community. Remember, the new universal health care law in Massachusetts only requires taxpaying citizens to purchase health insurance and does absolutely nothing to address the now customary use of our hospitals by illegal immigrants. As a result, the costs of medical care for immigrants are staggering and not sustainable for the long term. So, while legal residents of the Commonwealth are struggling to comply with the requirements of the health care mandates or face stiff fines, illegals continue to walk into hospitals across this state without hesitation.

For example, according to recent government reports (from the few states who dare to attempt to measure it) the estimated cost of unreimbursed medical care in California is approximately $1.8 billion per year. In Texas, the estimated cost was about $1.1 billion and in Arizona the comparable estimate was $500 million per year. Even a state such as Tennessee, which would not commonly be thought of as having an illegal immigration problem, estimates taxpayers spent about $15 million for health care services for illegal immigrants just last year alone, and this figure is growing. As far as I know, Massachusetts does not publish such a statistic. My guess is that it is some political hack bean counter's job to keep track, but it would not be politically correct to make such a figure public. After all, it might make people (taxpayers) angry...

I could go on and on about the increased taxpayer costs for education, housing, transportation, crime (including courts and prison), Social Security and welfare fraud, etc., but you should get the underlying point that the problems associated with illegal immigration are massive and complex. They literally touch every part of our economy and the American way of life. Unless we as Republicans are willing to stand up against the politically correct crowd and tell the people the way it is, the situation could easily balloon to a point of no return. In fact, some suggest that we are already there with up to twenty million illegal immigrants residing in the United States.

The hottest and most important political issue relative to illegal immigration is amnesty for those illegals who are presently residing in the United States. Legislative proposals are being constantly offered by the likes of Ted Kennedy and company. Senator Kennedy, who has been a United States Senator for more than forty years, has been very successfully promoting illegal immigration since he took office.

Our senior senator pushed the Immigration and Nationality Act or the Hart-Cellar Act of 1965. In signing that legislation into law, President Lyndon Johnson and supporters like Ted Kennedy promised the American public that his immigration reform would not be revolutionary or affect Americans in any meaningful way. During debate on the Senate floor, Senator Kennedy actually said, "...our cities will not be flooded with a million immigrants annually.... Secondly, the ethnic mix of this Country will not be upset...." I will leave it up to you to judge how wrong Senator Kennedy was or whether he ever actually believed what he was saying at the time. Time certainly has proven him to be completely wrong on both accounts.

For their part today, Ted Kennedy and his fellow liberal Democrats clearly see the amnesty recipients as potential new voters for their party and for their candidates to pander to. It has been a long standing successful political strategy of the Democrats to promote public policies which bring in new voters under their umbrella. Whether it is unions, welfare recipients, or now illegal immigrants, the Democrats have a solid history of constantly seeking to expand their base of voters and create a culture of increased dependence on government. With some estimates being in excess of tens of millions (in 2006, the total unauthorized population in the United States was estimated at 11,550,000 by the Department of Homeland Security) of potential new voting citizens should amnesty occur, the liberals feel they are on the verge of practically ensuring their electoral success for decades to come.

Barack Obama is right in line with the Ted Kennedy crowd. While certainly too new in office to have been tested on this issue, according to a U.S. News and World report article, Obama believes, "Give the 12 million people who are here illegally... many of whom have U.S. citizens for children...a pathway to legalization." A "pathway" to citizenship may sound harmless, but what it really means is amnesty for all those millions of illegals already here and thumbing their noses at the legal immigrants who obeyed our laws.

As a Republican, I wish I could say one-hundred percent of my fellow members of the GOP were always standing firm against any form of amnesty for illegal immigrants, but sadly I cannot make such an assertion. In fact, President Bush did not do himself or our party any favors with his positions on those currently residing illegally in America. Unfortunately, also joining forces with Ted Kennedy was GOP Presidential nominee Senator John McCain. He cosponsored in 2005, the now infamous Secure America and Orderly Immigration Act, as well as The Secure Borders, Economic Opportunity and Immigration Reform Act of 2007. Both proposals, while supported by President George W. Bush, ultimately failed to win approval on the floor of the United States Senate because conservatives from across America rose up and demanded that any form of amnesty be remove from the bills.

Obviously, neither the Bush Administration nor John McCain were interested in helping the Democrats register more voters. President Bush appeared to be most fearful about the impact a mass deportation effort would have on the agriculture industry and other big business concerns. While denying any association to the word amnesty, Bush's plan required that illegal workers must acknowledge that they broke the law and pay a fine to be eligible for a "Z" visa and thus be allowed to remain in the United States.

What Bush and McCain failed to mention when speaking about this subject is that after paying a fine and filling out some application forms, the illegal immigrant is now on a clear path for legal status. Such a scheme sends a clear message to those considering applying to emigrate to the United States. The clear signal to those watching America and considering whether or not to obey the immigration laws is to get here any way you can and stay underground for a while…sooner or later the government will make you pay a fine, fill out some paperwork and you will be all set!

What public policy message does that send to potential lawbreakers? Why would anyone wishing to come to America follow the rules when we forgive and forget those who break them? The answers are too obvious, but with the influences of the liberals needing new voters and a few Republicans protecting cheap illegal labor, we need to remain on guard and keep a close eye on Washington, D.C. My GOP must remain vigilant as the party of law and order. Republicans must say "no" to any and all special interest groups attempting to push elected officials in the opposite direction.

While primarily thought of solely as a federal issue, the United States Constitution does not specifically mandate states to ignore immigration. Certainly our federal Constitution does vest in Congress the authority to regulate it in several of the enumerated powers under Article I. For example, the Commerce Clause (Article I, Section 8, Clause 3) authorizes Congress to regulate commerce with foreign nations. The Migration and Importation Clause (Article 1, Section 9, Clause 1) addresses the limiting of migration and importation of "such persons as any of the States now existing shall think properly to admit." The Naturalization Clause (Article I, section 8, Clause 4) empowers Congress to "establish a uniform Rule of Naturalization." The War Power Act (Article I, Section 3, Clause 11) gives Congress the power to declare war, permits the federal government to stop the entry of every alien, and further permits the executive branch to apprehend, restrain, secure and remove alien enemies.

Additionally, the authority of Congress to regulate immigration has also been implied by the United States Supreme Court as both an incident of federal sovereignty and associated with their foreign policy powers. With all this said, there is absolutely no specific textually based exclusive denial of individual states to deal with illegal immigrants on state related issues and benefits. Granted, states cannot do anything contrary to the federal governments actions, but when the feds fail to act, states do not need to sit idly by, nor should they.

State lawmakers are increasingly and correctly stepping into the void created by the failure of Congress and the President to approve sweeping changes to our national immigration policy. Legislatures across America have passed bills dealing with a range of immigration issues, from employment laws and health care benefits to driver's licenses and the tragic consequences of human trafficking. While with good intentions, what has resulted is an uneven patchwork quilt of immigration laws across the country.

For example, Arkansas approved a law barring their state agencies from contracting with businesses that hire illegal immigrants. Louisiana has a new law forbidding the state from issuing driver's licenses to foreigners until their criminal background has been checked. Oregon made it illegal for anyone other than lawyers to perform immigration consultation work. In Texas, where human trafficking of illegal immigrants is a horrific problem through San Antonio and Houston, a new law increases the penalties and creates a more exact definition of human trafficking at the state level. These are all seemingly good public policies, but certainly there are no consistent patterns from state to state.

In 2007, over 175 immigration bills became law in some 41 states. This is more than double the 84 laws approved in all of 2006, according to the report by the National Conference of State Legislatures. More than half of the states have considered bills seeking to toughen or clarify laws related to driver's licenses or other identification as the feds continue to fail to pass anything of real substance regarding immigration reform.

While it would be impossible to discuss all of the impacts of illegal immigration in this single chapter, the foundation of the problem is that some employers are violating our existing laws by hiring inexpensive illegal labor. To make matters worse, the states are providing services and benefits to those of illegal status. With America's unclear stance on the plethora of issues surrounding this issue, it is difficult to place all the blame on the illegal immigrants themselves.

Without employment opportunities and access to public services and benefits, illegal immigrants simply would not be risking their lives to enter our borders. While dealing with actual people, it really is nothing more than the old law of supply and demand. If businesses did not hire illegals and government refused to allow access to entitlement programs, immigrants of illegal status would have virtually no reason to come to the United States in the first place.

There is no doubt that this is primarily a federal government issue; however, since our elected officials in Washington, D.C. have failed to successfully address this issue, states like Massachusetts have no other real choice but to attempt to deal with the increasing burden these illegal immigrants are placing on our health care providers, criminal justice system, educational facilities and employers who are following the rules.

In an effort to reduce the number of illegals coming to Massachusetts, I have joined a group of legislators and filed a comprehensive legislative proposal that would prohibit the Commonwealth from doing business with employers who willfully employ illegal immigrants. This bi-partisan measure is being pushed for passage in hopes of sending a convincing message that government will not condone the employment of illegal immigrants. One of those political disconnections that so many liberals seem not to be able to understand is that for each illegal immigrant who is employed, an American citizen does not have access to that job. Furthermore, wages for every unskilled worker is devalued, as illegals are almost always willing to accept wages which are less than the market rate.

Currently, there are no state requirements beyond the basic regulations of the Federal Immigration and Nationality Act for employers to verify the immigration status of someone seeking employment. Thus, employers are only required to comply with the current weak federal requirements, which provide little, if any verification of an employee's status. Our bill is entitled "An Act to Promote Fair Employment and Security in the Commonwealth" comes on the heels of disturbing widespread media reports of employers doing business with the state and the hiring of workers with questionable illegal immigration status. The bill requires the state and all businesses that contract with the Commonwealth to ascertain and verify the immigration or citizenship status of their employees through available federal mechanisms. Failure to verify will result in the suspension or loss of contracts with the state.

Additionally, the proposal targets the problem of false identification and imposes severe penalties for those who use false identification or falsify identification documents. Persons who use false identification to obtain or maintain employment from a business that contracts with the state will be subject to a fine of not more than $5,000 or by imprisonment for not more than 5 years in a jail or house of correction for not more than two years. Perhaps the threat of jail time will serve as a sufficient deterrent for employers not to hire illegal immigrants.

The legislative proposal will also require the Massachusetts Attorney General to enter into a memorandum of understanding with the United States Attorney General to collaborate with regard to the investigation and enforcement of alleged violations of Federal immigration law. This is a critical component, as the communication and cooperation between state and federal law enforcement agencies is key if our country is ever going to start to seriously address the real problems of illegal immigration. Importantly, the bill also stipulates that the Attorney General establish a toll free telephone reporting system for confidential reporting of unlawful employment of unauthorized aliens and state fair wage laws. Currently, there is virtually nowhere for someone to turn to report an illegal worker. If you think that the Immigrations and Customs Enforcement "ICE" agency will respond to such complaints, give them a try at 1-866-347-2423. Despite many hard working field agents, my own experience tells me those who run the agency are not really interested in the run-of-the-mill illegal immigrant working under the table.

The old argument that illegal immigrants are only taking jobs that American citizens don't want is at best only partially true. Over the past few years I have spoken to countless Cape Cod contractors who provide such services as painting, roofing, landscaping and masonry, who have sadly informed me that they are losing business to groups of illegal immigrants who are under bidding them. The reasons they can do so are many, including that most illegal immigrants are not paying income taxes, workers compensation, unemployment insurance or liability insurance. To make matters ever more difficult for legitimate contractors, most times illegal immigrants are paid a wage below minimum wage. This makes it virtually impossible for legitimate contractors to compete.

The bottom line is that illegal immigrants are hurting our businesses that are operating by the rules and it is time for the government at all levels to make certain that it does not directly or indirectly employ illegal immigrants. It is simply unfair to our citizens and legitimate contractors that the Commonwealth is in essence, subsidizing illegal activity by allowing tax dollars to be funneled to those who are working under the table and without proper documentation.

Some political figures, including yours truly, argue that the federal government has inadequate financial resources and manpower to enforce immigration laws and that state and local law enforcement should be empowered to reduce the effects of illegal immigration. In a positive step, several proposals have been introduced in Congress which would enhance the role of state and local law officials in the enforcement of immigration law. Unfortunately, these well intended ideas are failing to gain any political momentum and appear unlikely to pass, as many liberals and pro-amnesty types continue to question what role state and local law enforcement agencies should have in enforcing federal laws. While the federal government fails to do anything of substance, the situation grows more critical. In the time you have taken to read this chapter, about 160 more illegals have entered the United States. The Department of Homeland Security estimates 700,000 new illegal immigrants enter the United States and remain here each year. That's 1,917 per day, or 80 per hour!

Unfortunately, until the folks in Washington, D.C. get serious about this crisis, the Commonwealth and local communities will be forced to do what we can to protect our public services and legitimate business from the burdens that come with unchecked illegal immigration.

So, what would happen if by some miracle, the federal government was actually able to locate, process and deport the millions of illegal immigrants who are residing in the United States? My liberal friends will tell you that our economy will collapse as we will have a severe shortage of workers. I could not disagree more. I am confident that our employers somehow would find a way to replace the illegal workers with either legally permitted immigrants or American citizen employees. While illegal immigrant workers may increase profits for certain large employers, ultimately they are extremely costly to the American taxpayer and are harming our long-term economic strength as a nation.

The fact is that the majority of illegal aliens have few skills, little education and they work for low wages, often in the underground economy where they pay no taxes on their earnings. Would American workers, taxpayers and society in general not be far better off if we were able to decrease the number of illegal immigrants? Members of my GOP need to have the political courage to talk about such issues and make them a part of our campaigns and platforms. Not only do the vast majority of American voters agree with us, it is without question in the long-term best interest of our nation. During my 2008 reelection bid, we conducted a public opinion poll on many issues, including benefits to illegal immigrants. The poll of 769 registered votes asked: Do you feel that illegal immigrants should receive state benefits, such as tuition breaks, driver's licenses and other forms of financial assistance?

> No (580) 75.4%
>
> Yes (33) 4.3%
>
> Undecided (52) 6.7%
>
> Declined (104) 13.5%

In our enlightened Commonwealth and many other parts of America it is simply not politically correct to discuss such things, but just as my own poll, as well as countless others have demonstrated, the American people agree with conservative Republicans on this issue. We cannot be afraid to openly discuss it during campaigns or in our action as elected officials!

I would suggest that you ask yourself, what might happen to our crowded schools, busy hospital emergency rooms, accidents with unlicensed and uninsured drivers and low income housing shortage should illegal immigrants be asked to follow the law and return to their home county.

To respond specifically to the shortage of labor question, I believe that America's employers would adjust to the labor market and hire legal American citizens at a living wage. This is needed more than ever in the face of growing unemployment rates. By having fewer illegal workers, we would all benefit from more people paying their fair share of taxes because they wouldn't be working off the books. According to recent projections, this would result in an additional $400 billion in federal income taxes collected annually, and a significant revenue source for state income taxes as well.

Additionally, something that is rarely discussed outside of the financial markets, by dramatically reducing the number of illegal immigrants in America, over $100 billion annually in United States currency would not be crossing our borders via electronic fund transfers. One of Mexico's largest revenue streams consists of United States dollars being sent home by immigrants working in the United States. This is a massive and economically harmful transfer of wealth from America. Essentially, it is wealth from America's unskilled workers directly to Mexico. To make matters even worse, most of the time these funds have never been taxed by the federal, state or the Social Security Administration.

Currently, our Federal Reserve Bank appears to be working cooperatively with the Mexican government to make it even easier for illegal aliens to send money to their homeland, according to a Wall Street Journal article. "Directo a Mexico," is the name of the program which enables United States commercial banks to make money transfers for Mexican workers through the Federal Reserve's own automated clearinghouse, which is directly linked to Banco de Mexico, the Mexican central bank. While perhaps viewed solely as an administrative function by many bureaucrats, by facilitating the transfer of such a massive amount of United States wealth, we have seen the further devaluation of our own dollar and a decrease in the ability to tax earned income.

This taxpayer-subsidized Directo a México program seems to facilitate the transfer of wealth by illegal immigrants. Whether it is intended to do so or not is irrelevant, as this federal program undermines our nation's immigration laws and is a potential national security problem. There is no reason to believe that some of these millions of dollars are not going to groups that wish to harm America. Members of my GOP must demand that the Federal Reserve restrict this program to United States citizens and those who are working here legally. The Federal Reserve should also be more willing to work with law enforcement and taxation agencies to monitor all such transfers of funds. They should be allowed only when done so legally and when it makes monetary sense to our economic system.

American citizens have had enough of the broken promises from both sides of the political aisle regarding immigration reform. With a growing sense of frustration, citizen groups are forming and starting to take action. The most well known private citizen group is the Minutemen from Arizona. The Minuteman movements across the southwestern United States are grassroots efforts that seek to secure America's sovereign territory against incursion, invasion and terrorism. My GOP needs to reach out to and embrace such individuals who care enough about our nation to volunteer their time and energy to assist our Border Patrol agents. Speaking of our Border Patrol, the officers on the front lines are indeed American heroes for the most part. The problem resides in the lack of strong public policy and from a lack of funding coming from Washington, D.C.

Without a doubt, if my GOP is ever going to reconnect with the people we wish to represent, we need to wholly embrace the principles of our Party. Fighting against benefits for illegal immigrants and promoting a culture of law and order are certainly in line with what citizens want and need Republicans to stand for! Having said all this about illegal immigration, we need to do more than simply fight against the attempts by the liberals who will go on pandering to the illegals.

We need a comprehensive plan to address all aspects of the immigration issues. Discussed below are common sense positions GOP elected officials, candidates and activists should stand for:

First and foremost, we need to SECURE THE DAMN BORDER! Not with the liberals idea of "virtual technology," but with a real commitment to build an actual physical fence along the southern border. Yes, I mean Mexico! Now, I am aware we have a northern border as well which cannot be wholly ignored, but as a former police officer, if I knew of an area where the crimes were mostly being committed, I would be a fool to equally spread out my patrol time to other areas. Like any prudent law enforcement effort, we need to put our resources where the bulk of the problems are. The liberals might again accuse me of profiling, but I call it common sense law enforcement. Technology should also play a vital role in security, but come on folks, I don't care how many cameras and infrared motion detectors you have, for my money a twenty foot double fence with some barbed wire at the top and bottom is the first choice.

There is also a great deal of logic to the idea of using our National Guard units to safeguard the border. As a part of their annual training missions, members of our various National Guard units could be rotated on one-month training assignments at strategic areas of illegal migrant crossings and drug smuggling. This would provide our part-time soldiers with practical training opportunities, while providing a valuable and necessary service to the nation.

Secondly, Republicans must fight all efforts to reward illegal behavior with any form of amnesty. Amnesty policies are simply stated bad public policy and send the message that immigrants are better off breaking our laws rather than respecting them. An amnesty program like that supported by Ted Kennedy and Barack Obama is not a solution to the problem of illegal immigration. It creates a new and greater problem. This is too critical an issue and America must not repeat the mistakes of 1965 and 1986 by failing to truly reform our immigration laws and address those who are here illegally. I do not suggest that it is possible to round up every illegal immigrant and ship them back to their native country, but at the very least, when law enforcement or government officials come into contact with an illegal immigrant, it is simply wrong not to purposely enforce our laws.

Thirdly, along with a rejection of amnesty, the federal government should reduce, or eliminate if necessary, federal funding to any city or town that declares itself to be a "sanctuary" for illegal immigrants. In addition, should any city refuse to cooperate with federal law or refuse to assist federal law enforcement officials, such city or town should not receive federal assistance for a specific period of time. Reductions in federal appropriations can clearly be done under the Tax and Spending Clause of the United States Constitution and would serve a strong incentive for even our most liberal communities.

The reality is that the federal government already does this on a frequent basis, including the withholding of federal funding for highways and health programs until states comply with the "strings" which are almost always attached. If we as a nation are ever going to stem the tide of illegal immigrants flooding into our country, each and every level of government needs to be working together. My guess is that facing the threat of a loss of federal funds, even a bastion of liberalism like Cambridge, Massachusetts, which officially declared itself a sanctuary city for illegal immigrants in 2006, would likely give in. While political rhetoric and pandering is a favorite hobby for many leftists, money talks!

Fourthly, we need to invest more financial resources to enforce immigration laws. In addition to more manpower and resources for federal law enforcement authorities, this also means providing local and state police with the authority, tools and resources to enforce all of our laws, including the federal immigration laws. We also need to provide our state court judges with the ability to hold illegal immigrants who commit a felony without bail until the federal authorities assume responsibility and custody.

Bear in mind that the liberals hate this idea. In fact, when Governor Deval Patrick took office in 2007, he reversed the policy of former Republican Governor Mitt Romney which had allowed the Massachusetts State Police to arrest and detain someone when there was probable cause they were in the country illegally. Governor Patrick stated that the State Police were too busy to deal with illegal immigrants. Perhaps now we know what Governor Patrick had in mind, as in December, the Massachusetts Turnpike Authority reportedly set a $2.3 million speeding ticket goal for the Massachusetts State Police. This equates to a whopping $1.7 million increase over 2007.

The State Police on the turnpike anticipated $5.8 million in speeding ticket revenue for 2008. Income from speeding tickets for the rest of this year is estimated at $4.6 million. Quite an ambitious revenue goal, even for an ultra liberal like Governor Patrick. And don't forget that not only will you be ordered to pay the fine for the speeding ticket, but a speeding ticket will increase your insurance premium with a hefty surcharge. Thanks Governor Patrick! The insurance companies are grateful also for your service. Now I see clearly why Governor Patrick believes the State Police do not have time to arrest illegal immigrants!

Fifth, we need to enforce our wage and hour laws on employers who continue to hire illegals. Republicans should support stiffer fines and increased penalties, even incarceration of business owners for the most egregious cases. Former Presidential candidate Mitt Romney has a great idea on this subject. His plan would call for issuing a biometrically-enabled and tamperproof card to non-citizens and create a national database for non-citizens so employers can easily verify their legal status in this country. It is simple. If you don't have a card, you don't work in America. Employers who are caught employing illegal immigrants should lose any ability to contract with the government and face penalties large enough to serve as a deterrent against the financial attraction of employing illegal immigrants at sub-market wages.

States can and should also make an effort to discourage and punish employers from hiring illegal workers. The favorite liberal saying that illegal immigrants are, "only doing jobs that Americans don't want to do" is plain crap! The truth is illegals are doing work that Americans won't do for the wages the company is willing to pay. If we stopped employers from paying illegal immigrants sub-market wages, common sense and sound economic theory dictates more employment opportunities for legal residents at a more reasonable rate of pay.

Lots of things puzzle me about politicians and their relationship with labor groups, but the support of unions and organized labor of democratic candidates who support amnesty and employment of illegal immigrants is downright baffling. The rank and file union members are virtually fighting for their own jobs. Each and every time an illegal immigrant does any work (union or not), that union member has lost an opportunity to do the work themselves. Perhaps the dues paying members of America's unions will wake up one day and see what is really going on. By their continuation of supporting liberal Democrats who usually support amnesty, they are slowly but surely reducing their own wages and opportunities to support their families.

Members of my GOP should proudly walk into union halls across America and tell it like it is. Challenge the status quo. I suspect the hard working union members are only hearing one side of the story. We all too often fail to directly speak to unions as we expect them to be the opposition. While the union leaders are mostly pure partisan politicians, the members and workers are often more like my GOP than some liberal Dem any day of the week. But if they only hear one side of the story, who can blame them for believing it?

As mentioned earlier in this chapter, I have co-sponsored, "An Act to Promote Fair Employment and Security in the Commonwealth." The proposal requires the state and all businesses that contract with the state to ascertain and verify the immigration or citizenship status of their employees through available federal mechanisms. Importantly, the bill also stipulates that the Attorney General establish a toll free telephone reporting system for confidential reporting of unlawful employment of unauthorized aliens and state fair wage laws. Republicans need to embrace such proposals and talk about them everywhere they go in order to drive the political and media discussion. As stated previously, the people who are most angry with the illegal immigration are those who are here legally. I must admit that I am not optimistic this piece of legislation will pass any time soon, but we still need to keep pushing it. Republicans all across this nation, from Congress, to state houses, to local government, need to take a stand and demand our laws are enforced and obeyed. At the very least, even if we fail, we have done our duty to our nation and our Party.

The sixth area which Republicans need to promote is the improvement of our system of voting. There is clear evidence that a number of non-citizens are being registered and actually casting votes. Due to the laxity in checking the eligibility of registrants and voters, the full extent of the problem is really not known. A lack of attention by our government related to illegal immigrant voting and a total failure, or perhaps refusal to impose fines or jail time against those who cast votes illegally, should be an insult to every American legal voter. While it is both a federal and state crime to vote illegally, in all cases that I have researched for this book, I have not been able to find prosecutions of any significance.

Republicans need to demand that our voting laws are enforced and work against efforts for same day registration and instantaneous voting which clearly encourages illegal voters to participate. These proposals being constantly touted by liberals under the guise of "encouraging young people to vote" are nothing more than a smoke screen and yet another attempt to get a few more Democrat ballots cast. Registering to vote is already simple enough in America. Allowing someone to walk into a polling place on the day of the election without providing the clerk with a meaningful opportunity to verify whether the individual is a legal resident or not is simply bad public policy. Republicans must be vigilant in our promotion of legislation which will verify the eligibility of a potential new voter and support harsh penalties for those who register or vote fraudulently.

The seventh area of GOP effort should be to fight against any and all efforts to provide driver's licenses or any official governmental identification to someone of illegal status. Providing a driver's license to an illegal alien results in real and serious public safety risks. Those in favor of the proposals of issuing driver's licenses to illegal aliens have argued that it would improve national security and road safety. The security argument is outrageous on its face as many illegal aliens often use aliases and fraudulent documents in the first place. Just ask anyone who works behind the counter at one our Registry of Motor Vehicles offices about the continuous parade of illegal immigrants trying to pass documents which have obviously been fabricated. Let us not forget or dismiss too easily that any government issued identification card opens the door for other state sponsored entitlements, including food stamps, welfare and educational subsidies.

The argument offered by some liberals that safety on our roadways would increase if illegal immigrants were provided licenses, relies on the assumption that if illegal aliens are legally licensed to drive, they will all have auto insurance.

Even a state like Massachusetts, which requires automobile insurance as a condition of getting a vehicle registered, has not been enough to keep an illegal alien from canceling the policy the next day or from failing to pay the next premium. A better method is to require a valid driver's license to register any vehicle. Once again, I hate to state the obvious or be politically incorrect, but many illegals are not proficient in English, which for now anyway is the language our street signs are in. The road to citizenship must be paved with a requirement to learn English. Providing a drivers license to law breakers undermines our system of law and order.

It is not just roadway safety that should concern my GOP. Government issued identification cards of any type can and do lead to other serious consequences. For example, do you know what one of the first things that the September 11th terrorists did when they were allowed to enter our nation and start their planning to kill as many Americans as possible? They obtained a driver's license. Nineteen of the Muslim highjackers had no difficulty in collecting sixty-three driver's licenses from several states, including Florida, New Jersey and Virginia. At present, eleven states issue driver's licenses to illegal immigrants and many more, including Massachusetts have proposals to do so. My GOP must remain firm in our opposition.

The eighth area that Republicans must focus on to successfully address our nation's immigration crisis is reforming the rules concerning "anchor babies." An anchor baby results when an illegal alien woman gives birth to a child while illegally in the United States. Due to the constitutional provisions of the Fourteenth Amendment to the United States Constitution, which states that "All persons born or naturalized in the United States, and subject to the jurisdiction thereof, are citizens of the United States and the State wherein they reside," children of illegal immigrants born on United States soil have rights to remain in the United States.

What results under current law is that following the birth of that child, it also pulls the illegal alien mother, father, and siblings into permanent residency status simply by being born within the borders of the United States. As stated, anchor babies are true American citizens under our Constitution. They are thus instantly qualified for public welfare aid and the full menu of other entitlement programs.

Although birthright citizenship was never intended to be the law of the land by our Founding Fathers, and is perhaps a wrong interpretation of the Fourteenth Amendment, birthright citizenship now accounts for more than 380,000 children each year. These are children born to illegal alien mothers who become citizens automatically simply because their mothers gave birth after illegally breaking into our country.

The solution can be found in proposals such as the one offered by Representative Nathan Deal (R-Georgia) who introduced a federal legislative proposal, known as the Birthright Citizenship Act. If passed into law, it would eliminate birthright citizenship for the children born to illegal aliens in the United States by limiting the granting of such citizenship to the children of: "United States citizens or legal nationals; lawful permanent resident aliens residing in the United States; and aliens performing active service in the armed forces." Members of my GOP should make this issue a core part of all campaigns for Congress.

On the state level, in January of 2009, I filed a comprehensive legislation dealing with illegal immigration here in the Commonwealth. The package includes a measure to limit public taxpayer funded benefits to illegal immigrants; strengthen the laws as they relate to driving without a license; allow immigration status to be a factor in bail proceedings; and a bill to strengthen voter registration by requiring identification. This package has one overriding goal, which is to protect the rights, safety, and tax dollars of law-abiding Massachusetts residents from the onslaught of illegal immigration which is devastating our state's economy. My constituents have spoken loud and clear on this issue and I intend to push these pieces of legislation as a direct result to address their concerns.

The first proposal mandates that individuals applying for non-emergency state and local benefits provide identification verifying their legal residence in the Commonwealth. The legislation utilizes the Federal Employment Verification System known as the "SAVE program." Enacting this legislation would ensure that benefits go only to the citizens whose tax dollars have funded them and not to those that are here illegally. Every year we hear about the lack of funds and resources in the area of health and human services. This legislation will help limit further abuses of that system and ensure only those eligible to receive benefits will have access to them.

The second piece of legislation would increase the penalties for individuals operating a motor vehicle without a license. Current law limits fines to $100 for each conviction. This proposal would increase the penalties for repeat offenders to a fine of $500 to $1000 and allow a jail sentence of up to 30 days in the house of correction. These enhanced penalties are designed to deter such activity and penalize those who repeatedly violate motor vehicle laws by driving without a proper license and insurance. This proposal is vital in keeping our roadways and citizens safe from unlicensed operators. We as a Commonwealth have established laws to keep our roadways safe; however, many have disregarded these measures. As a member of the legislature's public safety committee and former police officer, I will not stand by and allow our traffic laws to be repeatedly violated by those engaging in illegal activity.

The third bill would allow judges to take into consideration one's immigration status when determining the amount of bail. The immigration status is currently not within the criteria for setting bail and has been problematic when illegal immigrants are released and never return for further proceedings. With the ability for judges to increase bail for those with a heightened flight risk, it is certainly likely our public safety will improve and more illegal immigrants will actually show up for their court appearances.

Lastly, but equally as important, is that we need to encourage legal behavior and provide for an orderly and efficient way to apply for legal residence and citizenship. America needs to streamline the paperwork and background checks. We need to welcome the best and the brightest from around the world to come and live the American dream. My GOP should support funding to improve and accelerate ICE processes. More than just arguing against illegal immigrants, Republicans need to be committed to building and maintaining an immigration services system that ensures integrity, provides services accurately and in a timely manner, and emphasizes a culture of respect for all who wish to abide by our laws. According to recent figures, it currently takes three years, or more in some cases, for the ICE to process immigration applications and petitions. In some areas of California, delays in processing adjustment of status applications have averaged over four years. This is an unacceptable processing period that is harmful to the applicants and the nation.

To improve ICE and the vast issues with delays in the processing of immigration applications, Republicans should support proposals for a single universal six-month standard for processing all immigration applications.

To meet this standard, the Bush Administration had requested a five-year, $500 million initiative to fund new personnel and introduce employee performance incentives to process cases more quickly. While doubtful Barack Obama will support such a plan, my GOP should make it a priority. Although certainly an expensive investment, the alternative of maintaining the current state of affairs is simply unacceptable.

There was once a day when we welcomed people from around the globe who possessed talents and ethics which would make America a better place for everyone. More than ever we need to get back to this formula today. There is no single or easy answer to solve our immigration crisis. It did not become a problem overnight and it cannot be repaired tomorrow, but the status quo of doing virtually nothing is dangerous to America and can no longer be tolerated by my GOP or the American people.

Chapter Six - Beyond "Welfare Reform"

Welfare Reform. Two words that often provoke an emotional response from both liberal social service advocates and conservative taxpayer groups. On many modern political issues voters often cannot see a clear difference between the policies and proposals of Republicans versus Democrats; however, on the issue of welfare entitlement benefits, my GOP is the clear choice for those among us who are most concerned about the role of government in our daily lives and the increasing costs of such social engineering programming efforts.

The issue of welfare benefits is the perfect example to demonstrate the fundamental differences between the goals of the two major political parties in America. While often times the media will paint Republicans as opposing welfare benefits in general, those who bother to take the time to study the specifics know full well that Republicans do not oppose welfare programs. But we do have a drastically different view of their purpose and duration than those on the left side of the political aisle.

To begin our discussion on this subject, I think we should all agree that government exists in part to provide a helping hand to those in serious distress. In other words, to help those who cannot help themselves. I further hope we can also agree that we have a moral obligation to protect our most vulnerable citizens in extreme times of need (as compared to times of want). But what happens when some of our citizens become dependent on government programs?

What should we do with those citizens who simply choose not to work and wait by the mail box for their monthly check funded by us hardworking taxpayers? Is it society's responsibility to support the unmotivated and if so, does this mean indefinitely? These questions clearly define the differing views of Republicans and Democrats on welfare and other entitlement programs. I think Republican President Abraham Lincoln described it best when he said:

> "You cannot bring about prosperity by discouraging thrift. You cannot strengthen the weak by weakening the strong. You cannot help the wage earner by pulling down the wage payer. You cannot further the brotherhood of man by encouraging class hatred. You cannot help the poor by destroying the rich. You cannot keep out of trouble by spending more than you earn. You cannot build character and courage by taking away man's initiative and independence. You cannot help men permanently by doing for them what they could and should do for themselves."

So, how do we as compassionate conservatives balance our desire to lend citizens (yes, once again I do mean only legal citizens) a helping hand, while not creating a society of generational dependence on government assistance? While this is a pretty straightforward question to ask, government has done a rather poor job at answering this question as well as implementing policies consistent with such a stated goal.

A little recent history on welfare reform is helpful to lay a foundation to our discussions. In 1996, under President Bill Clinton and a Republican controlled Congress lead by conservative House Speaker Newt Gingrich a bipartisan welfare reform law was enacted by Congress and has been credited with great success across the nation. The official title of the welfare reform measure was the "Personal Responsibility and Work Opportunity Reconciliation Act of 1996" and it replaced the failed social program known as "Aid to Families with Dependent Children" or AFDC with a new program called Temporary Assistance to Needy Families. The two key elements of the 1996 reform act were "Temporary" and "Needy Families."

Sometimes, the title of a piece of legislation is disingenuous as to the real impacts of a bill, but in this case, the title really said it all. "Personal Responsibility" and "Work Opportunity" are key to any real reform effort and the federal bill was an excellent step at reducing the lifetime entitlement mindset of the system of welfare benefits...not to mention saving the American tax payers billions of dollars.

The federal reform legislation had three stated and well intended goals. The first goal was to reduce welfare dependence and increase employment among those who were collecting welfare benefits. It is relatively undisputed that extended welfare dependence has severe negative effects on the development of welfare recipients and the children of parents receiving government subsidies. Welfare reform efforts should be intended to reduce the inter-generational dependence by moving families off the welfare rolls through increased work and education-related requirements.

Secondly, it was to reduce the number of children living in poverty. Children living in real poverty often results in a lack of nutritious food, clothing, educational material and habitable housing. As discussed later in this chapter, the definition and scope of poverty in America is certainly not what many Americans might think it is, but the goal of moving children out of despair is indeed one for my GOP to focus on.

The third stated goal was to reduce illegitimacy and strengthen the institution of marriage for those on welfare. The erosion of the institution of marriage has created enormous difficulties for children, parents and society in general. Recent statistics show that one child in three is born out of wedlock. Whether politically correct to speak about or not, compared to children born within a healthy marriage, children born outside of marriage are overwhelmingly more likely to live in poverty, depend on welfare and have significantly more behavioral problems. They are also more likely to suffer from depression and physical abuse, fail to succeed in school, abuse drugs and alcohol and sadly end up serving time in prison. While the left-leaning folks might not overtly support these worthy goals of strengthening marriage, in the general public's eyes, they are all worth the effort.

During the debate on the proposal to make it more difficult to remain on welfare for life, the liberals screamed that the poor would be in the streets and that America had lost its moral soul for those who were suffering a financial hardship. Ultra liberal Representative Charles Rangel, a New York Democrat, stated on July 31, 1996, as the bill passed against his strong opposition, "Nobody wants to be against welfare reform. I just didn't think that this bill dealt with the problem that we have with our children. It says that the mothers will have to find work for two to five years, and that's if there's no work available."

Representative Rangel and others who vehemently opposed a work requirement unsuccessfully used the weapon of fear to persuade other members of Congress to oppose the bill, suggesting the end of the world for the poor was just around the corner. Many other Democrats made similar claims of the pending despair, but of course, they were all 100% wrong. Even with the recent economic recession, conditions have greatly improved for the poor since welfare reform was enacted.

In the thirteen years since the welfare reform law was passed in 1996, the social conditions have changed in exactly the opposite direction from those predicted by Representative Rangel and his liberal friends in Congress. If you were to view the video clips from the talking heads on our televisions in 1996, you would believe that requiring those on welfare to look for work and to limit the duration of benefits was going to result in the death of millions of single mothers and their children. Like so many issues, the liberal media attempts to invade our homes via the electronic media and make us feel bad about ourselves for believing in the principles of Abraham Lincoln cited earlier in this chapter. For just once, I would like to see these news media outlets go back in time and hold their liberal commentators and politicians accountable when they end up being so terribly wrong.

There are not many things that President Clinton did in the oval office (or in that infamous connecting hallway) that I agree with, but his signature on the welfare reform bill was the correct decision for America from both a budgetary and public policy standpoint. Although my GOP did not have a President in the Oval Office at the time, they were still able to control the agenda on welfare reform by passing the issue in Congress and using the upward pressure from the American people to leave President Clinton with no other meaningful choice but to sign the welfare reform legislation. This is yet another example of Republicans staying true to core principles of their party and getting a necessary job done. When Republicans aggressively promote efforts such as this, the American people support our efforts on election day and America is a better nation for it.

History has proven that Newt Gingrich and his fellow conservatives were correct. Despite the liberals passionately criticizing the legislation and predicting that it would result in substantial increases in actual poverty, reforming our welfare entitlement benefit program has been extremely effective in meeting each of the previously discussed goals. Not only did the reform not result in throwing children onto the streets, welfare reform sent the child poverty rate tumbling, from 20.8 percent in 1995, to 16.0 percent in 2007, according to the National Center for Children in Poverty. More recent statistics discussed below, along with anecdotal evidence, strongly suggests that the trend is continuing downward some thirteen years since the bill was originally enacted.

In minority communities, where welfare dependence had done the most damage at maintaining a generational reliance on such programs, the decline has been even more dramatic. According to the Department of Health and Human Services, when a review of the legislation was last conducted, welfare reform has helped to move 4.7 million Americans (with a higher percentage success rate in minority communities) from welfare dependency to self-sufficiency within just a few years of its passage. In fact, the number of welfare caseloads has declined by 54% since the passage of welfare reform in 1996.

Having a serious discussion on welfare is not really complete without honestly looking at the issue of poverty in America. According to information supplied by the United States Census Bureau in their Annual Report on Poverty in the United States, there are approximately thirty-seven million "poor" people living in the United States, which is about the same number as in the preceding years. As a percentage of our total population, the report stated that 12.6 percent of Americans were poor. The percentage of poor people in America has varied from 11 percent to 15 percent of the population over the past few decades. In Massachusetts, the percentage of those living in poverty has remained around 10%.

Statistics are helpful to understanding any issue, including welfare and poverty, but there is almost always much more to be learned from looking at the particulars behind the raw numbers. As a starting point, Webster's Dictionary defines the word "poverty" as, "the state of one who lacks a usual or socially acceptable amount of money or material possessions" and to most Americans it also suggests that a person or family living in poverty likely has the inability to provide their family with nutritious food, proper clothing, needed medical care and reasonable housing.

When you go deeper, beyond the numbers of thirty-seven million persons classified as "poor" which certainly sounds disturbing as it represents a significant amount of our total population, and while real hardships certainly do occur, they are very limited in their scope and severity. In fact, the significant majority of those classified as "poor" live in situations that would have been considered to be middle class just a few generations ago. The following are facts about persons defined as "poor" by the United States Census Bureau and were taken from various government reports as compiled by the Heritage Foundation in August of 2007:

➢ Forty-three percent of all poor households actually own their own homes. The average home owned by persons classified as poor by the Census Bureau is a three-bedroom house with one-and-a-half baths, a garage and a porch or patio.

➢ Eighty percent of poor households have air conditioning. By contrast, in 1970, only thirty-six percent of the entire U.S. population enjoyed air conditioning.

➢ Only six percent of poor households are overcrowded. More than two-thirds have more than two rooms per person.

➢ The average poor American has more living space than the average individual living in Paris, London, Vienna, Athens and other cities throughout Europe. These comparisons are to the average citizens in foreign countries, not to those classified as poor.

➢ Nearly three-quarters of poor households own a car; thirty-one percent own two or more cars.

➢ Ninety-seven percent of poor households have a color television; over half own two or more color televisions.

➢ Seventy-eight percent have a VCR or DVD player; sixty-two percent have cable or satellite TV reception.

➢ Eighty-nine percent own microwave ovens, more than half have a stereo and more than a third have an automatic dishwasher.

While I am in no way suggesting that we should not be working to reduce poverty in America, we must do so honestly and recognize that the solutions are not simply about dropping money from the sky. Republicans have done a good job at fighting for employment and educational opportunities for those living in substandard conditions. "Lessons Learned the Hard Way" a book written by Newt Gingrich stated the effort this way:

> "I wanted that GOP majority to be a certain kind of majority, one based on ideas. I also wanted it to represent a party that would be open and beckoning to a majority of our fellow Americans not because we were handing out goodies to people but because we had better proposals for them and their families' futures. In short, I wanted to do nothing less than replace the welfare society with a society full of opportunity. I dreamed of a society that would begin to move the powers of a smothering, over centralized federal government back to the states and local governments back into the hands of volunteers much closer to the people and better aware of their real needs and wants."

So, with all the successes from the 1996 Act, why in 2009 would I bother discussing an old issue which has reportedly been successfully resolved? The answer is two-fold. First, not everything has been reformed that needs to be. The 1996 law positively affected only the basic welfare program. Other social engineering programs, such as food stamps and Medicaid still operate under the old rules, which continue to create and foster a long term dependency on government. Based upon the tremendous success of the federal government's efforts to reform welfare, our Republican members of Congress should take the brave next step and challenge all social entitlement benefits to ensure more citizens become self-sufficient contributing members of society.

Speaking directly to the food stamp program, the Government Accounting Office reported that over twenty-five million Americans received more than $16 billion in food stamp aid from the United States Department of Agriculture's Food and Nutrition Service, and this figure is likely to be higher with the recent economic downturn. Taken by itself, it is hard to know if these figures are significant or not. Certainly a program that provides food to those facing poverty is a worthy use of our tax dollars, but the problem is not the intent or goals of the program. The concern that Republicans should be most focused on are the abuses and fraud inherent in the system. The bottom line is we need to find a more efficient way to administer the program and ensure that the funding is actually going to provide nutritious food to those who are not able to provide it for themselves.

Certainly there has been some progress since the days of the paper coupons, which were often redeemed to food stamp traffickers, who bought them for cash at less than their value and sold them at full value. The cash received illegally for food stamps has been used to buy everything from drugs, alcohol, tobacco products, and cars to firearms.

In response to these abuses, the government instituted the mandatory EBT system. The EBT card is similar to an ATM card. A person receiving food stamps receives a card and a personal identification code. When a purchase is made the card is swiped, a personal identification number is entered and the available money is deducted electronically from a user's account leaving a balance to be spent later. The new system however, has not solved the problem of selling the value of the cards for other non-food items. People on the program can and do still sell their cards along with their identification numbers for cash or whatever they can find a buyer for. A WBZ television report in November of 2008 found some thirty-seven stores in Massachusetts had been found to be fraudulently providing cash for food stamp transactions. Nationwide the U.S.D.A. estimates that over $200 million annually is attributed to fraud and theft.

What is needed to decrease the abuse of EBT cards is simple. In association with a Republican backed proposal titled the Real ID Act, food stamp recipients should be required to present a new style of EBT card. The new card would include a digital photograph, anti-counterfeiting features and machine-readable technology to track the food stamp recipient's actual food purchases. The Department of Homeland Security would be charged with drafting the details of the regulation and the federal government could rightly withhold federal funding to any state that did not comply with the ID requirement.

The food stamp program remains as one of the largest "means tested" social welfare programs in America. The term "means test" refers to the government process undertaken to determine whether or not an individual or family is eligible to receive certain types of benefits from the government. The test consists of quantifying the applicant's income, or assets or a combination of both. While not a perfect test to determine whether government assistance is appropriate, Republicans should support such investigations prior to the approval of any entitlement programs.

Along with the initial income verification, periodic checks must be made to ensure the continued need of benefits. Although nearly all food stamp households contain working-age adults and most are able to seek employment, very few of these individuals are gainfully employed. There is no requirement that anyone seek employment as a condition to receive more food stamps. According to recent statistics, fifty percent of food stamp funding goes to individuals who have received them for more than eight years, and in many cases much longer. This is where my GOP should have the political courage to stand up and say enough is enough! Just like welfare reform, if anyone is going to receive food stamps and they are able to work, a good faith effort to seek employment, attend school or perform community service should be a requirement for the continuation of benefits.

This is yet another example of a well intentioned social program which has resulted in just the opposite desired effect. The current food stamp system has failed to realize the lessons learned from welfare reform. What we have is a system that provides one-way handouts, rewards non-work and ultimately fosters a long-term dependence on government for its food supply. Such programs are actually harming children and increasing the poverty levels by not providing an incentive to better ones own situation. Notwithstanding the disabled who are not able to work, Republicans should never support a social benefit program that does not at least require an attempt by the recipient to make verified efforts of getting off government support. Again, with the exception of citizens who are permanently disabled, all social welfare programs must be temporary in nature or we will never be able to break the system of generational dependence that faces so many who suffer in poverty.

To repair and improve the current food stamp program, and in order to actually provide a long term effort to raise people out of poverty and into productive taxpaying citizens, the GOP should lead a new reform effort in the same manner as the Aid to Families with Dependent Children program did in 1996. The people of Massachusetts and across this great country agree with Republicans on this issue; however, in recent years there seems to be a lack of political courage to talk about the poor. Our goal is not simply to reduce government expenditures. My GOP sincerely wants to provide people with the motivation and tools to take advantage of the opportunities that America offers.

The foundation on any entitlement benefit program must require that all able-bodied adults be required to work as a condition of receiving any form of aid. If an applicant cannot find a private sector job, he or she should perform community service work or other activities directed at self-sufficiency, including seeking approved educational opportunities. If any applicant refuses to engage in required activities, he or she should be denied access to the program. While perhaps viewed as harsh by some, by accepting the liberal policy of allowing someone to remain on food stamps for life, government is doing more harm than good by creating an incentive to stay home.

I believe that most Americans believe that food stamps or any other welfare type benefits should be temporary in nature. This is untrue when it comes to the food stamps program of today. In many cases, the majority of recipients is, or will become long term dependents of the system and if we believe the statistics, so will their children. The overwhelming majority of food stamp spending is received by individuals who have been or will be participants in the program for multiple years or even decades. As discussed, recent statistics show that nearly seventy percent of all food stamp spending went to households which have received food stamps for five years or more, and half of all food stamp spending went to individuals who received aid for eight or more years. Who do we really think we are helping by allowing this to continue?

Speaking directly to welfare benefits for Massachusetts residents, some in our state government are constantly working to exempt its residents from certain provisions of the federal welfare reform act. Specifically, some of my liberal friends are promoting ways to circumvent the tough work requirement sections of the federal law by expanding the loopholes which in many cases allow welfare recipients to avoid the legislative intent and successes of the Welfare Reform Act of 1996.

For example, you will likely be surprised to learn that Massachusetts is one of only five states in the entire nation without a lifetime limit regarding how long and how much recipients can collect benefits. In other words, assuming they qualify, a person can go on and off welfare throughout their entire lifetime, creating an economic incentive to become more dependent on government.

The conventional economic analysis of welfare benefits and similar entitlement programs is based on the work disincentive issue. For example, I would suspect that most people have heard someone state that they would like to work, but if they earn a certain level of income, their government benefits will be proportionately reduced. This is especially true for parents receiving welfare who have children and must also pay for childcare if they go back into the work force. From a purely economic point of view, it is often more of a cost benefit to stay at home. Republicans need to recognize this and lead the way toward new social welfare reforms that do not immediately penalize those who seek employment. Granted, we cannot afford to keep people on a government check indefinitely while they are also gainfully employed; however, we should do a better job at encouraging employment by allowing Americans to continue to receive government benefits while they get back into the work force. While somewhat more costly in the early stages, the long-term benefits to the welfare recipient and society will result in significant cost savings in the future.

My GOP should lead the way at reducing the unnecessary barriers to getting off welfare programs by helping families move toward self-sufficiency and financial independence, ultimately saving taxpayers billions.

In most cases, both the short-term and long-term incomes of families will be significantly enhanced if parents avoid welfare dependence and remain in the labor force or even work part time while seeking full-time employment.

By recognizing the sincere effort of people who are trying to provide for themselves and not withholding government assistance in the short term, we are better positioning these families to once again be self-sufficient taxpayers. To permanently move more citizens out of poverty, welfare recipients must be encouraged to be engaged in constructive work-related activities and not just some sham program. Today however, a substantial portion of government entitlement recipients are idle on the welfare rolls sitting at home watching television, which of course creates the continued dependence on Uncle Sam.

Despite welfare being thought of as primarily a federal program, the annual cost to the Massachusetts taxpayers is hundreds of million of dollars, and also despite the passage of the Federal Personal Responsibility and Work Opportunity Reconciliation Act of 1996, most Massachusetts welfare recipients are not required to comply with the intention of the federal act known as "Welfare to Work." Under the federal rules, welfare recipients are limited to a five-year lifetime benefit. When the act was passed, Congressional Republicans correctly understood that without a provision mandating work by all able bodied adults on welfare, we as a society are actually harming the very person we are trying to help. Just like F.D.R understood in the years following the Great Depression, Republicans today know that work is essential to any beneficial social welfare program.

Although it may "feel good" to my liberal colleagues to provide lifelong benefits to welfare recipients without requiring work, it is my own belief and should be a core value of my GOP, that we as a government are not doing the recipient or the taxpayers any favors by allowing such a dependence on government. The goal of government programs should be to provide citizens with a safety net until they can get back on their own feet and not create a lifetime free ride. To be clear, I am not referring to individuals with legitimate handicaps or our low-income senior citizens. But I think we all have heard about or actually seen someone abusing the welfare system. It should go without saying, but all of us should remember that each dollar provided to someone taking advantage of the welfare system is one less dollar we have to spend on those truly in need.

Fraud is certainly also a significant part of the problem. Entire books have been written about the egregious stories of creative scams to collect welfare checks. On a national level, the federal government needs to do more to combat fraud and my GOP should lead the way without hesitation. We cannot worry we will be labeled as being cold hearted, or whatever badge the liberals wish to pin on us, each time we attempt to discuss responsible improvements to social entitlement programs.

As previously discussed in this chapter, those who receive benefits should have an identification card with their photograph and other identifying information. In addition, all states should be required to use an automated fingerprint imaging system such as they do in New York. This technology is used to prevent and determine if someone is receiving assistance in two or more counties at the same time, many times under different names. All states should also have some form of an initial field investigation process before the benefit period begins. Investigators should conduct home visits to ensure the eligibility of an applicant and not rely solely on the information presented on an application. Believe it or not, there are criminally wanted people collecting welfare at post office boxes. States must have a system in place that matches their entitlement recipients to databases with the criminal justice system. This system should also check with the Department of Corrections for those individuals receiving any form of assistance and ensure that no one who is in our county jails and state prisons is receiving benefits. Unfortunately, there have been several media stories of people residing in jail while their welfare checks are deposited into their bank accounts waiting for their release.

Also, in a further effort to reduce fraud and bring credibility back to the welfare system, all states, including Massachusetts, should have a toll-free hotline to report cases of suspected entitlement fraud, including abuses of Medicaid, food stamps, housing and welfare benefits. I do not suggest that such efforts will lead to a one-hundred percent guarantee of ending fraud, but even my Democrat friends should realize that each and every dollar we save with sound fraud prevention is another dollar that is available to go to a truly needy family.

So, along with national efforts, how do we reform the welfare system in Massachusetts to both save taxpayers money and help those in need of assistance? When in office, Governor Romney had offered a few ideas which I believe have real merit and should become a platform and campaign issue for Republicans everywhere in the future. First of all, it must be the goal of welfare to get people (who are able) back to work. At its foundation, the welfare system must have a strong and real "welfare to work" requirement which should include educational opportunities, job training and subsidized child care. Any reform effort should include only an initial benefit period where a qualified individual or family is provided with financial assistance; however, this period should be relatively short.

Able-bodied individuals should be required to seek employment without delay and the continuation of benefits must be contingent upon proof that the recipient is actually seeking employment. Should someone not be able to locate employment within a reasonable amount of time, a welfare recipient should have the choice to enter a job training program or a public service program. There is absolutely no reason why an able-bodied healthy person should be able to receive tax payer dollars without demonstrating a sincere effort to improve their situation or providing a community service.

Perhaps we should look to the Democrat who is often criticized for creating many of the social programs we have today. We have much to learn from President Franklin Delano Roosevelt's work programs of the 1930's and 40's. His work programs were centered on putting people to work on community service projects and not simply mailing a welfare check. Roosevelt's efforts not only created countless community projects, but created a generation of productive and proud citizens. F.D.R.'s programs had the correct intent, as they focused on providing a paycheck for a day of work. These measures included the Works Progress Administration, which set up a national relief agency that employed two million Americans. Other programs, such as the Tennessee Valley Authority, built dams and power stations, controlled floods, and modernized agriculture and home conditions, especially in the poverty-stricken areas. All revolved around putting people to work in exchange for financial benefits.

The difference between F.D.R.'s programs of the Depression era and modern day Democrat efforts are drastic. I believe F.D.R. would be disappointed to see what his temporary job based programs have become today. While I believe Roosevelt truly intended his social programs to be a temporary helping hand to the most desperate in our society, the efforts of the liberals today are designed to promote a culture of dependence on government handouts, thus creating a base of voters who will only support candidates who vote in favor of an ever-expanding menu of benefits. After all, the more people who rely on a government entitlement program to support their family, the more available voters there are to pander to for the politicians who support more social welfare programs.

Whether we choose wage supplements, job training, community service work, maximum benefit time limits or participation mandates, which are all appropriate reform efforts and should be lead by Republican elected officials and those running under the GOP banner, we must creatively engage welfare clients with the goal of maximizing the total number who actually obtain employment while limiting the period of benefit collection. Doing anything less leads to excessive government spending, and equally important, does a tremendous disservice to the welfare recipient. The famous Chinese Proverb of, "Give a man a fish and you feed him for a day. Teach a man to fish and you feed him for a lifetime," accurately describes the GOP philosophy.

Perhaps it goes without saying, but Republicans should promote a mindset that does not encourage Americans to look to government first when faced with a legitimate need for a helping hand. Republicans should work towards and support concepts such as Presidents Ronald Reagan and George W. Bush's Office of Faith-Based and Community Initiatives, as well as other ideas designed to engage the local community and church leaders, instead of simply providing directions to the local welfare office.

In 1982, President Ronald Reagan created quite a controversy when, in the context of his welfare reform efforts, Reagan suggested that people should not look first to taxpayers and government for help. President Reagan held the position (one which I fully share) that charitable, including religious institutions, should be the primary source for assistance to those in need of temporary assistance. Reagan suggested that if every church in America would simply take care of ten families in need, we would be eliminating practically all government welfare programs. Of course, this is not a new concept. Not so long ago, neighbors helped neighbors and members of the church rallied around one of their own in need. Are these days over forever? I certainly hope not. With the encouragement of a more vocal voice from members of my GOP, government can provide incentives for local people to once again assume the responsibility of helping each other out in times of need.

Before my liberal friends get their feathers too ruffled, I agree that in order to comply with precedent of the United States Supreme Court, government must not promote any religious activity or fund any organization that discriminates on the basis of religion when providing taxpayer-funded services. Having said this, equally important is that no organization should be disqualified from receiving federal funds simply because it displays religious symbols, has a statement of faith in its mission statements or has a religious leader on its board.

When presented with such a proposition that faith-based institutions can and should be encouraged to take a more active role in the fight to reduce poverty, left-wing liberals usually counter the suggestion with a First Amendment Establishment Clause argument. They argue that those in need should not be forced to take financial assistance from a religion with which they do not perhaps share the same beliefs. It is kind of funny that these same liberals never seem to mind using tax dollars for funding their liberal social causes, many of which offend conservative minded taxpayers.

When rebutted with the fact that often times charitable and religious groups are more effective and efficient than government when it comes to providing assistance and delivering services, often times my left-wing friends will next go off into a Constitutional analysis, known as the "Lemon Test," which is from a famous 1971 United States Supreme Court case on government involvement with religion: <u>Lemon v. Kurtzman</u>. While often misquoted by the left as prohibiting any indirect relationship between government and religion, the decision held that government's action must have a legitimate secular purpose; the government's action must not have the primary effect of either advancing or inhibiting religion; and the government's action must not result in an "excessive government entanglement" with religion. If any of these 3 prongs of the court's test is violated, the government's action is deemed unconstitutional under the Establishment Clause of the First Amendment to the United States Constitution.

What those on the left are forgetting is that Ronald Reagan and George W. Bush were not advocating that government be directly involved or be excluded from the system, and that is exactly the point. President Reagan was completely correct in his view that simply because religion is indirectly associated with a social services program should not exclude any religious group from participating and making their community a better place. Faith-based groups that offer welfare-to-work programs are less dependent on government funds than secular organizations that offer the same services and do not have an incentive to keep participants addicted to the program. In fact, just the opposite is true.

Any discussion of welfare benefits and other entitlements is not complete without touching on the impact that illegal immigration is having on the overall cost to the taxpayers and fairness to United States citizens who are often told they cannot receive benefits as there simply is no funding remaining in the program's budget. While consensus estimates are difficult to ascertain, somewhere between $11 billion to $25 billion is spent on welfare to illegal aliens each year. In addition, approximately $2 to $3 billion a year is spent on food assistance programs such as food stamps, and about $4 to $6 billion a year is spent on Medicaid for illegal aliens. Of course we need to add in the $12 to $15 billion a year that is spent on primary and secondary school education for children here illegally. We could add in the costs of subsidized college tuition, transportation expenses and costs to your criminal justice system. Next time a tax, fee or toll is raised because government has a "revenue" shortfall, remember how much money is being wasted or inappropriately spent on illegals.

As a part of both future welfare and immigration reform efforts, Republicans must first work to revise the rules concerning "anchor babies." As discussed in a previous chapter, an anchor baby results when an illegal alien woman gives birth to a child while illegally in the United States. Due to the Federal Constitutional provisions of the Fourteenth Amendment, what results following the birth of that child is the law also pulls its illegal alien mother, father and siblings into permanent residency simply by being born within our borders. As stated, anchor babies are true American citizens and thus instantly qualify for public welfare aid. While primarily a problem that needs to be addressed under GOP immigration reform efforts, we must recognize that there are substantial impacts on our welfare spending, and more must be done by my GOP to ensure that only legal residents of the United States are accessing benefits funded by the American taxpayer.

We need to build on the successes of the 1996 reforms and continue to move more welfare recipients into jobs and off the welfare rolls. Elected office holders from the GOP must make sure that illegal immigrants never gain access to any of our taxpayer funded benefits. It is a betrayal to our platform of the party of law and order. Equally important, it sends the wrong public policy message to citizens and non citizens alike. America is the land of the free (and the brave), but "free" was never intended to mean "free" money from the government for everyone who wanted it. "Free" in

America should stand for the principal that along with the freedoms we all enjoy, comes a necessary personal responsibility to take care of yourself, your family and your neighbors. Welfare reform in 1996 was a strong step towards getting back to such principles, but much work remains to truly become a compassionate nation.

The bottom line is that there is absolutely no reason why an able-bodied welfare recipient should not be required to make an effort to become a productive member of society. Not only can we no longer afford lifetime welfare benefits, but philosophically my GOP should never be creating citizens who are dependent on government.

Chapter Seven - It is not just about the income tax roll back and gay marriage!

"We hold these truths to be self-evident, that all men are created equal, that they are endowed by their Creator with certain unalienable Rights, that among these are Life, Liberty and the pursuit of Happiness. That to secure these rights, Governments are instituted among Men, deriving their just powers from the consent of the governed, That whenever any Form of Government becomes destructive of these ends, it is the Right of the People to alter or to abolish it, and to institute new Government…"

As any casual student of history knows full well, the above words are directly from the United States Declaration of Independence as adopted on July 4, 1776, which declared that the thirteen colonies were now "Free and Independent States." Quite unmistakably, from reading the text of this founding document and further studying the writings of our Founding Fathers, we know it was their obvious and unequivocal intent that the power of government reside with the people and not with the government itself.

In fact, the Massachusetts Constitution, which is the oldest constitution in continuous use in the world, embraces these same principles. Authored by John Adams, the preamble outlines the true purpose of government:

"The end of the institution, maintenance, and administration of government, is to secure the existence of the body politic, to protect it, and to furnish the individuals who compose it with the power of enjoying in safety and tranquillity their natural rights, and the blessings of life: and whenever these great objects are not obtained, the people have a right to alter the government, and to take measures necessary for their safety, prosperity and happiness."

While not frequently discussed in today's political climate, included in these rights is the right of citizens to change or replace the current government all together when it no longer serves the best interest of the people it purports to be representing. Later in chapter nine we will discuss how the Second Amendment is about a lot more than just guns, but for now let us be clear, our Founding Fathers did not trust government and thus they loaded up the Constitution and the Bill of Rights with numerous protections concerning individual rights and limits on government's power.

It was not only the original Founding Fathers who shared this view of ultimate control of the government belonging to the people. Abraham Lincoln once said, "Our safety, our liberty, depends upon preserving the Constitution of the United States as our fathers made it inviolate. The people of the United States are the rightful masters of both congress and the courts, not to overthrow the Constitution, but to overthrow the men who pervert the Constitution."

Lincoln again reinforced this view while giving the Gettysburg Address on November 19, 1863, when he uttered the famous words, "…that this nation, under God, shall have a new birth of freedom and that government of the people, by the people, for the people, shall not perish from the earth."

From my experiences of serving as a state legislator, as well as being an observer of Washington, D.C. beltway politics, few too many elected officials today share the views as stated in the above quotes by honest Abe Lincoln. At its foundation there seems to be a drastic difference in political philosophy regarding what the proper role of an elected member of a legislative body is. For example, what should a legislator do when he/she does not agree with the articulated majority of voters in their respective district? In other words, does an elected official represent their own views or should they reflect the will of the majority?

John Adams, the author of the Massachusetts Constitution and second President of the United States, wrote extensively on the subject of a representative form of government, and while he may have ultimately preferred a pure republican form of government over a true democracy, Adams often wrote of his belief that the people must indeed be careful who they select to speak for them in the legislature or else be faced with unresponsive representation:

> "The principal difficulty lies, and the greatest care should be employed, in constituting this representative assembly. It should be in miniature an exact portrait of the people at large. It should think, feel, reason, and act like them. That it may be the interest of this assembly to do strict justice at all times, it should be an equal representation, or, in other words, equal interests among the people should have equal interests in it."

Some (mostly the extreme liberals) believe that once you have been elected by the voters of your district, you have carte blanche to follow your own views and opinions. In other words, since the electorate put someone in office assumably knowing what their political beliefs are or would be, such an elected official can now solely promote their own personal political agenda.

The alternative point of view and the one that I personally share is that the voters entrust in you a sacred relationship to represent their beliefs and interests. Under this school of political theory, you are primarily in office to speak, advocate and fight for their interests and the overall good of your district. Of course an elected representative can only do so when it is clearly known what the majority view of any given political issue is. Often times, there is no practical way to know how the majority of the constituents feel about many of the votes a legislator takes during their term in office.

When an issue does arise for which there is no apparent public interest or outreach to the elected official, he or she is left with little else to do except make a good faith assessment whether the particular measure is beneficial to their constituency. This is a part of the trust voters invest into their elected officials and the reason that the electorate is so quick to cast aside someone who turns out to be a flip-flopper, or even worse, someone who goes back on their promises. Did someone say, "No new taxes?"

However, many times the elected official does have a sense where the people of their district are on a given subject. There is no clearer indication of the will of the people as when they speak at the ballot box via a referendum question. While certainly not quite as frequently as states like California, Massachusetts' citizens have often exercised their constitutional right to redress their government by putting forth ballot questions and proposed amendments to the state's constitution for the voters of the Commonwealth to have their voices directly heard.

While this sounds logical and vanilla enough to grasp as a fundamental right of Americans to control and direct their government, the sad truth is that more often than not, despite what the majority of voters say at the ballot box, too many elected officials are disregarding the voting results and running rough shod over the enshrined constitutional rights of the voters.

The reasoning for the right to petition or redress government in the first place, is to provide citizens with a viable remedy when they collectively believe their government is oppressing them by violating their rights. This right exists as sometimes elected officials are simply not listening to the collective will of the people as to how government should be operated. When this occurs with either a small local issue or with major national concern, the people have a right to submit their grievances to the government, along with their request for redress. While many of the rights which allow for citizen petitions come from the text of our state constitutions, the First Amendment of the United States Constitution also enshrines this principle:

> "Congress shall make no law respecting an establishment of religion, or prohibiting the free exercise thereof; or abridging the freedom of speech, or of the press; or the right of the people peaceably to assemble, <u>and to petition the Government for a redress of grievances.</u>"

Usually, on the state or local level this means a process where people collect signatures to place a question before the voters which will either create a new law or change an old one. Sometimes the voters are trying to get an unresponsive legislative body to provide tax relief or fund a certain program. Perhaps there is an antiquated law on the books that a group of citizens would prefer to see repealed (the punishment for marijuana is the most recent example of a group of citizens voiding a law they disagree with).

In the Commonwealth of Massachusetts, our state constitution provides the right to change or alter state laws at the ballot box by the voters themselves. There are four types of petitions which may be used to place questions before the voters. They are: 1) An Initiative Petition for a Law (approval or rejection or to repeal or amend a particular section of an existing law); 2) Initiative Petition for a Constitutional Amendment; 3) Referendum Petition (repeal an existing law); and 4) Public Policy Petition (submit instructions to the senator or representative from a specific district on a non-binding question of public policy).

So the usual scenario is for citizens to stand outside of retail shops or conduct a door to door campaign seeking enough qualifying signatures (number depend on type of petition) to get their issue on the ballot. After receiving the necessary certifications from the Secretary of State and Attorney General, should the ballot measure win the approval of the majority of voters at the next regularly scheduled election, the government is then obligated to respond according to the will of the majority of voters. Seems rather simple and straightforward enough, but I remind you that while yet another wonderful idea of our Founding Fathers, in modern practice, this constitutional "right" is all too often disregarded by liberal elected officials who believe they know better what is good for you than you do for yourself.

Today, from issues ranging from taxation to gay marriage, the constitutional right as guaranteed by our forefathers is in serious jeopardy with political strong-arming and special interest influence becoming second nature. Procedural tactics are being used whenever necessary as "an ends justify the means" type of political justification. Generally speaking, I am extremely proud of my GOP's efforts to honor the rights and will of voters. Staying true to the underlying constitutional principles is something that generally I believe sets Republicans apart from many Democrats today. The more loyal we remain to these values, I believe the more the electorate will come to appreciate our political party.

In Massachusetts, the referendum petition process granted to citizens is found under the provisions of Article 48 of the Amendments to the Massachusetts Constitution. Without question, Article 48 provides an important vehicle for the public to participate directly in the lawmaking process and redress an out of touch government. This right was granted to the voters in the State Constitutional Convention of 1917-1918, and its goal was to provide for a balance between the role of elected officials in a republican form of government and the rights of individuals in a democracy. While certainly a delicate balance of power between the institutions of government and the people, it is a necessary one to keep government's power from overtaking the rights of the people.

Article 48 also provides the necessary protections against potential abuses of special interests groups or corrupt individuals who often times have great influence over some elected officials. From my perspective, Article 48 is a brilliant addition to the personal rights of the citizens as it reinforces other constitutional protections established by our Founders, including the separation of powers between the branches of government, frequent elections of legislators and the ability to impeach a governor. Article 48 is yet another of the checks and balances which attempts to keep an orderly balance between the different factions of government.

I doubt that too many people who hold elected office would have the political courage to publicly suggest that they oppose the rights under Article 48. However, when one conducts a review of what actually happens when the voters choose to exercise their constitutional right to redress their government, it is clear that a significant number of members of the Democrat Party believe that they know what is best for you when it comes to making public policy, even when you say differently at the ballot box.

Let's take a brief walk down memory lane and review the recent history of what actually happens when the people get motivated enough to organize, collect the necessary signatures, obtain the required certifications and vote a certain way at the ballot box. If you are thinking that the voters' will must prevail in such conflicts (after all, this is Massachusetts, the cradle of liberty where so many American patriots came from and guided the founding of our great nation) I sadly have to inform you that in modern history you would be mistaken.

For those of you who don't know the story of the income tax rollback, to set the stage for our discussion, I take you back to 1989. After the Commonwealth experienced a near collapse in the real estate market and difficult recession, then Governor and super-liberal Michael Dukakis, along with the Democratically controlled Legislature, raised the state income tax from 5 to 6.25 percent. Both Dukakis and the Democrats who controlled both the House and Senate with super majorities promised that after the economy improved, the tax rate would return to 5 percent. Promises, promises, promises...

Well, in just a few short years and thanks to the federal income tax cuts proposed and passed by President Reagan, the United States economy improved, including in our own Bay State where technology companies were doing very well and state revenue collections soared to record levels. But instead of rolling back the income tax as promised, the politicians broke their promise and the state's income tax remained unchanged. At the same, time as state revenue collections increased, the politicians in power said there just was not quite enough money to reduce the income tax and allow Massachusetts taxpayers to keep a few more of their hard earned dollars for their families. During this period of time the state budget was growing at a tremendous level. To make matters even more insulting to the taxpayers, the legislature also enacted a number of new targeted tax loopholes which were provided to some influential Beacon Hill lobbyists or special interests.

After years of promises, in 1998 a citizens' group attempted to reduce the state's income tax rate back to 5% by the use of the aforementioned initiative petition process found in Article 48. The campaign slogan for the effort was "Keep the Promise," which seemed quite appropriate considering the clear promises of practically every elected leader at the time of the "temporary" tax increase. Known as Question 4 on the 2000 statewide ballot, the proposed law called for setting the state personal income tax rate from 5.95% to 5.6% in 2001, then to 5.3% in 2002, and finally to 5% in 2003.

In 2000, Republican Governor Paul Cellucci joined forces with Barbara Anderson from Citizens for Limited Taxation and together they fought and won the battle against labor unions and a plethora of Beacon Hill special interest groups who worked tirelessly in an effort to defeat the ballot question. The strongest force against the income tax reduction was from the Massachusetts Teachers Association (MTA) who reportedly spent millions on media buys, lawsuits and challenges to the petition's signatures. Thankfully, the influences of the MTA, while having a great deal of political muscle in the halls and backrooms of Beacon Hill, did not translate to the general voting public. Of the 2,733,831 total ballots cast, 1,541,771 or 56.4% were in favor of the tax rollback. In areas like Cape Cod, the majority was close to two to one in favor of Question 4.

As mentioned, the voter approved ballot question required returning the income-tax rate to five percent over a three year period. Although the earlier tax increase was not a gradual one, the reduction by three steps was a common-sense approach to mitigate the opposition's main argument that the state budget could not absorb the reduction in a single fiscal year. The voters had spoken and the rollback was scheduled to be completed by 2003. So, this should be the end of the story, but regrettably it is not. The Legislature has frozen the rate at 5.3% since 2002, under various excuses, including once again, there simply is not enough revenue to do it.

While I am sure that there could never be enough money for some of my liberal friends to spend, the facts are in the Fiscal Year 2009, our state budget has never been larger, our revenues are at a record high level and the state budget continues to be loaded with earmarks and special interest spending. Not to mention that at one point prior to the recent recession, we had over $2 billion in the state's rainy day account. One does have to wonder when, if ever, will we have enough money in the hands of government to honor the will of the voters and stop making the same old lame excuses why now is not the right time!

Since 2002, the underlying political question at the heart of every campaign season is whether the state's income tax should be cut to five percent. That question has been answered by the voters in 2000. Even the most liberal politicians won't come out and suggest the vote should be ignored, but actions do speak much louder than words. The usual excuse is that this year (whichever year it might be) is just not the right year to do so. Despite the passage of the 2004, 2006 and 2008 elections, the more critical question remains: Should politicians respect the will of the voters when they speak at the ballot box or are such votes a mere recommendation that legislators can ignore with apparent impunity for their actions?

Also on the 2000 ballot was Question 7, which proposed a law to allow charitable donations to be deducted from Massachusetts' personal income tax returns. The Committee to Encourage Charitable Giving sponsored Question 7 estimating that the law would generate approximately $220 million per year in additional charitable gifts across Massachusetts. The proposed law would apply to any contribution that met the definition of charitable contribution used under federal income tax law. Republicans strongly supported this question as it is a fundamental tenant of my GOP to encourage the private sector to address the needs of society. The use of income tax policy is one of the time honored approaches that my GOP has supported to encourage positive economic behavior.

As of the 2000 election, thirty-three other states permitted tax deductions on their state income taxes (and of course the federal government) for charitable donations made to recognized and approved charitable organizations. When the votes were counted, 1,834,305 (67.1%) voted in favor of a state income tax deduction for charitable contributions. In political terms, this was a landslide victory, as you seldom see any ballot question or political candidate reach this level of support. This was yet another clear instruction from the citizens of Massachusetts to their state government regarding a straightforward public policy matter.

Despite more than two thirds of Bay State voters sending a very clear message to their state government, legislative leaders took this issue to the floor of the House and Senate and voted directly against what the people of Massachusetts wanted. No changes were made to the state income tax laws, leaving Massachusetts as one of only seven states who discourage charitable giving. While is seems hard to believe that this could occur in Massachusetts, as there is no other place in America that has a stronger history of freedom and liberty, there is a pervasive and disturbing trend of Massachusetts elected officials ignoring the will of the citizens they purport to represent. What makes the denial of the rights of the voters so disappointing is that Massachusetts has been the location of many historic events related to self-government. We are the home state of John Adams, who inspired many of our individual constitutional personal rights and is credited as the person who crafted the Massachusetts State Constitution. How can this be so?

According to several media sources at the time Question 7 was approved at the ballot box, the proposed law largely received a negative vote in the Legislature due to the alleged fiscal implications that Massachusetts would suffer if such law was allowed to pass. Once again, legislators claimed "we simply can't afford it." In 2001, 57.5% of the total state government revenue was from the individual income tax. The folks who run the show on Beacon Hill successfully argued to enough rank and file legislators that the tax cut would cause a fiscal crisis and would fail at encouraging new donations. This of course, is so illogical that even in liberal Massachusetts such an argument failed to convince the voters. Fidelity Investments, the largest supporter of the question, maintained that charitable donations in Massachusetts would have risen by hundreds of millions a year. While we will never know who would have been correct, it seems pretty likely that if you make something tax deductible, more people will take part. It seems to work rather well at the federal level and in most other states.

For some 88 years now, Massachusetts voters have enjoyed the textually based constitutional right to pass legislation at the ballot box through initiatives and referendum questions. For nearly all that time, voters' decisions were regarded as almost sacred by practically everyone holding elective office. The usual and expected procedure was that successful ballot measures took effect when the people exercised their right to redress their government, even if the political power base on Beacon Hill disagreed with them. It is only in the last few years that legislative leaders have had the political nerve to directly undermine the will of the people.

From my point of view, such behavior by elected officials is both outrageous and anti-democratic. Politicians who refuse to honor your vote are folks who clearly do not deserve to receive your vote in the next election, whether they are a member of the Democrat or Republican Party. That doesn't mean that candidates have to agree with the outcome of a ballot question. However, it should mean that whether they agree with it or not, they will abide by what the people in their districts want. After all, isn't the whole concept of elections to choose someone to represent the interest of the majority of people?

While my fellow Republican Caucus members and I do not always agree on each and every issue, one of the things that I am most proud of serving as a Republican legislator from Massachusetts, is the practically unanimous upholding of the will of the voters when they speak at the ballot box. Throughout my entire tenure in the House of Representatives, the GOP leadership, as well as the rank and file members have consistently fought for the voice of the electorate to be heard on Beacon Hill. While I am not overly optimistic that the majority party will change their ways any time soon, I remain confident that despite the low numbers of Republicans serving in the Massachusetts Legislature, we shall remain faithful to this most worthy cause.

Many frustrated Massachusetts voters often paint the entire legislature with a single broad brush, but a careful review shows that my GOP has done its very best to be on the side of the majority of voters and protect their constitutional rights of redressing their government. Being the minority party in Massachusetts, Republicans sincerely believe that ballot measures are a check and balance against the back room political deals that are the Beacon Hill culture. If we had more GOP members serving in the legislature, I am confident we could do ever a better job at exposing the abuses.

This essential constitutional vehicle for redressing citizens' grievances directly to elected officials is one of the foundational rights we have in America. Neither legislators nor governors should be allowed to disregard the peoples' grievances at their will without the electorate of this great state making them pay the political consequence of refusing to return them to office. Unfortunately, in recent memory there appears to be very little real consequence for such denial of our rights.

The Founding Fathers understood there would be times when elected officials neglected their constituents. During the constitutional debates a great deal of discussion was had on this subject and was one of the primary reasons for the process of frequent elections. The theory goes that when an elected official neglects the will of the people he represents, he would not likely be reelected. In modern day practice, there does not appear to be a consequence for such neglect by the politicians who occupy the State House. A situation our Founding Fathers would be greatly disturbed about.

The rights of voters to be heard are not limited to questions approved at the ballot box. Sometimes important proposed ballot questions never even make it that far. For example, whatever your position on the same-sex marriage issue is, you should be deeply concerned about the political and special interest groups influences which ultimately have kept the question and definition of marriage in Massachusetts from reaching the voters.

While many people understand that same-sex marriage is legal in Massachusetts, I have found that a majority do not have an appreciation of the history which set the stage as to where we find ourselves. Furthermore, we are a state where political leaders have steadfastly refused to allow the voters to be heard at the ballot box.

Like so many other issues which fail to gain political support from elected officials, this story starts with a few of what can only be described as activist minded judges. The court case that put Massachusetts on the forefront of the gay marriage issue was <u>Goodridge v. Department of Public Health</u>. In a tremendously controversial four to three decision handed down on November 18, 2003, the Massachusetts Supreme Judicial Court (SJC) held that the plaintiffs (gay couples) had successfully argued that denying gay couples equal marriage rights was unconstitutional under the language of the Massachusetts Constitution. The highest court in Massachusetts was the first state supreme court in the nation to reach such a conclusion. Immediately after the SJC's ruling, efforts by groups of interested citizens began to amend the state constitution to reaffirm the historical definition of marriage between one man and one woman that had existed since the beginning of recorded time.

Procedurally, in order to amend the state constitution, it is necessary for a proposed amendment first to receive sufficient support at two successive state constitutional conventions, which is a joint meeting of the House of Representatives and the Senate. If an amendment is put forward by a legislator, it needs the vote of a majority of the two-hundred members of the House and Senate at two constitutional conventions. For an amendment to move forward by the petition of citizens, it needs only a twenty-five percent vote.

There were several proposed amendments to redefine marriage as between one man and one woman, including an amendment that would have forbidden same-sex marriage, but established civil unions for same-sex couples. This proposal passed the first constitutional convention but was defeated in the second, which meant it was no longer before the joint constitutional convention and was effectively dead.

Another proposed amendment was later sponsored by an organization called VoteOnMarriage.org. This citizen-offered amendment stated, "When recognizing marriages entered into after the adoption of this Amendment by the people, the Commonwealth and its political subdivisions shall define marriage only as the union of one man and one woman." The VoteOnMarriage.Org supporters collected over 170,000 signatures before the December 7, 2005 deadline. It was clear from the overwhelming success of the petition drive and from several media polls that were conducted at the time, that the people of Massachusetts wanted to be heard on this divisive but important legal and cultural issue.

The first Constitutional Convention vote on the citizen petition amendment was scheduled for July 12, 2006, but was postponed until November 9, 2006, coincidently to take place after the next statewide election. While so many Democrats are pro gay marriage, it surprised virtually no one that many did not wish to push the voting button during an election season. When such divisive issues are injected into an election season, the liberals apparently are not confident that despite Massachusetts being one of the bluest states, the voters will actually agree with them on this issue.

A few days after the 2006 election day, the Legislature voted to recess the Constitutional Convention until January 2, 2007. Disappointingly, too many representatives and senators chose not to vote on the question and used procedural moves to avoid having to take what some legislators considered to be a difficult and controversial vote. In what I would describe as an abuse of democracy and a violation of Article 48 of our Constitution, the majority of legislators voted to recess until one day before the end of the legislative session. This question was brought forward by the people of the Commonwealth under Article 48 of the Massachusetts Constitution, which states:

> "Final legislative action in the joint session upon any amendment shall be taken only by call of the yeas and nays, which shall be entered upon the journals of the two houses; and an unfavorable vote at any stage preceding final action shall be verified by call of the yeas and nays, to be entered in like manner. At such

joint session a legislative amendment receiving the affirmative votes of a majority of all the members elected, or an initiative amendment receiving the affirmative votes of not less than one-fourth of all the members elected, shall be referred to the next general court."

Governor Mitt Romney led a very strong public effort against the procedural tactics that some of the members in the Massachusetts Legislature had used to delay and possibly prevent a vote on the same-sex marriage ballot initiative. Romney repeatedly suggested he would ask a justice of the state Supreme Judicial Court to put the initiative directly on the ballot if legislators failed to vote on the initiative on the last day of the Joint Session, January 2, 2007, as was clearly required by the Massachusetts Constitution's Article 48.

Mitt Romney firmly held the position that, "The issue before us is not whether same-sex couples should marry. The issue before us today is whether 109 legislators will follow the constitution." On December 27, 2006, the Massachusetts Supreme Judicial Court agreed unanimously with Governor Mitt Romney's repeated assertion that Article 48 of the Massachusetts Constitution explicitly and unambiguously requires that the Massachusetts Legislature take a final vote on any and all voter initiatives placed before them. While the SJC's opinion was straightforward, they also held that the courts had no legal remedy to enforce on the legislature due to principles that separate the judicial and legislative branches of government.

From my own personal and legal point of view, and as declared by our SJC in their Advisory Opinion on the subject, not casting a vote on any proposed constitutional amendment is not consistent with the intent and plain meaning of Article 48. The signers of these petitions have a right to have a vote, but once again this right had been denied. My fellow

Republican House members stood tall; and even though our Caucus does have a few supporters of same-sex marriage, we all stood firm on the principle that the petitioners had a right to a "yes" or "no" vote on this and every proposal properly brought before the Constitutional Convention.

With continued pressure from Governor Mitt Romney and the SJC, the legislature finally voted on the citizen proposal on January 2, 2007. The amendment received 62 (50 needed to move to next step) affirmative votes in Constitutional Convention and thereby passed an important first step toward reaching the people. However, the victory for those who wanted the chance to cast their vote was short lived, as a second vote was required during the next legislative session.

The second joint session of the Constitutional Convention was held on June 14, 2007. The marriage amendment was defeated by a vote of 151 against to 45 in favor. As stated above, at least 50 "yes" votes were needed for the measure to move on to a public referendum and appear on the 2008 ballot. Despite the fact almost every poll shows the people of Massachusetts want to vote on the definition of marriage, to date no such opportunity has been afforded to them and I seriously doubt ever will be.

It is not only conservative proposals that face the procedural abuses of the Beacon Hill political culture. A proposed health care constitutional amendment which would guarantee "comprehensive, affordable, and equitably financed health insurance coverage" for all state residents was not allowed to continue through the process and reach the voters. Let me be clear, I firmly oppose universal health care, but the underlying issue is not the point of this story. It is the integrity of the political process!

Supporters of the proposed amendment followed the rules and collected enough signatures to put the question before their representatives and senators. During the first vote on the question, ninety-two members voted in favor. If allowed to come to the floor again, the amendment needed the approval of just twenty-five percent of the legislature or fifty affirmative votes on a second vote to be placed before the voters. Unfortunately, when the proposed amendment came back to the Constitutional Convention for the required second vote, there would be no vote at all and the question died. Despite the fact the constitution requires a formal "yes" or "no" vote, those who control the process simply choose not to honor the system.

The Committee for Health Care for Massachusetts, which was the driving force behind the proposed amendment, filed a lawsuit. The complaint asked the Massachusetts SJC to consider the ninety-two votes from the first vote as votes in favor of the amendment during the first required vote to place it on the ballot in November of 2008. While the Massachusetts high court rejected the request, the court noted that this was the second time in the past three years that legislators failed to uphold their constitutional duty to vote on a proposed constitutional amendment after citizens had obtained the required signatures.

This question was brought forward by the people of the Commonwealth under Article 48 of the Massachusetts Constitution, and just like other issues, the rights of the people of Massachusetts to redress their government had been denied and apparently there was no remedy to be found. My own feelings, and as declared by our SJC, not casting a vote on a proposed constitutional amendment is not consistent with the intent and plain meaning of Article 48. The signers of these petitions have a right to have a vote, and once again this right had been denied. Wherever you stand on this issue or any proposal, you should be extremely concerned that the initiative petition process is being ignored by the majority of your elected officials. This is a dangerous precedent being set by your government, and I am fearful what abuse of the democratic process may be next.

On the underlying substantive question, I believe the people of Massachusetts should have the right to speak directly to this question at the ballot box. When the people speak at the ballot box, Republican principles strictly require that members of my GOP support whatever the decision of the voter might be. From a personal point of view, as the title of my position is "representative," this is my duty and I take my oath of office very seriously. While disregarding the will of the voters when they speak at the ballot box and politically maneuvering to keep certain questions off the ballot are certainly dangerous to our constitutional rights and freedoms, the abuses of the political process unfortunately do not end there.

Aside from the issue of voters not being heard via the referendum process, there are endless other examples of backroom deals and procedural tactics that occur on Beacon Hill which could be the subject of their own book. But my purpose here is to discuss why my GOP is still relevant in Massachusetts and to suggest some of the issues and principles Republicans should be talking about and fighting for. A prime example why more Republicans are needed in the Massachusetts Legislature occurred on the floor of the Massachusetts House of Representatives in January 2004. The events of that evening are both an insult to the institution of the Massachusetts Legislature as well as a direct assault on our democracy and rights to be represented by elected officials.

Just minutes after Governor Romney completed his State of the State Address, the Massachusetts House adjourned until the following day. This is pretty much a normal and customary procedure. At the close of business on any given day, there is an Order read by the House Clerk informing the membership when the next session will be and what type, either formal or informal, is scheduled. There was absolutely nothing unusual about this night, perhaps with the exception that it was the night the governor made his annual speech. After the Order was read, legislators said their good-byes and headed home to their respective districts.

But this night was indeed different from the normal course of business. After almost all of the members of the Massachusetts House of Representatives had left the chamber and departed the building, including myself, the House session was reopened with a declaration of the unanimous consent to do so. Unanimous consent from whom is the obvious question. There were just a handful of people remaining in the chamber. It was approximately 8:30pm and we had ADJOURNED until the following Friday!

When pressed on the House Rules, the House Clerk Steven James explained the sudden second meeting was somehow allowable under his interpretation of the House Rules. "The House may meet by unanimous consent at a time earlier than stipulated in an adjournment order," James was quoted as saying. He cited an instance in 1991, when the House apparently did so, but no one that I spoke to thought it was permissible or in any way fair.

Now, I do not claim to be an expert on every parliamentary procedure, and generally I have a positive impression of the House Clerk, but I can say with total confidence that no one in good faith believes that a handful of Representatives has the right to reopen a session that had formerly adjourned until the following day without some sincere attempt to notify the members. In this case, there was no announcement over the intercom, no e-mail, no memo, no phone call. So, what is next? Can a few members show up on a Sunday afternoon and vote to open a session and vote on pending laws?

So, one has to wonder why this would happen. The answer is really quite simple. The majority party wanted it to! This was a quiet and convenient method of getting something controversial done without the spotlight being on it. The legislation that was before the House allowed cities and towns to pass higher property tax bills onto owners of commercial and industrial properties. Business groups strongly opposed the legislation. I was also against the bill, but that is really not the point. The point is, once again, the liberals who control the Massachusetts Legislature ignored their own rules and in my opinion, their ethical responsibility to have a fair and open debate and vote on an important issue. As the Democrat Party holds a super-majority in both the House and the Senate, unless the rank and file Democrat members are willing to join the Republican Caucus and put a stop to such abuses, I see little reason to believe they will be discontinued.

In this case, Boston Mayor Menino had been pushing hard for this bill to pass during the session prior to the governor's speech, but he had been unsuccessful at bringing the issue to a formal vote. Many other legislators, including myself, had concerns with the proposal and wanted another debate and roll call to ensure that legislators who voted in favor of this tax increase were on record on the enactment vote. But as there was no roll call, there is no formal record of who did what when the session was reopened in the absence of most of the elected representatives.

I also believe that this happened when it did as a media tactic. All of this occurred on the very same night that the governor made his State of the State address. The story of the late night actions would likely be buried deep inside the newspapers, as the lead story would surely be the governor's comments on the condition of the Commonwealth. Such abuses occur in part because Massachusetts is such a one party state and the press does little to bring to light the abuses of the super-majority ruled and controlled system. If we had a more balanced political environment, it is only logical to assume that such abuses would not be tolerated by the rank and file members of the legislature or the media.

I am very proud to be serving the people of the Commonwealth and my district, but when things like this happen on Beacon Hill, I literally feel sick to my stomach. The people of our Commonwealth deserve much better from their government and its elected officials. At times, I may be only one voice, but I intend to use it and I shall continue to fight hard for reform and an open political system. Members of my GOP must shout from the roof tops each and every time abuses happen to our political system. When we do so on a consistent basis, it is my hope that the voters will ultimately hold accountable their elected officials who choose to blindly follow the instruction of their leadership, rather than what is in the best interest of the Commonwealth.

During certain times of the year, especially during the summer months, things are customarily a bit slow on Beacon Hill. Typically the House of Representatives meets only twice each week in what is called "informal sessions." These sessions are designed to keep the legislative process moving along on non-controversial bills, but sometimes efforts are made to pass legislation that does not share unanimous support of legislators.

The Republican Caucus closely monitors the action in these informal sessions to ensure any bill that we have an objection to is set aside and saved until a later date where a formal recorded vote can take place. During the summer of 2007, House Republicans, including yours truly, continuously objected to a piece of legislation which drastically changed how public unions are organized in Massachusetts. While my GOP is often unfairly labeled as being anti-union, and though this was a union related piece of legislation, that is not what this story is really all about. The real issue at hand is about the process of voting itself, something Republicans hold sacred.

I think most citizens realize the great benefits of the American tradition of the secret ballot. By voting in private, we all have the opportunity of expressing our opinions without any undue influences. The right to a secret ballot not only provides for a fair vote, but most importantly it protects the voices of a minority point of view. The secret ballot protects a voter from something as simple as peer pressure, to the extreme potential of physical intimidation.

The bill the Republican Caucus was objecting to and that was strongly being pushed by AFL-CIO and their Democrat friends changed the rules when it comes to employees considering joining a public collective bargaining unit. House Bill 2465, "A Petition relative to written majority authorization cards, petitions and other written evidence of collective bargaining results" no longer allows those considering forming a union to do so via a secret ballot. Instead of an employee expressing their honest and private opinion regarding the formation of a union by a secret ballot vote, the new law which passed pretty much along political party lines substitutes a new process where public employees considering the formation of a union do so by a majority of employees simply and publicly signing an authorization card. Gone is the day of a secret or anonymous ballot.

Can you imagine how this will play out in the future? A union organizer or perhaps a group of union officials come by your home or your work station and asks you to sign a card declaring to the world whether or not you wish to organize as a union shop. Perhaps union organization cards would be passed out to a select group in private. You might never even be aware or have an opportunity to voice your opinion if the union could obtain the signatures of fifty-one percent of your co-workers. The bill as passed has no requirement of notice or for an opportunity to be heard by any dissenting employee or even the employer.

The previous secret ballot process allowed the union and the employer to present their reasons or arguments for or against the formation of a union. It also allowed employees to speak to each other privately to weigh the pros and cons of making such a decision before a vote was taken by a secret ballot. Such an open process also provided an opportunity for a competing union to make a presentation to the employees.

So, what's the reason that we need to change the process that has worked well for a very long time? I, for one, see no justification for reducing the due process afforded employees and employers under the current system. This appears to be a move by union leaders to stem the tide of declining membership. According to the Bureau of Labor Statistics, 12.0 percent of employed wage and salary workers were union members, down from 12.5 percent a year earlier. The number of persons belonging to a union fell by 326,000 in 2006 to 15.4 million. The union membership rate has steadily declined from 20.1 percent in 1983. In an effort to stop the steady decline of union membership and with an "ends justify the means" mentality, the due process protections of a secret ballot were washed away in the area of the formation of labor unions.

Once again, I am proud that the Republican Caucus stood tall and fought the good fight. While we as Republicans on Beacon Hill do lose most of our battles more often than not, our efforts are based on solid principles. In this specific case at hand, the elimination of the secret ballot provision goes against all of the procedural due process principles of the American system of voting. Hopefully, one day in the very near future, the general electorate will realize the many abuses occurring are more than harmless political games: They are seriously eroding all of our rights and privileges we should hold so dear.

The media also has an important role in maintaining an open and honest political system. During my four terms serving in the House of Representatives, myself and a few others have been complaining about failing to honor the will of the voters, back room deals, consolidation of budget amendments and other abuses of the legislative process, but so few in the media actually seem to care. It seems as if the media does not report on such things as they accept it as part of the Massachusetts political culture.

Every abuse of the legislative process should be front page news. Each time this happens, democracy and the role of our elected legislators is diminished. The abuses of the process occur at least in part because the media in general fails to hold political leaders responsible for their individual actions; and also because of one party control of the process that is Massachusetts politics. If the media would more closely monitor the legislative sessions and report all of the abuses, it is likely there would be fewer occurring. When they did, perhaps the voters would ultimately have the necessary information to hold elected officials accountable.

I am extremely and sincerely concerned that the citizens' right to speak at the ballot box appears to be in serious jeopardy. The legislature has a disappointing record of ignoring the vote of the citizens and manipulating the process to serve the majority party's liberal-leaning agenda.

For our part, I am confident that my GOP will continue to offer bills and amendments to, at the very least, force the majority party to be accountable for their failures. Whether or not the collective general public will ever be engaged and care enough to remove elected officials who betray their own constituency is yet to be determined. The one thing that is for sure, if there is no political price to pay for dishonoring the voters, the status quo will continue.

Chapter Eight - Republican Economics are Reaganomics

In 1980, when Ronald Reagan challenged Jimmy Carter for the presidency, America faced an economy in great anguish and hardship. The recession of 2008 and 2009 was mild compared to the later 1970's. Interest rates were at record high levels, the country was suffering from a crippling energy crisis and consumer confidence was at modern-day low levels. During the late 1970's, even though I was still a grade school student and really lacked a perspective of the economic good or bad times, from the reports on the nightly news, as well as within my own home, I knew that things were not going well for America. I can recall the temperature in the house during the winter months being much colder than usual. As we lived across the street from a gas station, I remember the sign on the pumps indicating the station was out of fuel, and when there was gasoline available, the occasional long lines of frustrated customers waiting to fill up.

Thankfully, after winning the election, Ronald Reagan went right to work on a comprehensive economic program based on the theory of supply-side economics. Basically, supply-siders call for the reduction of income tax rates (and other taxes) in order that people can keep more of what they earn. Supply-side supporters, which I am one, firmly believe that lower taxation will encourage people to work harder and longer as they will be able to keep more of their income for themselves. As we all know from our own observations and perhaps our own behavior, when Americans have more money in their pockets, they usually spend it. This of course leads to increased economic activity, which then leads to higher government revenue collections.

Supporters of supply-side economics hold that when taxes of any type, especially income taxes, reach a certain level, despite a higher tax rate, the amount of the actual tax collected will decrease and thus fail to be sufficient to meet government's needs. The theory has been proven correct time and time again that cutting tax rates actually increases government income as more economic activity is generated by the incentive to be a more productive individual or business owner.

This economic proposition was first successfully advanced by French political economist Jean-Baptiste Say in the 19th Century. In modern history, supply-side theory has been discussed and promoted by the noted economist Milton Friedman in his 1962 book "Capitalism and Freedom." Friedman advocated minimizing the role of government in the free market as a means of creating more political and social freedoms. While liberals usually can't stand such thinking, it is indeed very logical and based on common-sense principles. If people are able to retain more of their income, they have a greater control over their own destiny and will work harder to achieve their personal goals. Dr. Friedman who also won the Nobel Prize in Economic Sciences in 1976, is likely the root of much of Ronald Reagan's economic strategies.

Simply stated, by putting more money into the hands of the hardworking American people, history shows that we see more people saving for their future needs (thus less need for government entitlements) and investing or spending into the stream of commerce (to stimulate our businesses and create employment). It is perhaps an overly obvious point, but one always worth pointing out, every time we get someone off a government assistance program and into a job, we gain in three distinct ways. First, government no longer has to subsidize the unemployed worker with unemployment or welfare benefits. Secondly, that same person is now a taxpaying contributor to government via his payroll taxes, sales taxes and social security contributions. And thirdly, and perhaps most importantly for the long-term, this individual is now a productive member of society with a sense of self-worth and pride.

As Ronald Reagan was cutting tax rates for all Americans, he was also attempting to reform social welfare programs and reduce entitlement spending overall. At the same time and due to eight years of the Carter administration depleting our military readiness, President Reagan recognized our military was in dire straits and needed a significant recommitment of resources. President Reagan successfully pushed Congress for big increases in defense spending. This also resulted in an increase in economic activity as defense contractors hired more workers, purchased increased raw materials, and more young people eagerly entered the military. This of course reduced the available labor pool, thus lowering the unemployment rate.

"Reaganomics" was the title given to President Reagan's supply-side economic strategy and it has achieved long lasting positive impacts on our economy and to our nation. Members of my GOP can learn a lot by studying the differences between the Carter and Reagan administrations and remaining true to our conservative economic policies. In case you need a refresher, President Reagan's economic plan had four separate and unique components, each of them equally and critically important and necessary to each other's success. The components or goals were:

(1)   To reduce the growth of government spending by reducing harmful social entitlement programs and eliminating unnecessary government agencies.

(2)   To reduce the marginal income tax rates and taxes on capital gains for Americans across the entire income spectrum.

(3)   To reduce unnecessary federal government regulation and wasteful spending, including "pet project" earmarks and special interest spending.

(4)   To reduce inflation by responsibly managing the growth of the money supply in our economy.

The critics of Ronald Reagan's economic plan correctly cite that the combination of tax cuts and higher military spending overwhelmed the more modest reductions in spending on domestic related programs and social entitlements. Simply put, members of Congress were not willing to go along with President Reagan's overall spending reduction requests. As a result of only part of President Reagan's economic recovery plan being implemented by Congress, the federal budget deficit grew to a level which was actually higher than during the recession of the Jimmy Carter years. Whether it is in Congress or in state capitols across America, politicians never seem to be able to reduce spending. We have developed into a political culture where any slow down in the pace of increasing expenditures is viewed as a "cut." As far as budgets actually being reduced, there are very few such occurrences at any level of government today.

The federal deficit which was approximately $74 million in 1980, when Ronald Reagan took office, reached a high of $221 million in 1986. Due to an ever expanding economy and some minor reforms to federal spending programs, the deficit was reduced back to $150 million in 1987, but then started growing again. Unfortunately, this trend has continued as members of Congress from both political parties continue to spend and spend and spend with little regard for the growing debt which is being passed along to future generations. Remember that President Reagan's first goal was, "To reduce the growth of government spending by reducing harmful social entitlement programs and eliminating unnecessary government agencies." As we all know from our history lessons, only Congress ultimately controls the spending.

Reflecting back to the elections of 2006 and 2008 for a moment, one of the primary reasons my GOP lost so many seats in Congress was our own failure to hold the line on federal spending. Remember, Republicans had control of the White House, the Senate, and the House prior to the 2006 election. Despite all that power, even my GOP failed to say "no" to increased spending. Disappointingly President Bush made little effort to frustrate the recent spending spree of Congress.

The voting public rightly expects Republicans to be firm on certain issues. Fiscal restraint and holding the line on increased government spending are certainly on the top of that list for most voters. Comparing 2006 to the 1980's, while the Republicans serving in Congress during the Reagan administration generally supported his tax cuts and the efforts of rebuilding our military, the Democrat majority simply was not willing to reduce spending of the social entitlement programs and the usual pork barrel spending earmarks. The American people recognized what Ronald Reagan was attempting to achieve with his budget reduction proposals, thus they supported his efforts with an overwhelming reelection victory in 1984. Ronald Reagan won every state, except Minnesota. Yes, even Massachusetts!

In 2006, it was the GOP who was in control of Congress. So, on election day with federal spending grossly out of control, the failure to reform Social Security and the growing illegal immigration problem, Republicans correctly bore the brunt of the blame and were kicked out of office. As discussed in chapter twelve, there is much to be learned from political figures who fail to embrace the principles of their chosen political party. But be certain that when Republicans fail to act like Republicans and control spending, voters will fail to reelect them. Ultimately, I guess that is the way it should be.

President Reagan was completely correct when he stated: "Only by reducing the growth of government, can we increase the growth of the economy." Without question, President Reagan delivered on each of his four major policy goals, but he simply could not get members of Congress to have the political courage to end their customary generous spending practices. While Reagan's economic efforts led to a substantial improvement in economic conditions for most Americans, especially compared to the days of Jimmy Carter, unfortunately, despite the President's best and sincere efforts, no major federal programs or agencies were eliminated.

The change to the federal income tax brackets has been one of Reagan's most positive legacies. This will forever impact Americans at every socioeconomic level, as long as some future liberal congress and president do not increase them. While it may seem hard to believe today, prior to Reagan's tax reduction efforts, the top marginal federal tax rate on personal income was seventy percent. The rate for income tax on corporations was reduced from forty-eight percent to thirty-four percent. While often described by the liberals as a windfall for the super rich, the fact is that most of the poor are completely exempt from the federal individual income taxes all together.

Speaking of federal income tax rates, all too often the liberals get away with suggesting that because of perceived tax loopholes and the marginal tax rate system, the wealthiest individuals pay little in income taxes. Well, the famous quote of John Adams, "Facts are stubborn things..." fits perfectly when telling the real story of who actually bears the income tax burden in America today.

Who Pays Income Taxes in America?

Percentiles Ranked by AGI	AGI Threshold on Percentiles	Percentage of Federal Personal Income Tax Paid
Top 1%	$364,657	39.38
Top 5%	$145,283	59.67
Top 10%	$103,912	70.30
Top 25%	$62,068	85.99
Top 50%	$30,881	96.93
Bottom 50%	<$30,881	3.07
Note: AGI is Adjusted Gross Income Source: Internal Revenue Service		

Sorry, wrong again liberals! The facts and chart do speak for themselves. Over ninety-six percent of the federal income taxes are paid by the top fifty percent of income earners, but I am certain that on some television or radio talk show we will all hear soon that it is the poor who pay the most in taxes. An even more telling statistic is that the top five percent of federal income tax payers are carrying almost sixty percent of the federal budget.

Reverting back to the economic statistics from the Reagan years also reveals quite a telling story about other key indicators. Under the leadership of President Reagan, the nation's unemployment rate declined from 7.0 percent in 1980 when he took office, to 5.4 percent in 1988, when he left the White House to his Vice President George H.W. Bush. Regarding the nagging problem of inflation which was inherited from the failed economic policies of President Carter, in the eight years of Reagan's terms the inflation rate was reduced from over ten percent to just four percent.

When Ronald Reagan departed the White House, the United States was again the premier economic and military superpower. Americans themselves were once again full of confidence in their economy and patriotism towards their country. Ronald Reagan stayed true to his conservative views on the economy and history has proven him to be correct. One does have to wonder how much more successful Reagan's fiscal policies would have been if Congress had listened to and acted on all of his requested reductions to federal spending.

Republican elected officials and candidates both at the state and federal level, should embrace supply-side economic theory and support all of the goals Ronald Reagan laid out in 1980. Most importantly, my GOP needs to hold a hard line on the spending component. Interestingly, the economic ideas of Ronald Reagan are once again garnering attention on the GOP campaign trail. Political messages of cutting federal spending and eliminating budget earmarks are hitting home with both fiscal conservative Republicans as well as with responsible independents. It is clear that more and more voters seem to be sincerely concerned about excess government spending, problems of the costs of illegal immigration and the soaring price tag of many harmful social entitlement programs.

So, it seems easy enough. Republicans need to remind themselves of the principles of Ronald Reagan and the successes of supply-side economic theory. If only it was that simple. The problem is not getting my GOP to acknowledge that such theories really do work or that they are matters of sound public policy, the real challenge is apparently getting my GOP to stand firm against the attractions of pork barrel spending and legislative earmarking. In case you are not familiar with what "earmarking" is, it is the practice of funding certain "pet" or special projects without going through the usual public hearing and voting process. During the annual budget process, this issue often rears its ugly head in some back room where most such deals are made.

The question remains, if a legislator is successful at convincing the political leaders to include a specific local earmark for that legislator, is such a legislator now committed to voting for the overall budget? What if the legislator believes the budget is irresponsible or does not include adequate funding for areas of concern, such as education, transportation or public safety? This question would likely be answered quite differently depending on how one views the legislative budget process itself. To me, there is never a valid excuse to cast a favorable vote for an irresponsible budget which contains unnecessary spending or increased taxes.

OK, I admit it, elected officials are in an extremely tough position on this issue. If a legislator gets in the budget line too often for their special local or pet projects, he is often correctly criticized for wasting taxpayer money. On the other hand, if a legislator decides to take a principled position and say no to "bringing home the bacon," it is entirely possible that a future political opponent will accuse him of being an ineffective elected official.

It certainly is a difficult question for some as to what the proper approach for an elected legislator should be, and one that has gone on in Washington, D.C. and state houses from sea to shining sea for a very long time. Republicans need to get off the gravy train of excessive spending and return to what the people expect and need us to be: The political party of fiscal restraint and only responsible government spending. For if my GOP simply continues to get in line with the Democrats for our share of the pork and earmarks, we are giving the American people another reason not to support our candidates, and even more importantly, we will be guilty of passing along an unsustainable pattern of spending for future generations to pick up the tab.

On the federal level, President Bush in his State of the Union address two years ago called on Congress to cut in half the amount of pork-barrel spending from the previous year's level of $13 billion. To no one's surprise, the President's request failed to result in any reductions in spending. In fact and disappointingly, Congress responded to his call by actually adding billions in new discretionary spending to the President's overall budget request. According to an editorial piece in the Cape Cod Times newspaper which quoted Taxpayers for Common Sense, a nonprofit Washington D.C. citizen action group, members of the Massachusetts Congressional delegation seem to have no problem getting in line for directing your tax dollars to their own special pork-barrel spending projects.

For example, the Congressman from my area, Representative William Delahunt, brought home $16.7 million to his district, which according to the article is $6 million less than the House of Representative average. I'm not sure if he should be complimented or criticized for that. Other Bay State Congressmen who were cited in the report were John Olver with $68.3 million; Marty Meehan who delivered $57.9 million; Michael Capuano brought home $29.8 million; James McGovern $27.7 million; Stephen Lynch secured $26.2 million; Ed Markey obtained $26 million; John Tierney $23.4 million; Barney Frank $15.4 million and Richard Neal delivered "only" $10.5 million in local earmarks.

As expected, our United States Senators did better than their counterparts in the House of Representatives with the Senior Senator, Ted Kennedy, delivering $198.2 million and Senator John Kerry with $183.9

million. According to the editorial, United States Senators each received an average of $178 million in earmarks. I am only listing Democrats, as that is all we have representing us in Washington, D.C. Sadly, many Republican House and Senate members from other states are really no better when it comes to pork barrel spending.

If we as a political party, or in fact, as a nation, are ever going to get control of our escalating budgets, restore faith in the political system and regain the high ground on fiscal responsibility issues, my GOP must take the bold step and "just say no" to earmarking and special interest pork. While initially politically painful, in the long run I am confident that the American people will understand and appreciate such efforts. We also need to honor the legislative process and only support measures which have gone through the committee hearing and public comment process. By their very nature, most earmarks and outside sections to an appropriations bill do not do so. It is my view, when my GOP cedes to the corrupt political system of back room deals during last minute budget earmarking or loading up appropriation bills with unrelated pork, we have lost our mission as Republicans and one of the core reasons people trust us with their votes in the first place.

On the federal level, if Congress has the political courage to actually eliminate all pork projects, according to the numerous media and watchdog interest group sources, the American taxpayer would save approximately $2,400 per year, per household over the next ten years. While much less on the state level, a significant reduction in taxes or reallocation of resources to more appropriate spending programs could be achieved by eliminating wasteful and unnecessary government spending. I am not naïve enough to believe that the Democrat Party will ever stop attempting to spend and spend our hard earned tax dollars; however, as they surely will continue to do, my GOP has a significant opportunity to stand tall on our core principles, make a real difference for the taxpayers and show the American people who Republicans are really all about!

George W. Bush got it one-hundred percent correct during his 2008 State of the Union address to the members of Congress and the American people when he declared he would, "veto any spending bill that does not succeed in cutting earmarks in half from 2008 budget levels." This is exactly the type of straightforward and firm leadership that will benefit my GOP and the nation in the long term! Perhaps a little bit late in his Presidency to start such a principled Republican stand, but I say better late than never. Now with Barack Obama in the White House, Congressional Republicans should focus in on the inappropriate nature of earmarking and special interest spending more than ever before.

President Bush also took a further and even bolder step concerning the use of earmarks by issuing an executive order "EO" outlining a new and aggressive policy. An EO is a specific directive issued by the president to his cabinet secretaries and managers of the executive branch of the federal government. Presidents have issued executive orders since 1789 and they have been used for a wide variety of purposes. President Bush with his EO authority specifically directed federal agencies to ignore and not fund any earmarks. These sometimes big dollar items usually do not have an open public hearing and many times are slipped into bills at the last minute.

If future presidents, which of course is doubtful under Obama, hold firm to the principle behind this EO, it will ensure a more proper use of taxpayer dollars and an honest political process. My GOP in Washington, D.C., in Boston, and all around the nation need to work to eliminate, or at the very least significantly reduce, the number and cost of earmarks. They need to open the process to our system of government for all to see what really goes on behind those infamous closed doors.

Along with vetoing any spending bills which have not been appropriated via an open process with individual votes on each substantive issue, it is time again for the Republican Party to advocate for a United States Constitutional Amendment providing the President with a line-item veto. Most state governors, including Massachusetts, have the line-item veto power regarding at least some kinds of legislative enactments. In basic terms, a line-item veto power is a form of veto which the president on the federal level or governor at the state level has the right to prevent certain components of a bill or budget from being enacted by the legislature without having to veto the remaining parts of the bill at the same time. Simply stated, it allows the executive to single out and reject specific line items while leaving the others to become law.

Many former presidents, including Richard Nixon, Gerald Ford, Ronald Reagan, George H.W. Bush and Bill Clinton have all endorsed the idea of granting the president line-item veto powers over appropriations bills as a means of controlling the budget deficit problem and making the political process more fair and transparent. While many members of Congress have either ignored or resisted the creation of a federal line item veto, it is really the only effective way to reduce the pork barrel spending projects and other special interest legislation that are often slipped into larger budget bills. This practice of adding non-germane items is termed "logrolling" and usually occurs when a legislator agrees to trade or concede his vote in exchange for the other's vote on a bill that he is personally interested in, sometimes because of a favorable spending earmark. This often occurs both at the state and federal level when a legislator is attempting to secure something for their own district while spreading out most of the costs to taxpayers of the entire state or nation, as the case may be.

As you might recall during the farewell speech to the American people by President Ronald Reagan, the outgoing President said there were two things he wished he had accomplished as President. Those two items were Constitutional amendments for the line-item veto and one to require congress and the president to balance the federal budget each year. Reagan's last day in office was not the only time he commented on these subjects. In Ronald Reagan's, State of the Union Address on January 25, 1984, he said:

"I also propose improvements in the budgeting process. Some 43 of our 50 states grant their governors the right to veto individual items in appropriation bills without having to veto the entire bill. California is one of those 43 States. As governor, I found this line-item veto was a powerful tool against wasteful or extravagant spending. It works in 43 states. Let's put it to work in Washington for all the people. It would be most effective if done by constitutional amendment. The majority of Americans approve of such an amendment, just as they and I approve of an amendment mandating a balanced federal budget. Many states also have this protection in their constitutions."

While two decades have passed since Reagan left office, the need for the line-item veto at the federal level is greater than it has ever been. Republicans, no matter who the current President is, should stand for renewing the call for a change in our federal constitution to embrace the line-item veto authority. It clearly reduces wasteful spending, pork-projects and most importantly it opens up the political process; goals which should be at the core of every Republican's heart. As it currently stands, if there is a wasteful spending item tucked deeply inside an otherwise worthy piece of legislation, the president must either sign the bill with the inappropriate earmark or wasteful item included, or veto the entire bill. This is simply not an acceptable system. It costs the taxpayers more money and fosters a culture of back room deal making.

A line-item veto is especially important to guard against abuses of a super-majority, such as what we have now in Massachusetts. Taking a look at the four state budgets that Governor Romney reviewed while serving as Governor of Massachusetts, you will quickly find that Romney used the line-item veto more than eight-hundred times. Over the course of the four annual budgets cycles, Mitt Romney made over three-hundred line-item spending reductions, three-hundred total line-item eliminations and struck harmful budget language over one-hundred and fifty times.

To be clear and accurate, a great many of these Romney vetoes were ultimately overridden by the Democrats (it takes two-thirds of both the House and Senate to override a Governor's veto); however, the real point here is that by having the authority to carve out negative items from the budget, the legislative leaders must then put the matter to an individual vote on the floor of both the House and Senate.

This results in legislators being more accountable for either supporting or opposing a specific item which is subject to formal votes on the record roll call. This process allows the voters the ability to learn exactly what their legislator is supporting or opposing. Often times, in the case of Mitt Romney's vetoes as Governor, the Democrat leaders would choose not to bring up the veto for a floor vote and thus the veto stood, saving taxpayers significant money. The bottom line is the line-item veto works well at the state level all across this nation and would add an important tool for any president, Democrat or Republican, to get a handle on the out of control spending of Congress.

Another important Massachusetts state economic issue is, while the legislature has allowed another term to pass without honoring the will of the voters and rolling back the income tax level to 5%, local property taxes have risen far beyond the increases in income of most people of modest income. All the while the Commonwealth had been enjoying approximately two-billion dollars in surplus cash with all sorts of new spending programs being proposed year after year.

If you will recall and as discussed in chapter seven, the voters statewide approved a ballot question calling for the rate to be rolled back to 5 percent in 2000. In Barnstable County for example, the vote was 81,254 in favor of the tax reduction and 36,558 against. Some political officials are suggesting that we should continue to ignore the citizens' votes and dedicate these funds towards property tax relief in the future. While I am all for lower property taxes, this position is flawed, overly simplistic and fails to apply any credible economic theory. Once again the liberals believe that by collecting more in income taxes at the state level, somehow property taxes will come down at the local cities and towns across the Commonwealth.

Over the past few years as the income tax rate has been stalled, property taxes have escalated. To assume that if we continue to hold the tax rate at 5.3% local property taxes will magically decline has proven to be wholly false, but that liberal argument persists at the State House. While all state revenue collections are indirectly related, there is no real evidence or historical precedent that suggests the more money the state collects in income taxes, the lower the property taxes imposed by the 351 cities and towns. In reality, exactly the opposite has occurred as we have record high property taxes and the largest state budget in the history of the Commonwealth.

The anti-income tax roll back folks also continuously neglect to inform us that even if (a really big if) all of the revenue from the difference between a 5.3% and 5.0% state income tax rate was sent directly to cities and towns, it would do practically nothing to reduce local property taxes. I think even the most casual government observer would correctly predict that when government at any level receives more money than it expected, it usually finds a way to spend it. Why should elected officials at city and town halls be any different from those in the State House? Remember, the state was enjoying record levels of revenue, but has failed to reduce the income tax!

As of the writing of the chapter, the taxpayers of the Commonwealth allocate more money to state and local services than in most other states. In the most recent available statistics, we ranked eighth in the country in total revenue generated by state and local taxes and fees per capita, which is 11.2% above the national average and ahead of every New England state except Connecticut. So, evidently the tax revenue stream is not the problem. It is the spending, spending, and spending.

The sad truth is that in many cases rising property taxes are forcing some seniors from their life-long homes. The values of residential properties despite the recent pull-backs, have risen much more rapidly than those of commercial properties. Tax bills for homeowners have been mounting despite the Proposition 2½ restrictions. According to the Municipal Finance Task Force, in cities and towns that lack residential exemptions, the average single-family tax bill rose from $2,679 to $3,589, or 36%, in recent years. In most Cape Cod communities, the increases have been even greater.

There are real solutions to reduce the burden of increasing property taxes; and while some suggest we should override the will of voters and not reduce the state's income tax, there is no reason we cannot and should not do both. To start with, I believe a significant portion of any surplus revenue should be distributed back to the local communities where it is needed the most for property tax reduction and increases in education and public safety spending.

While certainly in the minority in the Commonwealth, I am proud that our Republican House Caucus is constantly fighting to return more of the state's revenue collections back to our cities and towns. Local control and spending is a core GOP principle, and while our caucus might not always be successful in our efforts, it is not for any lack of effort. For example, as the Fiscal Year 2009 State Budget season was approaching, the House Republican Caucus filed a bill known as HD4651. If adopted, this proposal would return over $450 million in local aid to Massachusetts cities and towns. While not speaking for the Caucus, I believe they all would agree with my own view that Republicans believe the money is due to local communities because the state diverted $450 million away from them in recent years through a cap on lottery aid.

The money is due to cities and towns because the state sidetracked $450 million away from communities who use it to pay for police, schools, senior citizen centers and other essential local services. After all, the state made a promise to lottery players and local communities that 100% of the net lottery revenue would be sent back to cities and towns. That promise, like so many others in government today, was broken by the elected officials who are supposed to be the representatives of their local communities and the defenders of the people.

Under our proposed legislation, the $450 million would be returned to cities and towns as unrestricted local aid, so that communities could use the funds for their most pressing needs or lower local property taxes if they so desired. The money would be distributed through the same formula the state uses to distribute lottery aid every year. While as of the writing of this chapter our efforts do not look promising, my GOP is doing its best to keep this and related issues of local aid on the table during these difficult fiscal times. Hopefully, when the good people of the Commonwealth realize we could use a few more Republicans on Beacon Hill, then maybe we will be even more successful in such future efforts.

It can be practically guaranteed that when surplus revenues remain in the hands of the liberal-minded folks on Beacon Hill, it will be spent sooner rather than later and it is highly unlikely it will end up as real local property tax relief. The time for political posturing on taxes is growing old. Despite what some politicians of the left side of the political aisle will try to tell you, the state can afford to lower the income tax level and increase funding to our local communities, thus having a real possibility of reducing or at least slowing, the increasing of local property taxes. This is supply-side economics all the way!

Speaking of property taxes at the local level, Governor Deval Patrick made some pretty big promises to the voters during his 2006 campaign by declaring that if elected he would make it a priority to ease the growing tax burden on homeowners. To date, his promise has remained unfulfilled, but this has not stopped Democrats' attempt to pander to yet another group of voters. As of the writing of this chapter in December of 2008, Democrat Representative Ruth Balser of Newton has successfully pushed through the House of Representatives (Senate has yet to approve) a proposal which exempts senior citizens from the impacts of Proposition 2½ local property tax overrides.   While unlikely to pass this session, I suspect we will see it filed again.

In case you are not familiar with Proposition 2½, it limits the amount of taxes a city or town may generate from local property taxes each year to fund municipal expenses. Proposition 2½ was approved by Massachusetts voters in 1980, and first implemented in Fiscal Year 1982 after Massachusetts citizens grew tired of the never ending increases in their property taxes. While the legislation does limit annual increases in a city or town's budget to 2½ percent, voters can "override" the 2½ limitation by approving a ballot question. In the past, many seniors who are often the most knowledgeable and active segment of the electorate, would vote against most override attempts.

While seniors, just like the rest of us, are eagerly awaiting for the promised property tax reductions, Representative Balser's proposal does not lower property taxes at all. It simply shifts the burden of who pays them, and in theory it makes it easier for cities and towns to raise property taxes by voting for overrides to the Proposition 2½ limitations. The liberals' logic suggests that senior citizens will not get involved in a vote on a political issue if it does not impact them directly. From my point of view, seniors are better citizens than the liberals give them credit for. I believe seniors will continue to vote what is in the best interest of their communities and not be fooled into staying home when override votes occur.

A credible argument can be made that if anyone really needs a targeted property tax break, it is younger, first time homeowners, many of whom are facing the foreclosure crisis while doing their best to pay for their children, including day care, saving for college and experiencing rising health insurance and fuel expenses. The issue of property tax relief should not be about pitting one segment of society against another. Property owners of all ages are facing the burdens of local property tax increases and the solution should provide relief to everyone. Unfortunately, too many politicians know full well that senior citizens tend to vote in larger percentages, while many younger people do not.

As I see it, the real goal of this bill is to pander to seniors and provide them with an incentive to stay home when a Proposition 2½ override is on the ballot, thus making it more likely an override will pass and government will have more of your money! While we lost the battle on this issue in the House, I am proud that all nineteen Republicans stood firm and voted "no." We were also joined by fifteen good government-minded Democrats. This proposal was touted as "property tax relief for seniors," but it really just ends up to be a property tax increase for a majority of Massachusetts homeowners and a way to get more local override votes passed.

Sometimes things on Beacon Hill go a certain direction one day and another direction the next. As I am sure everyone has grown accustomed to by now, both the federal and state governments seem to have a sense of responsibility for how the overall economy is performing. Sometimes we are "stimulating" the economy with new tax breaks for certain industries, while at other times we are attacking other corporations for their previously provided tax "loopholes."

Depending on how you view the current state of affairs, one person's tax loophole is likely another's former economic stimulus attempt.

As I write this chapter, we in the House are working to find ways to balance the state's budget due to the current recession. Some people would have you believe that we can solve all of our fiscal problems by increasing taxes on our businesses or by closing alleged tax loopholes and that there would be minimal negative long-term impacts to our economy. In fact,

Governor Patrick has filed a number of complex pieces of legislation which actually increase the total taxes on various businesses.

At the same time that some liberal-minded folks are suggesting increasing targeted business taxes, Massachusetts finds itself near the bottom in the nation in our job growth. We are one of just a handful of states where our population growth is stagnant. Thus, while it may seem simple to raise taxes to increase spending for social programs, I remain deeply concerned about what the economic impact will be, especially as it relates to job creation and the long term stability of state revenue.

In general, state government seems to be sending conflicting messages to the business community. Just last year, the legislature passed an "Economic Stimulus" package spending hundreds of millions of dollars to create targeted tax incentives; some might correctly call these tax loopholes. Now, within just a few months of passing a bill creating tax incentives for certain businesses, we are talking about raising taxes on some of the very same businesses and eliminating other tax breaks for other industries, somehow alleging these are tax "loopholes."

This back and forth changing of positions sends a disturbing and uncertain message to businesses who may be thinking about coming to the Commonwealth. For example, if you are a business owner, either in this state or considering relocating to Massachusetts, and you are attempting to project your tax burden, the back and forth posturing of those in power on Beacon Hill makes it virtually impossible to predict what your tax liability will be in the long term. While you might chose to locate your business here because of a current tax incentive or loophole, one has to wonder if next year, some liberal politician might be targeting your very business as taking advantage of a tax loophole.

Republicans need to draw the line in the sand and vigorously oppose any greater burden of doing business in the Commonwealth. In this instance, when I speak of Republicans, I certainly mean elected officials at the state level, but even greater than just those who serve in the legislature. Business leaders, chambers of commerce and individuals need to oppose the efforts of the liberals on increased taxation.

All too often, it is only the GOP members of the House and Senate fighting against such efforts to increase taxes or regulations on businesses, while at best, the business community tentatively engages the Beacon Hill establishment. This must change if businesses want to have a real voice in state government. You can be certain when there is a union or labor issue before the legislature, there is an organized effort to be heard. The business community needs to exercise their own political muscle or else face the same negative and unpredictable consequences they have apparently grown accustomed.

One of the proposals by Governor Patrick, which I believe is extremely counter-productive, would be to place a new tax on communications networks, including on the telephone poles themselves. While it may appear that this new tax would create more net income to the state, when asked in a committee hearing at the State House, the Governor's staff admitted that there has not been a dynamic analysis on the long term net revenue to the state, nor what economic impact such a tax might have on the stability and growth of the industry.

While no credible projection has been forthcoming from the corner office, according to some experts around the State House, if the new tax passed, an estimated 2,200 jobs could be lost just in the telecommunications industry. I believe that our longstanding tax policy related to telecommunications actually encourages capital investment and job growth in the communications industry and has worked well.

To demonstrate this, according to a Boston Globe piece, just last year Verizon alone invested $600 million in Massachusetts to continue efforts to transform its network to a technologically advanced all-fiber network. At the same time it generated $180 million in state and local taxes. Counting payroll for its 14,000 employees, pensions, healthcare costs, and almost $500 million spent with Massachusetts companies, in 2006 Verizon alone poured over $2 billion into the state's economy.

Together, the major carriers generated almost $500 million in state and local taxes last year, including $221 million in sales taxes that are not assessed on other companies. If we were to increase the taxes on such companies, what would happen to their ability to hire or retain employees as well as continue to invest to upgrade our technology? What would happen to the rates for consumers?

While some want you to believe that we can lower our local property tax bills by increasing state taxes on businesses, I believe that view is shortsighted and often results in less revenue to the state and an overall negative business climate. This will result in the continued reliance on residential property tax payers. Once again, this is proven and pure supply-side economic theory.

The bottom line is that when taxes are increased on businesses, they either choose to locate their operations elsewhere or consumers end up paying the price as businesses raise prices to cover the new taxes. Rather than simply viewing our businesses as a revenue source, we should do more to work with them by having a fair and predictable tax system, which would encourage business to relocate and expand here in Massachusetts. This will also create greater employment opportunities for our citizens and ultimately more revenue for the state. If we do not change our view, I am afraid we will continue to see more businesses leave Massachusetts and take our good people with them.

While my GOP is often labeled as the political party of big business, my opposition to increased business taxes has nothing to do with my desire to protect corporations. Republicans need to remind people that supply-side economic theory does work when all of its components are honored, including the most important element of reductions to wasteful spending programs. When fully implemented, history tells us that people and business will pay less taxes as a percentage of their income, and government overall will have a greater amount of revenue due to the increased economic activity, which will actually provide more funding for necessary services.

The Republican platform and those who run for elective office as conservatives should support pro-growth style tax cuts, which undoubtedly boost economic performance and expand individual opportunity to provide for one's family. While the issue of corporate tax loopholes is a slightly different question than the appropriate effective tax rate for all businesses, the same principle does apply. The primary problem I see in Massachusetts is that there is little certainty as to what the tax policy will be in the future.

While some liberal politicians argue that taxes should be higher in order for government to provide more services, if these same folks would bother to study proven and sound economic policy, they should join my GOP and support more tax cuts like the ones adopted on the federal level by the Republicans in 2003. The root of the problem which continues in Washington, D.C. and on Beacon Hill is that despite record high levels of revenue collections, the spending remains unchecked and no matter how much government collects, legislators always seem to be at least one step ahead with their spending.

Chapter Nine – The 2nd Amendment means more than just guns!

"We hold these truths to be self-evident, that all men are created equal, that they are endowed by their Creator with certain unalienable Rights, that among these are Life, Liberty and the pursuit of Happiness. That to secure these rights, Governments are instituted among Men, deriving their just powers from the consent of the governed, <u>that whenever any Form of Government becomes destructive of these ends, it is the Right of the People to alter or to abolish it, and to institute new Government</u>…"

As any casual student of American history knows full well, the above words are directly from the United States Declaration of Independence as adopted on July 4, 1776, which declared that the thirteen colonies were now "Free and Independent States." Our Founding Fathers had taken the bold and dangerous step of declaring their independence from King George, III and from the British Empire. These brave men knew full well of the treason they were committing towards their mother land as they desired to create a new nation of limited government and personal freedoms.

Quite unmistakably, from reading the text of this founding document and further studying the actual writings of our Founding Fathers, we know that it was their clear and unequivocal intent that the ultimate power of this new American government was to primarily reside with the actual people and not with the government itself.

This fundamental principle of the people retaining the power is wholly consistent with the Republican Party's platform. As discussed in chapter seven, my GOP is the political party which stands for the rights of the people when they speak at the ballot box, prefers local control of government and stands firm on individual rights, including the Second Amendment right to keep and bear arms. This is the focus of this chapter. I could have chosen any of the individual rights included in the Bill of Rights to make such a point, but by thrusting the issues of the Second Amendment into a discussion of constitutional interpretation, I hope to demonstrate the need for Republicans to continue to fight for conservative judges and only a strict interpretation of law, which certainly includes the Constitution first and foremost.

Today, some left-leaning folks would have us believe otherwise, but America is supposed to be about personal freedoms and personal responsibilities, not about the powers of a large and centralized government. While it is not frequently discussed in the modern political climate, included in these rights granted and guaranteed by our Founders, is the right for citizens to change or alter the government altogether when it no longer serves the purposes enshrined in the Preamble of the Constitution:

"We the People of the United States, in Order to form a more perfect Union, establish Justice, insure domestic Tranquility, provide for the common defence, promote the general Welfare, and secure the Blessings of Liberty to ourselves and our Posterity, do ordain and establish this Constitution for the United States of America."

Remember that George Washington, John Adams, James Madison, Thomas Jefferson and many other of our Founding Fathers had risked everything they owned to rebel against their mother Country. They knew full well that sometimes governments become unresponsive and cruel towards their citizens and thus the ultimate power must be retained by the people and not with the institution of the government itself. The inclusion of such a constitutional provision to allow the change or complete elimination of this new government if it no longer serves the best interest of the people it purports to be representing is entirely consistent with the concerns of many of our Founders.

While the Framers of our Constitution were indeed the elite citizens of their time, they were purposely driven to create a new and free nation: One not controlled by a group of elite nobility, but one of the common man. Remember, this is exactly what they were revolting against. The Founding Fathers had risked their reputations, their fortunes and even their own lives to rid themselves of an overreaching monarchy. In this chapter we will discuss how the Second Amendment is about a lot more than just guns. It stands along with all the other personal rights provided to us in the Bill of Rights. These rights were provided to protect us from an abusive government and not to grant additional power to the government.

In fact, the Founders displayed how important this right was by placing it second among the rights and liberties included in the Bill of Rights. Our Founding Fathers did not trust government, whether it was the old one in England or the new government forming in the American colonies. They undoubtedly understood that if the ultimate power to alter an unresponsive government was to be retained by the people, that these very same people must possess the right to keep firearms to defend themselves against a tyrannical government that could possibly develop at some point in the future.

The Second Amendment of the United States Constitution may only be the twenty-seven words of: "A well regulated Militia, being necessary to the security of a free State, the right of the people to keep and bear Arms, shall not be infringed," but the meaning of the Second Amendment is one of the most misunderstood and most frequently disputed in our constitutional history.

With liberals today suggesting that the Founding Fathers only wanted to protect the states' ability to maintain a militia or national guard, the comments of our Founders clearly indicate otherwise:

"The true importance of the Second Amendment will not be fully understood, until they begin to usurp its power."

Thomas Jefferson

"The said Constitution shall never be construed to authorize Congress to prevent the people of the United States who are peaceable citizens from keeping their own arms."

Samuel Adams

"Americans need never fear their government because of the advantage of being armed, which the Americans possess over the people of almost every other nation."

James Madison

"The great object is that every man be armed. Everybody who is able may have a gun."

Patrick Henry

"No free man shall ever be debarred the use of arms. The strongest reason for the people to retain their right to keep and bear arms is as a last resort to protect themselves against tyranny in government."

Thomas Jefferson

"I ask sir, what is the militia? It is the whole people, except for a few public officials."

George Mason

"Arms in the hands of citizens may be used at individual discretion...in private defense."

James Madison

"Firearms stand next in importance to the Constitution itself. They are the American people's liberty teeth and keystone under independence...From the hour the Pilgrims landed, to the present day, events, occurrences, and tendencies prove that to ensure peace, security, and happiness, the rifle and pistol are equally indispensable, The very atmosphere of firearms everywhere restrains evil interference, they deserve a place of honor with all that's good."

George Washington

The Framers of our federal constitution and the subsequent Bill of Rights, who unmistakably feared government's potential abuses, knew full well that if the real power of government was going to ultimately be retained by the people, the people must be guaranteed an individual right to keep and bear arms for private purposes. As compared to the liberal interpretation of the Second Amendment as being some sort of collective or group right to keep and bear arms only in connection with state militia service, the right of citizens to bear arms is an important personal right. The official Republican Party's Platform embraces this principle:

"Republicans and President Bush strongly support an individual's right to own guns, which is explicitly protected by the Constitution's Second Amendment. Our Party honors the great American tradition of hunting and we applaud efforts by the Bush Administration to make more public lands available to hunters, to increase access to hunting clinics and safety programs for children and adults, and to improve opportunities for hunting for Americans with disabilities. We believe the Second Amendment and all of the rights guaranteed by it should enable law-abiding citizens throughout the country to own firearms in their homes for self-defense."

The Father of our nation, George Washington himself personally owned over fifty firearms including both handguns and rifles. As we know full well, he led the fight for freedom and liberty with thousands of other citizen soldiers who brought their own firearms to the battles against England. To make the suggestion, as so many liberals do, that the Second Amendment does not apply to an individual right would be laughable, if it were not so dangerous.

As tensions mounted between England and the colonists, the British military had attempted their own form of gun control with a raid on the guns and supplies stored in Concord, Massachusetts. During the early morning hours of April 19, 1775, British troops assembled with plans to destroy military supplies in an effort to inhibit the colonists' ability to resist the orders of the British regarding taxation. Fortunately, the colonists had received word of the impending British assault and had moved most of the arms supplies to safety at another location. The subsequent battles of Lexington and Concord were the first military engagements of the American Revolutionary War and changed the course of freedom and liberty forever in America.

One does have to wonder if the British had started the process of destroying and confiscating firearms belonging to the colonists at the very first sign of the pending conflict, whether the outcome of the Revolutionary War might have been different. It is hard to imagine that our Founding Fathers would have been able to muster any effort for independence at all without firearms.

So, I would hope at this point in the discussion on the Second Amendment that we can at least agree that our Founding Fathers recognized the necessary right of citizens to own firearms. While this fact along with the actual text of the Second Amendment is enough for most conservative-minded folks, my left-leaning friends are likely to suggest that even if the right existed at the founding of America, today the constitution does not mean the same thing as it did over two-hundred years ago. Many liberals believe the Constitution is a "living and breathing" document, one subject to interpretation by modern-day standards. My GOP must remain firm on the principle that the Constitution is not a mere guideline for expected behavior. It is a law and must be honored and followed according to its actual language. Unlike many other countries where constitutions are merely a statement of ideals or aspirations, our constitution is the supreme law of the land.

To start where any good constitutional analysis should begin, is with a careful review of the plain text of the amendment itself, which in this case guarantees in part "the right of the people to keep and bear Arms." Throughout the entire Constitution and Bill of Rights, individual rights are guaranteed to "the people" and only the Tenth Amendment specifically refers to the rights of the states. So why should the Second Amendment be read differently? Obviously it should not, but as we know, sometimes liberals like to give alternative or modern definitions to things.

Some folks like President Clinton sadly amused us with his statement: "It depends on what the meaning of the words "is" is," during his 1998 grand jury testimony regarding his Monica Lewinsky "incident." It's all a matter of interpretation. All throughout the language of the Bill of Rights, it is clear the rights of the people were being protected, not the rights of the government itself and no modern-day interpretation should be allowed to alter the true meaning.

Remember that the power of government itself to declare war is found in Article I of the Constitution and the powers of President as Commander in Chief are authorized in Article II. Why would the Framers of the Bill of Rights feel the need to spell out further rights of government in the Bill of Rights where the underlying purpose of the first ten amendments were to protect individual rights from government intrusion?

In some cases, there can be a reasonable disagreement as to the meaning of a phrase or provision of any document, including the Constitution itself. In those rare instances where there is room for multiple meanings to a sentence or phrase, the next appropriate step is to look to the historical context and the intent of the people who actually drafted it. Either way, the Second Amendment is about the individual right to keep and bear arms!

Without the Bill of Rights being adopted, many of our sacred personal rights, such as: religious freedom; the right to a free press; the right to be free from warantless searches; the right of the accused to a trial by jury or to confront their accuser, right to a jury trial; and the right against cruel and abusive treatment may not have been ultimately provided. Throughout world history many people have been abused by their own governments and our Founding Fathers wanted to ensure that the ability of this new Federal government to abuse Americans would not be allowed.

The personal right to keep and bear arms is just one of those many rights our Founders configured to restrain a would-be tyrannical central government. Again, we must remember that King George, III was squarely on the Founder's mind. The right to keep and bear arms is as equally important as all of our other freedoms. My GOP has a long and proud history of protecting the Second Amendment. We must continue to do so, for if we allow the erosion of any one of our liberties, it won't be long before none of them remain.

In drafting the Constitution, the Framers desired to define and narrow the role of the federal government, protect the sovereignty of the states and protect the individual rights of the people. Just like the main body of the Constitution itself, the Bill of Rights is all about limiting the power of government, not granting it additional power. The Founding Fathers also recognized that it would have to be changed from time to time. Rather than encourage judges or politicians to apply their own contemporary beliefs, the Framers of the Constitution expressly included a provision directly in the Constitution allowing for amendments. Article V of the Constitution provides in part:

> "The Congress, whenever two thirds of both Houses shall deem it necessary, shall propose Amendments to this Constitution, or, on the Application of the Legislatures of two thirds of the several States, shall call a Convention for proposing Amendments, which, in either Case, shall be valid to all Intents and Purposes, as part of this Constitution, when ratified by the Legislatures of three fourths of the several States, or by Conventions in three fourths thereof...."

While our Constitutional Framers recognized that the young nation needed a stronger central government than the one that existed under the Articles of Confederation, they also wanted to make sure that at some point later that the federal government would never be able to infringe upon the very freedoms our Founding Fathers had risked so much to establish in this new nation.

While there is little disagreement as to the historical intent of the Bill of Rights, the interpretation of the Second Amendment remains a subject of much debate. Fortunately for those of us who hold the Bill of Rights sacred, on June 26, 2008, by a 5 to 4 decision in the case of <u>District of Columbia, et al. v. Dick Anthony Heller</u>, the Supreme Court handed down the most important decisions in modern history concerning the meaning of the Second Amendment.

Justice Scalia, writing for the majority, addressed the issue of a complete firearms ban in Washington D.C., "In sum, we hold that the District's ban on handgun possession in the home violates the Second Amendment, as does its prohibition against rendering any lawful firearm in the home operable for the purpose of immediate self-defense." The court based its decision that the operative clause of the Second Amendment, "the right of the people to keep and bear Arms, shall not be infringed." Finally, over two-hundred years after the ratification of the Bill of Rights we now have a firm statement from the Supreme Court telling us what all conservatives have always known: Americans have the personal and individual right to own a firearm!

"This is a great moment in American history. It vindicates individual Americans all over this country who have always known that this is their freedom worth protecting," declared National Rifle Association Executive Vice President Wayne LaPierre. "Our founding fathers wrote and intended the Second Amendment to be an individual right. The Supreme Court has now acknowledged it. The Second Amendment as an individual right now becomes a real permanent part of American Constitutional law."

Our Founding Fathers sought to guarantee the right of private ownership of firearms and not simply restate some right of the government itself to form or maintain a national guard. The Second Amendment guarantees an individual's right to possess a firearm unconnected with service in a militia, and to use firearms for traditionally lawful purposes, such as self-defense within the home. Thankfully the original meaning of our Constitution has not been altered by the four liberals on the court. All too often, activist judges want to apply a modern meaning to the constitution. When they do so, they are not only ignoring the available amendment process to change the constitution, they are lessening the public's confidence in our system of government itself. Our laws and constitution can and should at times be changed, but not by a court.

When considering the Founders' state of mind and intent, we must also recall the historical context in which the Constitution and Bill of Rights were created. During America's Revolutionary War with England, it was the citizen soldiers who took up their own arms and formed an army. When the colonists finally defeated the British troops, these firearms were not collected by the new government. The individual former soldiers took them back home from where they had come. To now make an argument that the Second Amendment only applies to our modern version of a national guard is ignoring history and the clear intent of our Founding Fathers.

We also have to remember the language of the Declaration of Independence as cited at the opening of this chapter, "...that whenever any Form of Government becomes destructive of these ends, it is the Right of the People to alter or to abolish it, and to institute new Government..." The Second Amendment right of private ownership in essence prevents the federal government from effectively disarming the general populace and thus eliminating their ability to protect themselves from an abusive government or even abolish it if necessary.

Were our Founding Fathers correct about such a fear of an overreaching central government or was it simply a case of extreme paranoia from the years of suffering under King George III? While not the focus of this chapter, a quick review of what has occurred in other nations around the globe leads one to better appreciate the fears of government repression and the underlying reasons why the Second Amendment was included in the Bill of Rights.

Probably the most well known and horrific historical account of a government first disarming its citizens and then abusing them occurred when Germany established a gun control program in 1938. It all started when the Nazi government required the immediate surrender of all firearms and other weapons by the Jewish people. For those people who were caught with such a weapon, a sentence of death or twenty years in a concentration camp was summarily imposed. When Adolf Hitler later made the decision to round up all the Jewish people, they were left unarmed and powerless to resist. We all know too well what occurred next.

I could go on with additional sad historical accounts from the Soviet Union where millions of dissidents were disarmed and exterminated in the late 1920's or in China in the late 1940's, where over twenty million political activists were stripped of their firearms and later killed. History tells us that the disarming of citizens has often been the first step of a subsequent loss of other rights and freedoms, or even worse. Our Founding Fathers knew full well that if the British Army had been able to disarm the colonists, the Revolutionary War would not have been won. In fact, it is doubtful it would have ever been fought.

This real constitutional debate today on the true meaning of the Second Amendment is not left to simply guess work. The alternatives to the Second Amendment we know were actually discussed by our Founding Fathers. If the Framers' of the Bill of Rights intent had been to protect only the states' ability to organize a militia or national guard, as some liberals now suggest, the Second Amendment would have been worded much differently.

For example, the delegates to the Constitutional Convention in Philadelphia could have adopted a proposed amendment by the Virginia delegation, which stated, "each State respectively shall have the power to provide for organizing, arming and disciplining its own militia, whensoever Congress shall omit or neglect to provide for the same," but our Founding

Fathers rejected this proposal and supported the language that still remains today of guaranteeing a right to "the people." Republicans today need to continue to honor the text of the Constitution itself and resist any effort to give new or modern meanings to otherwise well settled textual based personal rights and freedoms.

During their own respective period of time in history, the Framers of the Second Amendment knew full well that a significant part of America's population heavily depended upon the private ownership of arms to provide for and protect their families. While so many left-leaning Democrats today might attempt to argue this point, they are at a loss as to what they think would have happened if the federal government, after ratifying the Bill of Rights, had attempted to ban the citizens of America in the 18th Century from owning firearms.

What would have been the response if the new federal government of 1791 went traveling around the American countryside telling everyone that the Second Amendment only provided a right to form a government militia? Ask a liberal how they think George Washington, John Adams or Thomas Jefferson would have responded if some federal marshal arrived at their door stating the government was collecting, and would be maintaining in the government's custody, all privately owned guns.

Contrary to what some liberals try to get you to believe, the Constitution is not some living and breathing document, nor is it a broad statement of general principles, guidelines or suggestions. Unlike many other nations, our Constitution is given the full force of law. It is the highest and most honored law that is above all others. The Supremacy Clause or Article VI, Clause 2 of the United States Constitution states this founding principle:

"This Constitution, and the Laws of the United States which shall be made in Pursuance thereof; and all Treaties made, or which shall be made, under the authority of the United States, shall be the supreme Law of the land; and the Judges in every State shall be bound thereby, any Thing in the Constitution or Laws of any State to the Contrary notwithstanding."

If our nation is going to remain one of respect for our courts and legal system, the actual text of the document and the Founding Fathers intentions must always be honored. As noted previously, while there is a provision to allow for limited change in the form of amendments, the body of the Constitution and it's meaning was not meant to be changed by modern thinking. Rather, to be a unwavering set of rules and standards that could be relied on and maintained with continuity from generation to generation without being watered down or twisted into some unrecognizable statement of a current politically popular platform. My GOP must never allow the Constitution to be tampered with for political sake. Whether it benefits the conservatives or liberals, our first allegiance must always remain to the Constitution itself!

The interpretation of the Second Amendment, or any other constitutional provision, must be done so with an honest and strict construction of the actual text. When judges usurp our Framers' intention and read their own personal meaning into the document, it most often has lead to disastrous results throughout United States history. The theory of the living and breathing constitution or a broad interpretation theory of the constitution has also been responsible for many of this nation's worst Supreme Court rulings.

For example, in the case of <u>Dred Scott v. Sanford</u> of 1857, the Supreme Court ignored the actual words of the constitution and declared that free blacks were not citizens. To make matters worse, the majority of justices held that they were protecting the property rights of slave owners. By not strictly reading and interpreting the actual words of the constitution, the Supreme Court basically manufactured a property right of human beings where plainly the constitution did not provide one.

In 1896, the <u>Plessy v. Ferguson</u> case was decided where the United States Supreme Court upheld the "separate but equal" doctrine of segregation of black Americans. Of course they did so despite the fact that segregation is squarely at odds with the language and clear meaning of the 14th Amendment. I would suspect that the seven justices who voted in favor of segregation did so not because of their own fair interpretation of the words of the constitution, but more likely, they read into it their own personal prejudices and beliefs.

I could spend this entire chapter, or perhaps a whole other book, outlining the harmful mistakes when liberals give their own personal political definition to the constitution. The point is clear that if our constitution is going to truly mean something, it must be strictly interpreted as written and our judges and elected officials must remain more dedicated to the constitution than to any cause, issue or any political party. No matter where someone stands on any given issue, my GOP must always be the political party to uphold our constitution. In the wise words of Abraham Lincoln:

> "Don't interfere with anything in the Constitution. That must be maintained, for it is the only safeguard of our liberties."

The Constitution says, "The right of the people to keep and bear arms shall not be infringed" and the Founding Fathers and now our Supreme Court unmistakably set forth what I believe is the position of most of the members of my GOP. The Second Amendment means more than just guns, it is about honoring our constitution and the individual rights which make us all free.

Chapter Ten - Why I am a Republican

Well, if you have stayed with me for the first nine chapters, I hope you know why I am a Republican. There is surely no single issue or motivation for labeling myself as a member of the GOP, but without question Ronald Reagan first put the idea into my head in 1980. From there, and primarily based on the values with which my mother and grandparents raised me, it was an easy road to travel. Today, some twenty-nine years later, I proudly remain a conservative Republican. I continue to believe my GOP is the best hope for America to be as safe, free and prosperous as possible.

For sure, I do not share each and every belief of the official Republican Party's Platform and there certainly have been many times when a GOP elected official has disappointed me. But this has never dissuaded me from using my best efforts to push my chosen political party to where I believe it needs to go. To wit, the motivation for this very book...

In the previous pages, I have exposed my own personal thoughts, opinions and beliefs. Now it is time to provide some space for the words of others. This chapter is simply a compilation of statements and quotes from some well known and some not so well known individuals for whom I have an underlying respect. Many quotes are from historical figures that have long since departed this earth. Some are offered by my fellow Republican office holders of today. A few others are provided by citizens who have volunteered their reasons for being a Republican. To start off, let us review the official oath of my GOP.

The Republican Oath

> ➢ I believe that the proper function of government is to do for the people those things that have to be done but cannot be done, or cannot be done as well by individuals, and that the

most effective government is government closest to the people.

➢ I believe that good government is based on the individual and that each person's ability, dignity, freedom and responsibility must be honored and recognized.

➢ I believe that free enterprise and the encouragement of individual initiative and incentive have given this nation an economic system second to none.

➢ I believe that sound money policy should be our goal.

➢ I believe in equal rights, equal justice and equal opportunity for all, regardless of race, creed, age, sex or national origin. I believe that persons with disabilities should be afforded equal rights, equal justice and equal opportunity as well.

➢ I believe we must retain those principles worth retaining, yet always be receptive to new ideas with an outlook broad enough to accommodate thoughtful change and varying points of view.

➢ I believe that Americans value and should preserve their feeling of national strength and pride, and at the same time, share with people everywhere a desire for peace and freedom and the extension of human rights throughout the world.

➢ Finally, I believe that the Republican Party is the best vehicle for translating these ideals into positive and successful principles of government.

The following pages are quotations from various individuals from different periods in history who share their statements and beliefs as to why they call themselves Republicans:

"The Founding Fathers knew a government can't control the economy without controlling people. And they knew when a government sets out to do that, it must use force and coercion to achieve its purpose. So we have come to a time for choosing... I didn't leave the Democratic Party. The party left me."

"I am a Republican. But I am a Republican without a hyphen. I am neither a Left, nor a Right, nor a Mainstream, nor even an over-there-in-the-ripples-and-shallows-Republican. It is my belief that the Party which I represent is polarized around a policy of adherence to constitutional limits on the power of government and fiscal responsibility, and that government, to be effective and to be just, must be kept close to the people..."

"I believe our Republican Party is the true party of the future because our vision, ideas, and proposals seek to bring out the best in America by challenging the best in our people. The Great Opportunity Party believes in challenging people to do better. The Democratic leadership still insists on challenging government to grow bigger."

Ronald Wilson Reagan, the 40th President of the United States

---

"I am a Republican, as the two great political parties are now divided, because the Republican Party is a national party seeking the greatest good for the greatest number of citizens...But I am a Republican for many other reasons. The Republican Party assures protection to life and property, the public credit, and the payment of the debts of the government, State, county, or municipality, so far as it can control. The Democratic

party does not promise this; if it does, it has broken its promises to the extent of hundreds of millions, as many Northern Democrats can testify to their sorrow. I am a Republican, as between the existing parties, because it fosters the production of the field and farm, and of manufactories, and it encourages the general education of the poor as well as the rich."

Ulysses S. Grant, the 18th President of the United States

"I am a Republican because, like you, I want to relieve the American people of the heavy hand of a government. I am a Republican because, like you, I believe government must defend our nation's security wisely and effectively . . . I am a Republican because I believe, like you, that government should tax us no more than necessary, spend no more than necessary . . . I am a Republican because I believe the judges we appoint to the federal bench must understand that enforcing our laws, not making them, is their only responsibility..."

John McCain, Senior Senator from Arizona and candidate for President

---

"I am a Republican because we are the party committed to lessening the burden of taxes, cutting government regulations and reducing government spending, all for the purpose of generating the higher economic growth that will bring better jobs, wages and living standards to all our people."

Colin Powell, Secretary of State under George W. Bush

"We Republicans seek a government that attends to its inherent responsibilities of maintaining a stable monetary and fiscal climate, encouraging a free and a competitive economy and enforcing law and order. Thus, do we seek inventiveness, diversity, and creative difference within a stable order, for we Republicans define government's role where needed at many, many levels -- preferably, though, the one closest to the people involved."

Barry Goldwater, five-term United States Senator from Arizona and the Republican Party's nominee for President in 1964. Goldwater is often credited for sparking the resurgence of the conservative political movement in the 1960s

---

"I am a Republican, a black, dyed in the wool Republican, and I never intend to belong to any other party than the party of freedom and progress."

Frederick Douglass, one of the foremost leaders of the abolitionist movement which fought to end slavery. Douglass served as an adviser to Abraham Lincoln during the Civil War

---

"I'm a Republican because I have lived the American Dream. The American Dream might take different forms for different people. To the young families who are the roots of our society, it might mean owning their very first home. To the single mom who needs medicine for herself and her child, it might mean health care you own and can take with you when you switch jobs. To the small family business owner who dreams of growing his

business, it might mean lower taxes and less regulation. To our seniors, including members of that Greatest Generation, it might mean knowing that they can control their own retirement. But to all of them, it means opportunity, and a limitless future. And that is what our Party is all about."

Mel Martinez, United States Senator from Florida and former Chairman of the Republican Party

---

"I recognized government was not the answer to every problem. I learned that personal responsibility and a government closer to the people was supremely better for businesses and individuals than an intrusive federal government that lead to a personal dependency through liberal programs. The grand power of the United States hinges on a competitive, free market economy in order to protect life, liberty, and the pursuit of happiness."

Orrin Hatch, United States Senator from Utah

"There are several reasons why I am a Republican." First and foremost, I believe that it is the people not government that is granted the power by God to make a difference in the world...As the Declaration of Independence declares, 'governments are instituted among men, deriving their just powers from the consent from the governed.'"*

Chuck Norris, actor and political supporter of former Presidential Candidate Mike Huckabee

---

"We remember those great Republican Presidents who sustained American leadership through the decades, ended the Cold War and lifted our nuclear nightmare. Thank you Gerald Ford, Ronald Reagan and George Herbert Walker Bush."

Condoleezza Rice, Secretary of State for President George W. Bush

---

"Why am I a Republican? I am a Christian who believes in the right to say 'Under God' in our Pledge of Allegiance or have a prayer in school, but my party respects the right to not have to say a prayer or to face East at the appropriate time to pray to Allah if that is your belief. My party is committed to helping the poor, while at the same time encouraging all Americans to do more without punishing them with higher taxes and excessive regulation."

Lynn Swann, former wide receiver with the Pittsburg Steelers

"Why am I a Republican? Two words, Ronald Reagan. I became interested in politics as President Carter led our country into a malaise that Ronald Reagan led us out of. He was inspirational, an incredible orator and a man of conviction. He didn't just talk the talk, he truly walked the walk. He had a way of delivering news, good and bad with cautious optimism, speaking bluntly but eloquently and most importantly he bled red, white and blue. A true patriot and a man of his word, there is no better reflection of the greatness of the Republican Party than Ronald Reagan."

Rep. Bradley H. Jones, Jr., Republican Minority Leader

"I am a Republican because it is the party which stands most closely for what the Founders envisioned for America; individual liberty and individual responsibility."

Michael O'Keefe, District Attorney, Cape Cod & the Islands

"As someone who has been in Law Enforcement, Public Safety and Corrections my entire life I couldn't help but have a Republican/Conservative mind set."

James Cummings, Barnstable County Sheriff

"When I first registered to vote, I was a student at a Massachusetts public college. So, of course, I went along with the crowd and registered as a Democrat. I didn't know anything about politics, or the history and traditions of either political party. Looking back, I can say I was definitely "under the influence" of some very outspoken liberal college professors. I even voted for Mike Dukakis for President! I know, I know. They had done a good job of indoctrinating me.

I credit several important people with my evolution into a Republican: My parents, Don & Alberta Humason, were never particularly political at home. But they taught by example. They were consistent voters and supported some good local candidates for office. They also taught me to think independently, critically. And they instilled in me the values of hard work, independence, and frugality.

My friend Steve Pierce deserves the lion's share of credit for my transformation. Steve was Westfield's State Representative and the Minority Leader of the Massachusetts House of Representatives when I had my political coming of age. He entered the race for Governor in 1990 and I volunteered to help him. I decided I would change my party registration to Independent in order for my signature to count toward the total he needed. The more I listened to Representative Pierce on the campaign trail that year, the more I came to realize that I agreed with many of his Republican ideas. Ideas like fiscal conservatism, small and efficient government, individual responsibility unhindered by intrusive government, and the like. I went on to work for Steve's successor, Republican State Representative Mike Knapik.

If anything, my Republican and conservative credentials have only been strengthened, even at a time when much of this country, state, and legislature have turned their backs on the Republican philosophy in favor of a Democratic party that promises to take care of all their troubles if only they will surrender their money and freedoms."

Donald F. Humason, Jr., Westfield's State Representative

"I am a Republican because I do not believe government has all the answers."

Taylor White, Chief of Staff to Rep. Jeffrey Davis Perry

"People all too often ask me: Are you extinct yet? Although the question is posed with light humor, it is a serious matter that the Republican Party is almost non-existent in Massachusetts. I am committed now more than ever to returning our Commonwealth to a place where two-party government is real as this benefits all of our citizens. Our first steps include re-defining what it means to be Republican and inviting with modern technology, more young, female and minority voters to consider being a part

of our Party. Republican principles of low taxation, personal responsibility and small government resonate with lots of people. Let's make it cool to be Republican, not an embarrassment."

Representative Karyn Polito, R-Shrewsbury

"*I am a Republican because I believe that conservatism represents mainstream America and that liberals and moderates are the ones who are out of step with our country's values. I am a Republican because I believe in the wisdom of our forefathers. I do not try to rewrite history just because history is not politically correct or contradicts liberalism.*

I am a Republican because I believe in assisting the truly disadvantaged; recognizing the need for personal responsibility rather than a never-ending stream of handouts without accountability. I am a Republican because I believe that hard work and entrepreneurialism should be rewarded and not disdained and taxed to death.

I am Republican because I see what is great about America and do not continually search for what is wrong just to malign our country.

I am a Republican because I believe that there is a difference between truth and lies. Just because a lie is repeated over and over and the masses believe it, doesn't make it true.

I am a Republican because I believe there's more good in America than bad, that optimism trumps pessimism any day of the week, and that what is good and right will win in the end.

I am a Republican because I believe that as individuals we have the right to bear arms and defend our homes, our families, and ourselves with deadly force.

I am a Republican because I believe that as a country we must honor and recognize the great sacrifices that our military makes every day and allow them to do their jobs without the interference of ridiculous political correctness.

I am a Republican because I believe in the rule of law and that we cannot sanction the breaking of laws by drug users, illegal aliens, or anyone and to do so undermine the fabric of our nation.

I am a Republican because I believe in the sanctity of life from the point of conception. I am a Republican because I believe that our country was founded on Judeo-Christian principles that recognize and honor God yet allows us to worship Him as we wish.

I am a Republican because I believe that government is not the solution to our problems as a nation, in fact, the less government intrudes into our lives the better off we are."

Dennis Fonseca, Chairman of Sandwich Republican Town
Committee and Campaign Chairman for Jeff Perry's Campaign
Committee

"I am a Republican because I firmly believe that no man is free until all men are free and the Republican Party possesses the best philosophy to achieve this goal. We Republicans believe that man is basically good and that government should be limited. Democrats believe that man needs to be governed with more and more restrictions and laws that only serve to restrict individual freedoms."

Dave Neal, political activist

"Naturally, one's political philosophy and orientation come from a variety of sources, but for me, the modeling, mentoring and parenting of my Mom and Dad, especially Dad, were the very foundation of my current thinking. To be sure, adolescence, college years, young adulthood, and working in the field of education were challenges for me but the strong voice of Dad never disappeared.

He was a smart, hard working business man who believed success was the direct result of personal hard work, discipline and focus. Our life's playbook is determined not by the government but by how we live our lives, what we give back to the community (that includes lots of campaigning) whether we were patriotic and whether we lived honest lives with a strong commitment to family and friends.

In addition, his support for lower taxes, smaller government, and individual responsibility were other sources of my current Republican orientation."

Fran Manzelli, President of the Cape Cod Republican Club

"I'm a republican because I enjoy freedoms and personal liberties at my own expense. If I were a democrat I would enjoy liberties at the expense of others' freedoms."

Jonelle Gingrich, Legislative Aide

"Having lost all faith in the Democrat Party during decades of membership, I joined the GOP when Ronald Reagan came on the scene and have never looked back. I'm deeply committed to the solidly conservative, pro family and moral values which are embedded in the GOP

philosophy; in the concept of smaller government and people-power over their own lives and income; in an educational system which teaches children HOW to think, not WHAT to think; in upholding the virtues of honesty and truth. Mostly, I value the loyalty to and defense of our Constitution and the rights it provides. This is why I am a Republican."

Patricia Stebbins, President, Cape Cod Family Life Alliance

"I am a Republican as I believe Americans should keep more of what they earn, have more control of their private lives and less government involvement in business. As a Republican, I believe the family is first. While neither party is perfect, I believe the Republican Party most closely represents the men and women who get up every day, go to work, and raise their families."

Chris Perry, son of Jeff Perry

"I am a member of the Republican Party because I have believed that their basic philosophy of small government, low taxes, encouraging entrepreneurship, capitalism, and strict interpretation of the Constitution would help keep the spirit of freedom and patriotism alive and well in our Country. I am now beginning to wonder if the Republican Party that I once knew, is transforming its ideals of conservative values to those of being more politically correct so that we will be 'more liked'. If this is so, I am fearful that it will bring about its own death and destruction."

Carol Fonseca, GOP campaign volunteer and activist

"Being a member of the Republican Party in Massachusetts is in many ways a purely symbolic way of expressing the conservative ideal; that our government must be one of limited powers if we are to be free to pursue our dreams and achieve the type of greatness only found in America."

Brent T. Warren, Esquire

"To live in the greatest Nation is truly a privilege and an honor. To this we owe a great debt of gratitude to our forefathers and those who have perished in the time of war; those who unselfishly made tremendous sacrifices while standing up for freedom and what they felt was right. I am a Republican because I believe that each and every individual has the responsibility to strive toward preserving the personal freedoms we are so fortunate and blessed to have been given by those who came before us and fought for our future. We are the future of freedom."

Lisa Perry, 1st Lady of the Fifth Barnstable District

Chapter Eleven - Rendezvous with Destiny

Address by Ronald Reagan on behalf of Senator Barry Goldwater
October 27, 1964

There are certain "must reads" in every profession. Just as every lawyer has a copy of Black's Law Dictionary and every medical doctor surely has a Physicians' Desk Reference always nearby, any serious Republican should take a few moments and read Ronald Reagan's 1964 speech, "A Time for Choosing" or a "Rendezvous with Destiny."

While writing this book and considering what portions of the speech to quote, it became obvious that any attempt at editing would end in a severe injustice and thus what follows is a verbatim account of a nationwide televised program on behalf of Barry Goldwater, who was the Republican candidate for the presidency. The speech was given by Ronald Reagan who actively supported Goldwater during the entire campaign. Just two years prior to this speech, Ronald Reagan was a Democrat. As he formally switched to the Republican Party, Reagan was famously quoted as saying "I didn't leave the Democratic Party. The party left me."

Every member of my GOP should take the time to read Ronald Reagan's speech and reflect on his words. They are as true today as they were when the Great Communicator first uttered them!

"Thank you very much. Thank you and good evening. The sponsor has been identified, but unlike most television programs, the performer hasn't been provided with a script. As a matter of fact, I have been permitted to choose my own ideas regarding the choice that we face in the next few weeks. I have spent most of my life as a Democrat. I recently have seen fit to follow another course. I believe that the issues confronting us cross party lines. Now, one side in this campaign has been telling us that the issues of this election are the maintenance of peace and prosperity. The line has been used "We've never had it so good."

But I have an uncomfortable feeling that this prosperity isn't something on which we can base our hopes for the future. No nation in history has ever survived a tax burden that reached a third of its national income. Today, 37 cents of every dollar earned in this country is the tax collector's share, and yet our government continues to spend $17 million a day more than the government takes in. We haven't balanced our budget 28 out of the last 34 years. We have raised our debt limit three times in the last twelve months, and now our national debt is one and a half times bigger than all the combined debts of all the nations in the world. We have $15 billion in gold in our treasury, we don't own an ounce. Foreign dollar claims are $27.3 billion, and we have just had announced that the dollar of 1939 will now purchase 45 cents in its total value.

As for the peace that we would preserve, I wonder who among us would like to approach the wife or mother whose husband or son has died in South Vietnam and ask them if they think this is a peace that should be maintained indefinitely. Do they mean peace, or do they mean we just want to be left in peace? There can be no real peace while one American is dying some place in the world for the rest of us. We are at war with the most dangerous enemy that has ever faced mankind in his long climb from the swamp to the stars, and it has been said if we lose that war, and in doing so lose this way of freedom of ours, history will record with the greatest astonishment that those who had the most to lose did the least to prevent its happening. Well, I think it's time we ask ourselves if we still know the freedoms that were intended for us by the Founding Fathers.

Not too long ago two friends of mine were talking to a Cuban refugee, a businessman who had escaped from Castro, and in the midst of his story one of my friends turned to the other and said, "We don't know how lucky we are." And the Cuban stopped and said, "How lucky you are! I had someplace to escape to." In that sentence he told us the entire story. If we lose freedom here, there is no place to escape to. This is the last stand on Earth. And this idea that government is beholden to the people, that it has no other source of power except to sovereign people, is still the newest and most unique idea in all the long history of man's relation to man. This is the issue of this election. Whether we believe in our capacity for self-government or whether we abandon the American Revolution and confess that a little intellectual elite in a far-distant capital can plan our lives for us better than we can plan them ourselves.

You and I are told increasingly that we have to choose between a left or right, but I would like to suggest that there is no such thing as a left or right. There is only an up or down, up to a man's age, old dream, the ultimate in individual freedom consistent with law and order, or down to the ant heap totalitarianism, and regardless of their sincerity, their humanitarian motives, those who would trade our freedom for security have embarked on this downward course.

In this vote harvesting time, they use terms like the "Great Society," or as we were told a few days ago by the President, we must accept a "greater government activity in the affairs of the people." But they have been a little more explicit in the past and among themselves--and all of the things that I now will quote have appeared in print. These are not Republican accusations. For example, they have voices that say "the cold war will end through acceptance of a not undemocratic socialism." Another voice says that the profit motive has become outmoded, it must be replaced by the incentives of the welfare state; or our traditional system of individual freedom is incapable of solving the complex problems of the 20th century. Senator Fullbright has said at Stanford University that the Constitution is outmoded. He referred to the president as our moral teacher and our leader, and he said he is hobbled in his task by the restrictions in power imposed on him by this antiquated document. He must be freed so that he can do for us what he knows is best. And Senator Clark of Pennsylvania, another articulate spokesman, defines liberalism as "meeting the material needs of the masses through the full power of centralized government." Well, I for one resent it when a representative of the people refers to you and me, the free man and woman of this country as "the masses." This is a term we haven't applied to ourselves in America. But beyond that, "the full power of centralized government," this was the very thing the Founding Fathers sought to minimize. They knew that governments don't control things. A government can't control the economy without controlling people. And they know when a government sets out to do that, it must use force and coercion to achieve its purpose. They also knew, those Founding Fathers, that outside of its legitimate functions, government does nothing as well or as economically as the private sector of the economy.

Now, we have no better example of this than the government's involvement in the farm economy over the last 30 years. Since 1955, the cost of this program has nearly doubled. One-fourth of farming in America is responsible for 85% of the farm surplus. Three-fourths of farming is out on the free market and has known a 21% increase in the per capita consumption of all its produce. You see, that one-fourth of farming is regulated and controlled by the federal government. In the last three years we have spent $43 in feed grain program for every bushel of corn we don't grow.

Senator Humphrey last week charged that Barry Goldwater as President would seek to eliminate farmers. He should do his homework a little better, because he will find out that we have had a decline of 5 million in the farm population under these government programs. He will also find that the Democratic administration has sought to get from Congress an extension of the farm program to include that three-fourths that is now free. He will find that they have also asked for the right to imprison farmers who wouldn't keep books as prescribed by the federal government. The Secretary of Agriculture asked for the right to seize farms through condemnation and resell them to other individuals. And contained in that same program was a provision that would have allowed the federal government to remove 2 million farmers from the soil.

At the same time, there has been an increase in the Department of Agriculture employees. There is now one for every 30 farms in the United States, and still they can't tell us how 66 shiploads of grain headed for Austria disappeared without a trace and Billie Sol Estes never left shore.

Every responsible farmer and farm organization has repeatedly asked the government to free the farm economy, but who are farmers to know what is best for them? The wheat farmers voted against a wheat program. The government passed it anyway. Now the price of bread goes up; the price of wheat to the farmer goes down.

Meanwhile, back in the city, under urban renewal the assault on freedom carries on. Private property rights are so diluted that public interest is almost anything that a few government planners decide it should be. In a program that takes for the needy and gives to the greedy, we see such spectacles as in Cleveland, Ohio, a million-and-a-half-dollar building completed only three years ago must be destroyed to make way for what government officials call a "more compatible use of the land." The

President tells us he is now going to start building public housing units in the thousands where heretofore we have only built them in the hundreds. But FHA and the Veterans Administration tell us that they have 120,000 housing units they've taken back through mortgage foreclosures.

For three decades, we have sought to solve the problems of unemployment through government planning, and the more the plans fail, the more the planners plan. The latest is the Area Redevelopment Agency. They have just declared Rice County, Kansas, a depressed area. Rice County, Kansas, has two hundred oil wells, and the 14,000 people there have over $30 million on deposit in personal savings in their banks. When the government tells you you're depressed, lie down and be depressed.

We have so many people who can't see a fat man standing beside a thin one without coming to the conclusion that the fat man got that way by taking advantage of the thin one. So they are going to solve all the problems of human misery through government and government planning. Well, now, if government planning and welfare had the answer and they've had almost 30 years of it, shouldn't we expect government to almost read the score to us once in a while? Shouldn't they be telling us about the decline each year in the number of people needing help? The reduction in the need for public housing?

But the reverse is true. Each year the need grows greater, the program grows greater. We were told four years ago that 17 million people went to bed hungry each night. Well, that was probably true. They were all on a diet. But now we are told that 9.3 million families in this country are poverty-stricken on the basis of earning less than $3,000 a year. Welfare spending is 10 times greater than in the dark depths of the Depression. We are spending $45 billion on welfare. Now do a little arithmetic, and you will find that if we divided the $45 billion up equally among those 9 million poor families, we would be able to give each family $4,600 a year, and this added to their present income should eliminate poverty! Direct aid to the poor, however, is running only about $600 per family. It would seem that someplace there must be some overhead.

So now we declare "war on poverty," or "you, too, can be a Bobby Baker!" Now, do they honestly expect us to believe that if we add $1 billion to the $45 million we are spending, one more program to the 30-odd we have and remember, this new program doesn't replace any, it just duplicates existing programs do they believe that poverty is suddenly going to disappear by magic? Well, in all fairness I should explain that there is one part of the new program that isn't duplicated. This is the youth feature. We are now going to solve the dropout problem, juvenile delinquency, by reinstituting something like the old CCC camps, and we are going to put our young people in camps, but again we do some arithmetic, and we find that we are going to spend each year just on room and board for each young person that we help $4,700 a year! We can send them to Harvard for $2,700! Don't get me wrong. I'm not suggesting that Harvard is the answer to juvenile delinquency.

But seriously, what are we doing to those we seek to help? Not too long ago, a judge called me here in Los Angeles. He told me of a young woman who had come before him for a divorce. She had six children, was pregnant with her seventh. Under his questioning, she revealed her husband was a laborer earning $250 a month. She wanted a divorce so that she could get an $80 raise. She is eligible for $330 a month in the Aid to Dependent Children Program. She got the idea from two women in her neighborhood who had already done that very thing.

Yet anytime you and I question the schemes of the do-gooders, we are denounced as being against their humanitarian goals. They say we are always "against" things, never "for" anything. Well, the trouble with our liberal friends is not that they are ignorant, but that they know so much that isn't so. We are for a provision that destitution should not follow unemployment by reason of old age, and to that end we have accepted Social Security as a step toward meeting the problem.

But we are against those entrusted with this program when they practice deception regarding its fiscal shortcomings, when they charge that any criticism of the program means that we want to end payments to those who depend on them for livelihood. They have called it insurance to us in a hundred million pieces of literature. But then they appeared before the Supreme Court and they testified that it was a welfare program. They only use the term "insurance" to sell it to the people. And they said Social Security dues are a tax for the general use of the government, and the government has used that tax. There is no fund, because Robert Byers, the actuarial head, appeared before a congressional committee and admitted that Social Security as of this moment is $298 billion in the hole. But he said there should be no cause for worry because as long as they have the power to tax, they could always take away from the people whatever they needed to bail them out of trouble! And they are doing just that.

A young man, 21 years of age, working at an average salary, his Social Security contribution would, in the open market, buy him an insurance policy that would guarantee $220 a month at age 65. The government promises $127. He could live it up until he is 31 and then take out a policy that would pay more than Social Security. Now, are we so lacking in business sense that we can't put this program on a sound basis so that people who do require those payments will find that they can get them when they are due that the cupboard isn't bare? Barry Goldwater thinks we can.

At the same time, can't we introduce voluntary features that would permit a citizen who can do better on his own to be excused upon presentation of evidence that he had made provisions for the non-earning years? Should we allow a widow with children to work, and not lose the benefits supposedly paid for by her deceased husband? Shouldn't you and I be allowed to declare who our beneficiaries will be under these programs, which we cannot do? I think we are for telling our senior citizens that no one in this country should be denied medical care because of a lack of funds. But I think we are against forcing all citizens, regardless of need, into a compulsory government program, especially when we have such examples, as announced last week, when France admitted that their Medicare program was now bankrupt. They've come to the end of the road.

In addition, was Barry Goldwater so irresponsible when he suggested that our government give up its program of deliberate planned inflation so that when you do get your Social Security pension, a dollar will buy a dollar's worth, and not 45 cents' worth?

I think we are for an international organization, where the nations of the world can seek peace. But I think we are against subordinating American interests to an organization that has become so structurally unsound that today you can muster a two-thirds vote on the floor of the General Assembly among the nations that represent less than 10 percent of the world's population. I think we are against the hypocrisy of assailing our allies because here and there they cling to a colony, while we engage in a conspiracy of silence and never open our mouths about the millions of people enslaved in Soviet colonies in the satellite nation.

I think we are for aiding our allies by sharing of our material blessings with those nations which share in our fundamental beliefs, but we are against doling out money government to government, creating bureaucracy, if not socialism, all over the world. We set out to help 19 countries. We are helping 107. We spent $146 billion. With that money, we bought a $2 million yacht for Haile Selassie. We bought dress suits for Greek undertakers, extra wives for Kenyan government officials. We bought a thousand TV sets for a place where they have no electricity. In the last six years, 52 nations have bought $7 billion worth of our gold, and all 52 are receiving foreign aid from this country.

No government ever voluntarily reduces itself in size. Government programs, once launched, never disappear. Actually, a government bureau is the nearest thing to eternal life we'll ever see on this earth. Federal employees number 2.5 million, and federal, state, and local, one out of six of the nation's work force is employed by the government. These proliferating bureaus with their thousands of regulations have cost us many of our constitutional safeguards. How many of us realize that today federal agents can invade a man's property without a warrant? They can impose a fine without a formal hearing, let alone a trial by jury, and they can seize and sell his property in auction to enforce the payment of that fine. In Chico County, Arkansas, James Wier overplanted his rice allotment. The government obtained a $17,000 judgment, and a U.S. marshal sold his 950-acre farm at auction. The government said it was necessary as a warning to others to make the system work. Last February 19 at the University of Minnesota, Norman Thomas, six-time candidate for President on the Socialist Party ticket, said, "If Barry Goldwater became President, he would stop the advance of socialism in the United States." I think that's exactly what he will do.

As a former Democrat, I can tell you Norman Thomas isn't the only man who has drawn this parallel to socialism with the present administration. Back in 1936, Mr. Democrat himself, Al Smith, the great

American, came before the American people and charged that the leadership of his party was taking the part of Jefferson, Jackson, and Cleveland down the road under the banners of Marx, Lenin, and Stalin. And he walked away from his party, and he never returned to the day he died, because to this day, the leadership of that party has been taking that party, that honorable party, down the road in the image of the labor socialist party of England. Now it doesn't require expropriation or confiscation of private property or business to impose socialism on a people.

What does it mean whether you hold the deed or the title to your business or property if the government holds the power of life and death over that business or property? Such machinery already exists. The government can find some charge to bring against any concern it chooses to prosecute. Every businessman has his own tale of harassment. Somewhere a perversion has taken place. Our natural, inalienable rights are now considered to be a dispensation of government, and freedom has never been so fragile, so close to slipping from our grasp as it is at this moment. Our Democratic opponents seem unwilling to debate these issues. They want to make you and I believe that this is a contest between two men that we are to choose just between two personalities.

Well, what of this man that they would destroy? And in destroying, they would destroy that which he represents, the ideas that you and I hold dear. Is he the brash and shallow and trigger-happy man they say he is? Well, I have been privileged to know him "when." I knew him long before he ever dreamed of trying for high office, and I can tell you personally I have never known a man in my life I believe so incapable of doing a dishonest or dishonorable thing.

This is a man who in his own business, before he entered politics, instituted a profit-sharing plan, before unions had ever thought of it. He put in health and medical insurance for all his employees. He took 50 percent of the profits before taxes and set up a retirement program, a pension plan for all his employees. He sent checks for life to an employee who was ill and couldn't work. He provided nursing care for the children of mothers who work in the stores. When Mexico was ravaged by floods from the Rio Grande, he climbed in his airplane and flew medicine and supplies down there.

An ex-GI told me how he met him. It was the week before Christmas during the Korean War, and he was at the Los Angeles airport trying to get a ride home to Arizona for Christmas, and he said that there were a lot of servicemen there and no seats available on the planes. Then a voice came over the loudspeaker and said, "Any men in uniform wanting a ride to Arizona, go to runway such-and-such," and they went down there, and there was this fellow named Barry Goldwater sitting in his plane. Every day in the weeks before Christmas, all day long, he would load up the plane, fly to Arizona, fly them to their homes, then fly back over to get another load.

During the hectic split-second timing of a campaign, this is a man who took time out to sit beside an old friend who was dying of cancer. His campaign managers were understandably impatient, but he said, "There aren't many left who care what happens to her. I'd like her to know I care." This is a man who said to his 19-year-old son, "There is no foundation like the rock of honesty and fairness, and when you begin to build your life upon that rock, with the cement of the faith in God that you have, then you have a real start." This is not a man who could carelessly send other people's sons to war. And that is the issue of this campaign that makes all of the other problems I have discussed academic, unless we realize that we are in a war that must be won.

Those who would trade our freedom for the soup kitchen of the welfare state have told us that they have a utopian solution of peace without victory. They call their policy "accommodation." And they say if we only avoid any direct confrontation with the enemy, he will forget his evil ways and learn to love us. All who oppose them are indicted as warmongers. They say we offer simple answers to complex problems. Well, perhaps there is a simple answer, not an easy answer, but simple.

If you and I have the courage to tell our elected officials that we want our national policy based upon what we know in our hearts is morally right. We cannot buy our security, our freedom from the threat of the bomb by committing an immorality so great as saying to a billion now in slavery behind the Iron Curtain, "Give up your dreams of freedom because to save our own skin, we are willing to make a deal with your slave masters." Alexander Hamilton said, "A nation which can prefer disgrace to danger is prepared for a master, and deserves one." Let's set the record straight. There is no argument over the choice between peace and war, but there is only one guaranteed way you can have peace and you can have it in the next second surrender.

Admittedly there is a risk in any course we follow other than this, but every lesson in history tells us that the greater risk lies in appeasement, and this is the specter our well-meaning liberal friends refuse to face that their policy of accommodation is appeasement, and it gives no choice between peace and war, only between fight and surrender. If we continue to accommodate, continue to back and retreat, eventually we have to face the final demand--the ultimatum. And what then? When Nikita Khrushchev has told his people he knows what our answer will be?

He has told them that we are retreating under the pressure of the Cold War, and someday when the time comes to deliver the ultimatum, our surrender will be voluntary because by that time we will have weakened from within spiritually, morally, and economically. He believes this because from our side he has heard voices pleading for "peace at any price" or "better Red than dead," or as one commentator put it, he would rather "live on his knees than die on his feet." And therein lies the road to war, because those voices don't speak for the rest of us. You and I know and do not believe that life is so dear and peace so sweet as to be purchased at the price of chains and slavery. If nothing in life is worth dying for, when did this begin just in the face of this enemy? Or should Moses have told the children of Israel to live in slavery under the pharaohs? Should Christ have refused the cross? Should the patriots at Concord Bridge have thrown down their guns and refused to fire the shot heard 'round the world? The martyrs of history were not fools, and our honored dead who gave their lives to stop the advance of the Nazis didn't die in vain. Where, then, is the road to peace? Well, it's a simple answer after all.

You and I have the courage to say to our enemies, "There is a price we will not pay." There is a point beyond which they must not advance. This is the meaning in the phrase of Barry Goldwater's "peace through strength." Winston Churchill said that "the destiny of man is not measured by material computation. When great forces are on the move in the world, we learn we are spirits, not animals." And he said, "There is something going on in time and space, and beyond time and space, which, whether we like it or not, spells duty."

You and I have a rendezvous with destiny. We will preserve for our children this, the last best hope of man on Earth, or we will sentence them to take the last step into a thousand years of darkness.

We will keep in mind and remember that Barry Goldwater has faith in us. He has faith that you and I have the ability and the dignity and the right to make our own decisions and determine our own destiny. Thank you very much."

Ronald Reagan's presentation was so powerful that rather than simply benefiting the Goldwater campaign, Reagan became the political powerhouse of the Republican Party from that point forward. Although Goldwater ultimately lost to Lyndon Johnson and subsequently Richard Nixon captured the nomination and the Presidency in 1968, Ronald Reagan's reputation and leadership had been firmly established in GOP circles. Ronald Reagan revived the spirit of the Republican Party with his victory in the presidential election of 1980 and will forever be remembered as one of our greatest presidents and members of my GOP! Personally, but for the presidency of Ronald Reagan, I doubt my family would have become Republicans.

Chapter Twelve - We have a Proud History

It certainly is wise to take some time to review how and why the Republican Party came to be in the first place, as well as look back at our successes and failures. Let me be clear from the very start of this chapter, the following discussion of Republican history is not an attempt to be a history lesson of the United States. My purpose in writing the chapter is to show the proud history of my GOP. It is a completely biased story of the Republican history. As a foundation of this chapter, I used resources from the Republican National Committee and filled in the gaps with additional credible sources. Of course, I added lots of personal editorial comments to emphasize my points.

Without a doubt the old saying: "Those who ignore history are bound to repeat it" is as true in political history just as much as any review of American history in general. In fact, it is surprising how often modern political leaders and candidates repeat the same old mistakes their predecessors made and then experience the same negative consequences. There is certainly much to be learned from those who have gone before.

After reading this chapter and perhaps the entire book (if they can stomach it), I expect my liberal critics to suggest that I am telling only half of the story, leaving out the accounts of the great leaders and successes of their Democrat Party. To this, I plead guilty! This chapter and book are not a non-biased, bi-partisan treatise of American history nor is it intended to be a fair and balanced discussion on political history overall. My goals are clear, I am only telling half the story on purpose.

First, I wish to remind you of the greatness of our party, its leaders and why my GOP came into existence in the first place. Secondly, it is apparent from recent political events that some within my GOP need to be reminded of the core values and beliefs of the Republican Party. And finally, we need to explore, discover and implement what Republicans need to do now in order to regain the popularity and connection we should have with the American people.

The GOP is the party of many of the greatest of the great in America's proud history, including presidents Abraham Lincoln, Teddy Roosevelt, Dwight D. Eisenhower and Ronald Reagan. Certainly, not all of Republican or United States history surrounds those who have served as president; however, much of the review of political history is appropriately put into the context of who was serving as president at the given period of time. For example, the founding of our great nation is always associated with George Washington. World War II cannot be thought of without the vision of F.D.R. coming to mind. The pages which follow attempt to mesh the history of the GOP with not only who was serving as president, but other significant historical and political events which were occurring.

Despite some missteps along the way, Republicans have historically been the faithful believers and promoters of limited government, the rule of law, individual freedom and responsibility and a free market economy. These beliefs are the key elements which have made America the greatest nation to ever have blessed this planet.

To start with, political parties did not even exist in America when in 1789, George Washington became our first president following the Constitutional Convention in Philadelphia. In fact, Washington despised the concept of political parties altogether. The father of our nation saw the extreme danger of partisan political organizations, as their goal was usually to pit one group of citizens against another. Inherent in such a system of organized group efforts brings the negative campaigns and a structural division of people based along political lines and not on specific issues. In his farewell speech in 1796, Washington discussed his dislike for partisan political groups in general:

"They (political parties) serve to organize faction, to give it an artificial and extraordinary force; to put, in the place of the delegated will of the nation, the will of a party, often a small but artful and enterprising minority of the community; and, according to the alternate triumphs of different parties, to make the public administration the mirror of the ill-concerted and incongruous projects of faction, rather than the organ of consistent and wholesome plans digested by common counsels, and modified by mutual interests."

George Washington was right on target, considering the partisan nature of the political scene today. Even though Washington himself never embraced a political party structure personally, his hope and desire for our young country to reject a party system was short lived by the political leaders that followed. Since our first president's departure from office, the United States has always had at least two significant political parties. Long gone are the Federalists Party, Union Party, Democrat-Republican Party, and the Whig Party. In fact, since 1868, the White House has been occupied by a Republican eighteen times and a Democrat on thirteen occasions. While many other minor political parties and independent candidates have come and gone, they have usually been nothing more than a distraction, rather than a meaningful choice for the voters to consider.

The word "Republican" appeared early in the founding of our nation and was first used in conjunction with the word "Democrat" to denote a single political party during the formative period of the United States. In fact, four presidents have called themselves Democratic-Republicans, including Jefferson, Madison, Monroe, and John Quincy Adams. These Founding Fathers did not use the term Republican or Democrat as we think of them today, but their principles and beliefs in the role of government are certainly consistent with those of Abraham Lincoln and Ronald Reagan.

Jefferson and Madison created the Democrat-Republican Party with the goal of opposing the expansive central government policies of the Federalists, which was the party created a year earlier by then Treasury Secretary Alexander Hamilton. The Federalists desired a strong central government and had little interest in states' rights, which has developed to be an important core Republican value. The Federalist Party advocated a loose construction of the United States Constitution based on Article I, Section 8 of the Constitution which states that Congress shall have the power "to make all laws which shall be necessary and proper for carrying into execution...powers vested by this Constitution in the government of the United States." This clause, known as the "Elastic clause," was and remains, a point of significant contention between those who favor a loose reading of the Constitution and those who favor a strict interpretation.

The Federalists had the view that political power was best held by a well-educated elite who would serve all interests of people. One of John Jay's (who was an ardent Federalist) most common public statements was, "The people who own the country ought to govern it." In fact, during the Constitutional Convention of 1787, Hamilton and Jay took the floor of the Convention and suggested that the formal organization of states themselves would not be necessary following the establishment of a central government and new Constitution. Fortunately, the other delegates rejected Hamilton's plans as they recognized the dangers of creating a potentially new version of the British system with an overly powerful central government.

The Democrat-Republican Party of Jefferson and Madison insisted on the strict construction of the Constitution and denounced many of Hamilton's proposals as unconstitutional and against the spirit of freedom and liberty. Hamilton's views of lifetime tenure for the new "Monarch" as well as lifetime appointments for members of the Senate raised serious concerns that America could be headed down the road toward simply forming another England with a king and all the associated trappings.

The Democrat-Republican Party promoted a more decentralized form of government which was most concerned with states' rights and the idea that the free market should take care of most economic matters, including the formation and ownership of banks. Certainly the values of a free market and states' rights are closely aligned with the modern Republican Party's platform and the principles which Jefferson and Madison fought for during these early days of our nation.

The Democrat-Republican Party officially disbanded in the 1820's, splintering into different factions. The term Republican standing alone was not prominently used again for the next thirty years. The country experienced a period where the political scene was dominated by the Whig and Democrat parties. During this time, America was expanding its territory westward and the primary domestic conflict was the battles with native American indians on the western-most frontier.

A Republican Party as a formal organization did not become a major political force in the United States until it appeared on the presidential ballot for the first time in 1856. This election occurred under the cloud of increasing tensions and a looming conflict between the northern and southern states.

The 1856 Democrat's convention in Cincinnati, Ohio had James Buchanan as the clear front-runner. Buchanan was nominated on a platform which supported the Compromise of 1850. According to the infamous compromise, the territories of New Mexico, Nevada, Arizona and Utah would be organized without a mention of slavery and thus the decision would be made by the residents at a later time, but only after they formally applied for statehood. The slave trade would be abolished in the District of Columbia, although slavery itself would still be permitted. California was to be admitted without any form of slavery. The Compromise of 1850 did accomplish what it set out to do as the United States remained united, but as we know, the solution was only temporary. Over the following decade, Americans became further and further divided over the moral and legal issues of the institution of slavery and other reasons.

There were many events of the 1850's that lead ultimately to the Civil War, but historians most generally agree that the United States Supreme Court's 1857 Dred Scott decision is the most infamous. Chief Justice Roger B. Taney, a Democrat, wrote the often described "worse decision in United States History" that a slave was to be considered property and thus not a person. This resulted in the right of slave owners to move their "property" to other states, including "free" states. Obviously, this was highly unacceptable to those states who rejected slavery and was in total conflict with the principles of our Constitution.

Over the following decade and largely based on the backs of the leaders from the Democrat Party, the country's citizens became further divided over the issues of slavery. The tensions would continue to grow until the nation itself divided as brothers took up arms against each other. It was quite clear that Buchanan and the Democrats supported the status quo on slavery and offered political protection to the plantation owners of the South. These businessmen were clearly the most powerful special interest group of their day.

The traditional parties were growing more and more untrustworthy by the voters, not unlike what is happening in today's political environment. The special interest slave owners had a grip on many leaders of the

Democrat Party and it was clear the Democrats would do whatever was necessary to maintain the ownership and exploitation of slaves in order to protect the powerful industries that profited from the institution of slavery.

This growing lack of confidence in the existing political parties and their elected leaders created an opportunity for a new political party to emerge. Those who opposed slavery realized that neither of the political parties (Democrats and Whigs) had the courage or interest to meaningfully challenge the status quo on the question of slavery. The anti-slavery movement had only one real choice, and that was to organize a new political party, the Republican Party. While recent political history has not resulted in the presence of a significant third political party, the growing number of unenrolled or independent voters does indicate a general dissatisfaction or mistrust of the current two major political parties. Whether or not our modern political climate will result in enough voters splintering off to form a substantial third political party does not appear to be on the immediate horizon, but it certainly is a possibility...

The other major political party of the day, the Whig Party, had also disintegrated in the minds of Americans due to its own internal conflicts. Originally organized by opponents of President Andrew Jackson, whom they called "King Andrew," the Whig Party took its name from the British antimonarchist party. The Whigs claimed four United States presidents, including William H. Harrison, John Tyler, Zachary Taylor and Millard Fillmore. As the issues of slavery heated up, the Whig Party began to split into the "conscience" (antislavery) and "cotton" (proslavery) groups. The Whigs became even further divided by the Compromise of 1850. Their nominee in the 1852 election was Winfield Scott, who failed to win the needed support as most southern Whigs who joined the Democratic Party were in support of slavery. In 1854, most northern Whigs joined the new

Republican Party to oppose slavery, and for the most part, the Whigs were done and gone.

Thus my GOP primarily grew out of a desire to organize politically to oppose the expansion of slavery into new territories that were being added to the United States as we expanded westward. Generally, when people are disillusioned with their political organizations and leaders, opportunities are created for men of principle to come forward and return the voice of the people to government. Because of the fear of expanded slavery and a growing recognition that owning slaves was inconsistent with our founding Constitutional values, meetings started to occur in several states across the country to organize and fight for such beliefs. One such meeting occurred at Ripon, Wisconsin on March 20, 1854. This is often credited as marking the birthplace of the Republican Party.

According to the Wisconsin Historical Society, the attendees of the Ripon meeting resolved at this first Republican meeting, "That we accept this issue (freedom or slavery) forced upon us by the slave power, and in the defense of freedom will cooperate and be known as Republicans." The Wisconsin Republican Party was dominated by former Whigs who were sincere believers in freedom and opportunity for all Americans, black or white. Many early Republicans decided to concentrate solely on the issue of slavery, which at the time was the one issue they knew all Republicans could agree on. It was also the issue which undoubtedly showed the voters the differences between the Democrats and the Republicans.

In the first organized electoral effort of 1854, in Wisconsin, the new Republican Party had captured one of the two United States Senate seats, two of the three United States House of Representatives' seats, a majority of the state assembly seats and a large number of local elected offices. The very next year, Wisconsin even elected a Republican governor. It was clear the people of Wisconsin and many other parts across this great nation desired a new political party, a political party which stood firmly for freedom and for the principles of the Bill of Rights. This need was met by the new Republican Party.

So was Wisconsin actually the birthplace of the Republican Party or perhaps just the best documented in our history books? Whether one accepts Wisconsin's claim depends fundamentally on how one interprets the words "birthplace" and "party." Several modern reference books, while acknowledging other Republican organizational efforts, usually cite Ripon, Wisconsin as the birthplace of the formal movement to first organize the new Republican Party.

Along with the organizational efforts in Wisconsin, there are many historical accounts of local meetings held throughout the North in 1854 and 1855. The first national convention of the new party was held in Pittsburgh, Pennsylvania on February 22, 1856. Once again, the driving issue before the convention delegates was their firm desire to end slavery and promote freedom for all Americans.

The name "Republican" first publicly appeared in the media in a June 1854 editorial by Horace Greeley. Greeley's New York Tribune was one of America's most influential newspapers of the time. Greeley said the new party called "Republicans" will "fitly designate those who had united to restore the Union to its true mission of champion and promulgator of liberty rather than propagandist of slavery." From the founding of my GOP, we have been focused on the freedoms which are at the heart of the American dream, and while not always receiving the credit from some historians, my GOP has a lot to be proud of!

The issue of slavery was developing in every state in the nation in one way or another. In Massachusetts, Republican Senator Charles Sumner, who was both morally opposed to slavery and a believer that slavery was harming the American economy, was one of the most vocal politicians to oppose slavery in the United States Senate. Sumner delivered his most famous antislavery speech titled, "The Crime against Kansas." Sumner, in his usual passionate and personal style of debate, singled out fellow Senator Andrew Pickens Butler of South Carolina, who by the way was not present in the Senate Chamber to rebut Sumner's comments.

Just two days later Senator Sumner was brutally assaulted in the Senate chamber by Preston S. Brooks, who coincidently was Senator Butler's nephew. It took Sumner more than three years to fully recover from the brutal attack. Massachusetts residents appreciated Sumner's courage and commitment to the issue of freedom and reelected Sumner to continue the fight against slavery. By his example of bravery and standing firm on his principles, despite the serious personal dangers, Charles Sumner was critical to the success of the early organizational efforts of the new Republican Party in Massachusetts. It was clear that the Republican Party stood firmly for freedom, and this principle resonated with the voters as more and more people labeled themselves Republicans. The party has been a major political force in the United States ever since.

In the first chance for the newly founded Republican Party on a national stage, during the 1856 race for President, the Republicans put forth their first ever presidential candidate. His name was John C. Frémont, a former explorer of the West who also served from 1850 to 1851 as a Senator from California. Frémont was nominated under the slogan: "Free soil, free labor, free speech, free men, Frémont." Even though Republicans were considered a "third party" as the Democrats and Whigs solidly represented the established two-party system, Frémont received a surprising thirty-three percent of the vote. Although ultimately unsuccessful (Buchanan was elected), the Republicans carried eleven of the sixteen northern states and the political landscape was forever changed.

With the following complete fracturing of the remaining Whig party organization and on a platform of freedom and justice, the Republican Party was well positioned for Americans to embrace. All it needed was a leader who people could trust. Often times in our history, events and circumstances have required a certain style of leadership. One can wonder where our country would be today if Abraham Lincoln had not been elected when the Civil War was raging. Fortunately, we shall never know the answer, but assuredly America would not be as free or as great as we are if Abe Lincoln had not been president. In 1860, as tensions between the North and South escalated into Civil War, Abraham Lincoln emerged as perhaps the only person who had the vision, courage and tenacity to lead America during the most turbulent time in America's history since the Revolutionary War.

Lincoln became the first Republican to win the White House. It was the Civil War that firmly identified the Republican Party as the promoters of freedom for all Americans. The Republican Party's reputation as the party that had freed the slaves and saved the Union is certainly well deserved. Abraham Lincoln was perhaps the only person who could have successfully presided over this time period of American history and ultimately retained the United States as one nation. Lincoln did so in no small part because of his commitment to his principles and those of his relatively new political party. In the face of the horror of war, with brother fighting against brother, Lincoln had plenty of excuses to lose his focus and determination; however, he stayed true to his principles and made the necessary tough decisions, ultimately paying with his life.

During the war, Lincoln was highly regarded for taking the bold step of signing the Emancipation Proclamation that freed the slaves. Well at least on paper it did. The Republicans of their day worked to pass the Thirteenth Amendment, which constitutionally outlawed slavery; the Fourteenth, which guaranteed equal protection under the laws; and the Fifteenth, which helped secure voting rights for African-Americans.

Abraham Lincoln never let the country forget that the Civil War involved an even larger issue than the actual fighting itself. In dedicating the military cemetery at Gettysburg, Lincoln stated, "That we here highly resolve that these dead shall not have died in vain, that this nation, under God, shall have a new birth of freedom and that government of the people, by the people, for the people, shall not perish from the earth." Even though it had been over seventy years since the approval of such Constitutional principles, Lincoln was the first person, and the Republican Party the first political party, willing to pay the real price to ensure our freedoms and rights would be applied to all Americans regardless of the color of their skin. Without question, America would not be as great as it is today, but for the formation of the Republican Party and the work of our leaders.

The war years gave the Republican Party a unique opportunity to propose and pass a comprehensive menu of legislation without any meaningful opposition from the Democrats. Of course, this was due to the fact that states from the Democrat South had already seceded from the United States and thus were not a part of the current political system. During this period, Republicans passed a number of critical economic programs, including the Homestead Acts and the authorization and funding to build the transcontinental railroad.

Lincoln won reelection in 1864, as Union military victories signaled a hopeful end to the war. In his planning for peace and reunification of the states, President Lincoln was flexible and generous, encouraging his former enemy to lay down their arms and reestablish a single nation. Lincoln recognized that there was no real victory to be proclaimed, in the traditional military sense, from a Civil War. This spirit of reunification with the South was a central theme of his Second Inaugural Address, "With malice toward none; with charity for all; with firmness in the right, as God gives us to see the right, let us strive on to finish the work we are in; to bind up the nation's wounds..."

On Good Friday, April 14, 1865, Lincoln was assassinated at Ford's Theatre in Washington, D.C. by John Wilkes Booth, who somehow believed he was promoting the continuation of slavery and helping the South's war effort. When President Abraham Lincoln died the following day, the Civil War was in its final stages. Lincoln was never able to see the benefits of the many sacrifices he paid as President. In the weeks to follow, the remaining Southern troops were defeated and Confederate President Jefferson Davis was finally captured in Georgia on May 10, 1865. This was less than a month after Abraham Lincoln's assassination. Although President Lincoln never did see the actual end of the war, he is forever remembered as a wise and humane person who is properly credited with ending the legal institution of slavery. Lincoln set the stage for reuniting the country and will always be thought of as the father of the Republican Party.

The man who had to fill Lincoln's shoes and take up his unfinished work was Vice President Andrew Johnson of Tennessee, who officially was a member of the Union party. When the Civil War began, Andrew Johnson was the only Senator from a Confederate state who did not leave Congress to return to the South. During the war, Johnson joined Republicans in their efforts, but officially remained a member of the Union party. In 1864, Abraham Lincoln selected Johnson as his Vice Presidential running-mate most likely in an effort to show his interest and concern for issues of the southern states.

Without any real preparation for what he was up against, the new president was suddenly called upon to handle the most complicated problems our nation has arguably ever encountered. There was the pressing and obvious problem of how to deal with the defeated South and, more importantly, to reunite a people who had been torn apart by four years of horrific war.

President Johnson's policies made Congress distrustful of his motives, mostly for his growing leniency toward former confederates and obvious lack of concern for the former slaves. Johnson demonstrated his lack of interest in protecting the blacks by his veto of civil rights bills and his strong opposition to the Fourteenth Amendment. Johnson not only ignored the advice of his cabinet, but he replaced them as quickly as he could, surrounding himself with like-minded individuals.

To protect the remaining Lincoln Republicans who were now a part of Johnson's Cabinet and administration, Congress passed the Tenure of Office Act in 1867, which prohibited the president from dismissing office holders without the Senate's consent. The Republicans knew that the military victory was but one step in the long process needed to endure if we were to really be a land with liberty and justice for all people.

An angered President Johnson tested the constitutionality of the Tenure of Office Act by attempting to remove Lincoln's Secretary of War, Edwin M. Stanton. President Johnson's violation of the Tenure Act became the basis for his impeachment in 1868 by the House of Representatives. The Senate was one vote short of the two-thirds majority needed to convict Johnson, thus he was ultimately acquitted. Despite a lack of a conviction,

Johnson's political life was in effect over and the Republican Congress pressed on with their efforts despite Johnson's public and private objections.

The Republican Congress was able to pass meaningful legislation, over Johnson's vetoes of course, to aid in the reconstruction of the South. Republicans extended the life of the Freedman's Bureau, which was a federal agency established during the war to provide assistance and comfort to thousands of black refugees. Under Republican control, the Bureau attempted to protect the rights of the former slaves by assisting in labor issues, arbitrating disputes with whites and establishing some freedman's schools. While surely not as successful as many would have liked, the Bureau's presence in the South certainly did much good and prevented at least some of the violence against the newly freed black citizens.

The Republicans' power in Congress was furthered by an overwhelming victory in the midterm elections of 1866. Firmly under the GOP control, Congress continued to push for their reconstruction and reunification efforts with the South. During this time, Republicans also started to gain prominence across sections of the South. The growth of the GOP was primarily based on the votes of now free black Americans. In fact, over eighty percent of the votes that were cast for Republican candidates were from black Americans.

Following Johnson's difficult term in office, former Civil War hero and now Republican candidate General Ulysses Grant received a unanimous vote on the first ballot at the Republican convention in 1868 and was subsequently elected as our eighteenth president.

Grant's Democrat opponent was Horatio Seymour of New York. The Republicans promised continued radical reconstruction in the South and the protection of the former slaves. The Democrats attacked the Republicans for reconstruction and attacked Grant as being a drunk (yes, another personal attack from the Democrats). Ultimately, it was Grant's personal popularity, earned for his character, integrity and willingness to stand firm on Republican principles that resulted in his two strong victories.

The Republican control of the southern state governments following the end of the Civil War unfortunately was short lived. By 1875, most of the southern states were once again firmly under Democrat control.   This was not because of a shift in the values of the residents of these states, but with the growing influences of the Ku Klux Klan and the passing of "Jim Crow" laws by local white Democrats, blacks in the South effectively loss their electoral influence.

Poll taxes and intimidation tactics resulted in fewer and fewer black citizens having the ability to actually cast their ballots for Republicans. Over the next seventy years the South became solidly under the control of the Democrat Party. Regrettably, many of the advances made to ensure freedom for all men regardless of the color of their skin would be slowly and steadily reversed by the still strong prejudice and bias of the political bosses of the South.

It was also around this time that the symbol of the elephant for the Republican Party was created by Thomas Nast, who was a famous illustrator and caricaturist for the New Yorker Magazine. The correlation of the Republican Party with the elephant first occurred in 1874, when a rumor that animals had escaped from the New York City Zoo coincided with concerns about a possible third-term run for Grant. Nast chose to characterize the Republicans as elephants as they were clever, steadfast and controlled, yet somewhat unmanageable when frightened, especially when done so by a rather strange looking jackass.

In a subsequent cartoon, when Republicans had suffered severe loses in Congress, Nast followed up the idea by showing the elephant in a trap, illustrating the way the Republican voters had been fooled. It appears that the stories and lessons from Nast's cartoons are still true today. Reflecting back on the chapter concerning the 2006 and 2008 elections and the lessons to be learned from the Republican defeats, it appears that in many ways my GOP fell into a similar Washington, D.C. beltway political trap.

Other cartoonists and commentators picked up the use of the elephant symbol and it soon became the logo of the Republican Party. As we know, the jackass, now in a more politically correct fashion referred to as the donkey, made a natural transition to representing the Democrat Party. The elephant has continued as the well recognized symbol of the GOP because of its representation of power and grace.

Embracing a tradition established by George Washington and later the Republican Party as a whole, President Grant did not run for re-election in 1876. Instead, in one of the most bitterly disputed elections in American history, Republican Rutherford B. Hayes won the Presidency over Democrat Samuel Tilden by the margin of only one electoral vote, and this was only after what has been called the "Great Compromise of 1876." Under seemingly endless claims of voter fraud and intimidation, where blacks who were voting Republican had literally been physically prevented from getting to the polls, a deal was made to give Hayes the White House with the promise he would withdraw federal troops from the South. Just like so many other political compromises gone wrong, this one resulted in political setbacks for the GOP and, more importantly, significant steps backward for black Americans.

After the election dust had settled, cooperation between the Republican White House and the now Democratically controlled House of Representatives was nearly impossible, as relentless partisan bickering reached levels which would make today's political battles seem like an afternoon tea. Despite the conflicts, President Hayes managed to keep his campaign promise and withdrew federal troops from the South. The white politicians of the South slowly began to resume control of their state and local governments.

While perhaps a politically expedient solution, it was shortsighted. While many Americans favored the withdrawal of troops from the South in an effort to settle down the political conflicts and geographical divisions that remained following the end of the Civil War, many Republican faithful lost interest in the challenges of the now free blacks. African Americans slowly but surely lost much of the freedoms and political gains they had achieved during the period of Reconstruction. We must be honest as a political party when we look back at this turning point when black voters who were fully in the Republican camp, started the long and steady process of abandoning their affection for GOP candidates.

The Republican Party continued its success of winning the White House in 1880, when the party won its fourth consecutive Presidential election with the victory of another Civil War hero, James Garfield. As the last of the log cabin style (a very different meaning today) presidents, James Garfield attacked political corruption, which had been an increasing problem in Washington. D.C. Unfortunately, after just approximately six months as President, on September 19, 1881, Garfield died from an infection and internal hemorrhage resulting from a bullet wound inflicted by Charles Julius Guiteau.

Following President Garfield's assassination, Republican Chester A. Arthur succeeded him to the Oval Office. President Arthur had some political successes as he oversaw the passage of the Pendleton Act through Congress. This legislation classified about ten percent of all government jobs and created a bipartisan Civil Service Commission to prepare and oversee competitive examinations. As mundane and unimportant, to Republican or American history as this might seem, it was important as it made at least part of the government bureaucracy a professional work force. While history may not look fondly upon the current status of the civil service system, it was completely necessary as corruption was rampant and the Pendleton Act did a great deal to improve the efficiency of the federal government and decrease political favors in exchange for employment.

Suddenly, after four consecutive Republicans in the White House, the GOP's fortune changed with a loss in 1884. President Arthur attempted to receive the Republican nomination, but had little support from the party faithful, many of whom had been ousted in his government job reform efforts. Arthur had effectively broken up the "old boy's network." But by doing so, the political base of campaign workers was also gone, as many had previously come from the patronage jobs that had been eliminated. Today, while we do not see government workers directly supporting candidates, it is organized labor who has taken their place.

Grover Cleveland was the front-runner for the Democrats. Cleveland's opponent in the election was ultimately Republican James Blaine of Maine. The major political issue in the election was the integrity of the candidates themselves. Blaine was attacked for his close relations with the railroad interests and allegations that he received financial benefits. Cleveland was attacked for being immoral for an affair, before his marriage, which produced a son. Cleveland's opponents chanted "Ma Ma Where's my Papa?" Grover Cleveland was able to defuse the story by telling the truth, a political tactic that some future politicians might also wish to give a try. While personal negative attacks continue to invade almost every election, just like in 1884, the tactic failed and Cleveland received the support of many government reformers including several leading Republicans. During this period of time and until the early 1890's, Congress was about evenly split between the two parties. The Democrats generally enjoyed a majority in the House and Republicans were for the most part in control of the Senate.

The GOP had firmly established itself as a permanent force in American politics by not only preserving the Union and leading it through the Reconstruction period, but also by striking a chord of greater personal autonomy within the hearts of Americans. Republicans had successfully portrayed themselves as the party founded on principles of freedom and responsible government spending. Yet, while the Presidency was regained for the next term with the 1888 election of Republican Benjamin Harrison, just four years later in the election of 1892, the Democrats won control of the House, the Senate and the presidency by again electing Grover Cleveland.

While the Democrats may have been pleased to be back in power, the following economic depression of 1893 resulted in a frustrated, desperate and politically disappointed nation. Cleveland's administration and the Democrat Congress failed miserably to offer any meaningful assistance or support to struggling farmers or unemployed workers in the inner cities. As time passed, Americans were once again looking to make a change in their governmental leaders.

History shows us a common theme that when one political party has control and fails to perform as expected, the American people are more than willing to kick them out of office and give the other party a chance. Similar to the elections of 2006 and 2008, when Republicans failed to successfully promote their agenda and were removed from office, the Democrats in the mid-1890's experienced a similar fate.

Republican voters returned their party to power with the 1896 campaign, electing William McKinley to the White House. His term was the start of another consecutive four-term Republican possession of the White House. The Republican Party had again emerged as the party of free enterprise, reasonable government regulation and the best prospect for prosperity for all Americans.

During this period of American history, the GOP also played a leading role in securing women the right to vote. In 1896, Republicans were the first political party to formally support the women's suffrage movement. When the 19th Amendment was finally added to the Constitution, twenty-six of then thirty- six state legislatures that had voted to ratify a woman's right to vote were solidly under Republican control. In addition, the first woman elected to Congress was Jeanette Rankin from Montana in 1917, who by the way was a Republican.

The Republicans' political strength was reinforced by the return of prosperity under William McKinley and by the successful military actions of the Spanish-American War. President McKinley was initially hesitant for the United States to assume any role in the long-standing war between Spain and Cuba. However, when the USS Maine was sunk in Havana Harbor in 1898, killing over two-hundred and fifty American sailors, McKinley knew America must respond firmly and swiftly. The following war with Spain united Americans with a tremendous sense of patriotism and love of their country. Like so many other Republican Presidents, McKinley did not choose war, but understood America could never sit idly by when our own people or friends were under a serious threat.

It was also during this time that a young and energetic Teddy Roosevelt came forward to serve his country. Roosevelt gave up an assignment as an assistant secretary of the Navy to lead a volunteer military unit called the "Rough Riders." While the future President faced several battles in Cuba, the most notable occurred on July 1, 1898, when the Rough Riders and elements of the Ninth and Tenth Regiments "buffalo soldiers" took Kettle Hill. After that hill was captured, Roosevelt who was now on foot, led a second charge up the San Juan Heights. Following its capture, the city surrendered, and the war was over for the most part. Teddy Roosevelt's public image became widely known across America and his reputation of being a strong and successful leader would serve him well in future political efforts.

Assuming the office of President in 1901, after McKinley became the third Republican President to be assassinated, President Theodore Roosevelt focused the United States directly on the Republican principle of real competition in a free market system. To do so, Roosevelt used the Sherman Anti-Trust Act, which had originally passed in 1890 under the leadership of Republican President Benjamin Harrison. The goal of the Act was to successfully prosecute and break up several large business monopolies, which were undoubtedly harming the American worker, small business owner and ultimately the consumer.

To be clear, the GOP was still the political party favored by the business community, but Roosevelt recognized that the influence of a few monopolies had simply gone too far. While many today wish to unfairly label the GOP as the protector of big business, Teddy Roosevelt's actions tell a much truer story. Republicans generally believe that government should stay out of the business of business, but there are those limited times that Uncle Sam needs to step in when abuses are taking place. The Sherman Anti-Trust Act was appropriately one of those limited times.

Simply stated, Teddy Roosevelt was a man of principle. He believed as president he had a duty to make government more responsible, while also ensuring that it was as limited as possible. In his second term as President, he uncovered a number of scandals involving special interest groups and deals made with certain legislators. President Theodore Roosevelt is also credited with the popularity of the term "muckraking" and defined it accordingly:

> "There are, in the body politic, economic and social, many and grave evils, and there is urgent necessity for the sternest war upon them. There should be relentless exposure of and attack upon every evil man whether politician or business man, every evil practice, whether in politics, in business, or in social life."

While not a partisan matter at all, Republicans are expected to conduct themselves at a higher ethical level than Democrats. The real life examples are endless. In fact, we don't have to look beyond our own Senior Senator from Massachusetts. Do you really think a Republican could have survived the issues, personal mistakes and alleged wrongdoings of Ted Kennedy?

Like so many other successful political leaders, Teddy Roosevelt used the "Bully Pulpit" to take his case to the American people and fight for reforms when Congress refused or neglected to act. Roosevelt was not a single issue President. In fact, during his two terms as President he fought for regulations of the meat packing industry, established the United States Forest Service, signed into law the creation of five new National Parks and signed the 1906 Antiquities Act under which he established some eighteen new national monuments. The land area of the United States placed under public protection by Theodore Roosevelt totals approximately 230,000,000 acres. Once again it was a Republican taking the lead on a critical issue, such as environmental protection and preservation. The Republican efforts on creating national parks and preserving open space have had a long standing positive impact on our nation, once again without much credit.

Roosevelt also became deeply involved with foreign policy, supporting revolutionaries who were forming the Republic of Panama. His actions in Panama resulted in the treaty that permitted construction of the Panama Canal, which is widely credited with the expansion of free trade. "Speak softly and carry a big stick" was Roosevelt's modus operandi to explain his views and tactics on foreign policy matters. In addition, Teddy Roosevelt successfully negotiated the Treaty of Portsmouth, ending the conflict between Russia and Japan. Roosevelt's accomplishments as a peacemaker earned him the Nobel Peace Prize and the distinction of being the first American to receive this award. Appropriately so, "TR" as he was sometimes affectionately called, often appears on the list of those Americans and historians considered to be one of the most recognized, popular and finest presidents.

On the political momentum of an ever-expanding economy at home and great diplomatic success abroad, Teddy Roosevelt easily won a second term and continued to stand by his principles and those of his GOP. Consistent with the Republican history of promoting freedom and diversity, Roosevelt appointed America's first Jewish member to the cabinet of a United States President. Oscar Strauss was selected by Roosevelt to the important position of Secretary of Commerce and Labor. Once again, it was the Republican Party breaking down a barrier for yet another disaffected group of Americans.

While I understand that perceptions do change with time and with the influences of the left-leaning media and revisionist historians, often times the truths and realities of a certain event or period of time are not fairly attributed. When history is sincerely and fairly reviewed, the successes of race, gender and religious equality are primarily a result of the efforts of Republicans. This fact is practically forgotten today due to the modern day Democrat support of Affirmative Action and other social programs they designed to target certain groups of Americans.

While I am in agreement that such programs are not to be favored by Republicans, our success at providing opportunity to all people, regardless of race, gender or religion is often lost in the recounting of America's history and it should not be so. Somehow the practice of liberal pandering to targeted groups has resulted in a public perception that the Democrats are actually working in the best interest of minority groups. The truth of the matter is that Republicans in reality have done more to offer equal opportunity to all Americans.

Without question, Teddy Roosevelt's tremendous popularity would have practically guaranteed that he would be elected to a third term, but following history and precedent of our Founding Fathers, Roosevelt did not seek another term and encouraged his friend, William Howard Taft, to seek the office of president. Unfortunately, things did not go as Roosevelt and the Republicans would have preferred. Although Taft was elected in 1908, problems within the Republican Party began to rise to the surface and just four years later, Teddy Roosevelt, dissatisfied with President Taft's performance in office, led his supporters to create the new "Bull Moose" political party ticket.

With the obvious advantage of a splitting of the base Republican vote between the Taft and Roosevelt camps, Woodrow Wilson and the Democrats won. Four years later in 1916, Wilson was re-elected promising to keep the United States out of World War I. Despite Wilson's campaign pledge, the United States stepped onto the European battlegrounds and entered the war. By 1918, the Republican Party won control of Congress as Wilson's popularity began to decline while World War I dragged on.

Much like today's political climate, at the time of the raging battles of the "Great War," many people could not justify the need to fight a war on foreign soil. Reflection and history has a way of appreciating the efforts of leaders who understand that despite the difficult task of sacrificing human life, war is sometimes necessary to preserve our freedoms and our way of life.

At the end of World War I, Woodrow Wilson pushed for America to enter the League of Nations. Republican Senator Henry Cabot Lodge, who was born in Boston and was the great-grandson of Senator George Cabot successfully lead the charge against joining the League by arguing:

> "The United States is the world's best hope, but if you fetter her in the interests and quarrels of other nations, if you tangle her in the intrigues of Europe, you will destroy her powerful good, and endanger her very existence. Leave her to march freely through the centuries to come, as in the years that have gone. Strong, generous, and confident, she has nobly served mankind. Beware how you trifle with your marvelous inheritance; this great land of ordered liberty. For if we stumble and fall, freedom and civilization everywhere will go down in ruin."

Much of Lodge's argument parallels our current dissatisfaction with the United Nations. Just as in 1920, today we as a nation must be protective of our sovereignty and not allow the right to make decisions which impact America's security, freedom and economy to be transferred to anyone other than our own elected leaders. The responsibility of such decisions that are in the best interest of American citizens must always rest with those accountable to the voters of the United States.

Americans were tired of the policies of the Woodrow Wilson administration and with liberal progressivism following the end of the War. This dissatisfaction allowed the Republicans to reassert their electoral dominance during the decade to follow. The GOP was able to elect Warren G. Harding as president following the end of Wilson's term of office. Unfortunately, Harding's tenure in office was riddled with a number of questionable ethical dealings, including the infamous Teapot Dome scandal. Republicans are always held to a higher standard than Democrats, and when they make ethical missteps in their political or personal life, not only does that particular Republican politician pay the price, but the entire party bears the burden.

Harding's backroom dealings included certain oil reserves that had been set aside for the Navy by former President Wilson. In 1922, Albert Fall, Secretary of the Interior for Harding, leased without a competitive bidding process, the Teapot Dome fields. This backroom deal became the focus of a United States Senate investigation which resulted in a cloud of suspicion hanging over President Harding's head.

When Harding died of an apparent heart attack, Calvin Coolidge, the former Republican Governor of Massachusetts, became our thirtieth President. Coolidge gained a reputation as a small-government conservative and was elected to his own term as President in 1924 with the slogan "Keep Cool and Keep Coolidge."

Coolidge's style of governance did much to restore public confidence and he left office with considerable popularity, as he upheld his own honor and promoted the principles of the Republican Party for the overall benefit of the nation. We could certainly use more men like Calvin Coolidge in Massachusetts politics today.

Next in the line of Republican Presidents was Herbert Hoover. He was elected in 1928 by a comfortable electoral margin as the Republicans retained a majority of the members in Congress. Republicans were in power, the world was at peace and America was enjoying the roaring 1920's, but the good times would not last forever. Under Presidents Harding, Coolidge and Hoover, Washington, D.C. had taken a laissez-faire attitude and allowed the country to enjoy a post-war period of relative peace and prosperity.

There were, however, signs that the Republican dominance in certain areas of the North was declining. For example, in the 1928 elections, the Democrats faired very well in Massachusetts and Rhode Island where Catholic voters did not support Herbert Hoover. The election marked the first time since the Civil War that the voters of Massachusetts did not vote for the Republican ticket. As we now know, this was a signal of a slow and steady decline for the GOP in many northern urban areas.

The stock market crash of 1929, and the subsequent Great Depression, brought an end to the era of Republican dominance as Herbert Hoover failed to respond promptly enough to the subsequent and devastating economic suffering. The significant change in the economy's outlook resulted in Hoover being soundly defeated by the positive and inspiring message of Franklin D. Roosevelt in 1932.

After supporting the Roosevelt administration's initial emergency measures to get America on a steadier fiscal path, the Republicans became hostile toward the social programming of Roosevelt's "New Deal" programs. Republican members of Congress correctly observed that many well-intended programs resulted in a federal government that was growing at an unsustainable pace.

In 1935, the Supreme Court unanimously ruled three times against FDR and his New Deal programs. The next year, the Supreme Court held that several more of FDR's economic recovery laws violated the constitution. The court also overturned some state reform efforts which mirrored federal work statutes.

This series of decisions by the Supreme Court greatly disappointed President Roosevelt. Thus, he decided the best method of dealing with the Court would be to add more justices, ones that he would appoint and in theory, control. Thankfully, the Republican members in congress, along with a number of common-sense based Democrats, put a halt to the plan in the Senate Judiciary Committee. The bipartisan committee issued a negative report against the President's proposal. "This Bill," the report declared, "is an invasion of judicial power such as has never before been attempted in this country."

Despite the seriousness of the economic conditions of the time, conservative Republicans understood that certain principles must always be adhered to and the constitution should never be disregarded for political convenience. While it may often "feel good" for government to rush in and save the day from whatever crisis we are currently experiencing as a society, my GOP must always remember that each time government expands its influence into our lives, we give up some of our personal responsibility and freedom.

The American people were indeed desperate for a solution to their economic struggles and embraced the charismatic Roosevelt's efforts to provide more and more social programs. From my point of view, the difference between the worthy goals of F.D.R. in the face of desperate times and the current principles of the modern Democrat Party, is that Roosevelt intended his programs to be temporary and based in an employment setting.

The liberals who pervade F.D.R.'s party today appear to be more interested in creating a culture of dependency on government rather than simply providing a temporary helping hand to those in real need.

Not since the founding of the GOP, had Republicans been so irrelevant in national politics as when F.D.R. was in the White House. Republicans of the era either merged with the New Deal Democrats or turned into strict conservatives to fight against the expansion of the size and scope of Roosevelt's programs. (Sometimes, this is similar to how I feel serving in the Massachusetts House of Representatives) This split among Republicans primarily occurred on a regional basis. Progressive Republicans were mostly from the northeastern United States and conservative Republicans tended to be more rurally based. Much of this segmentation of philosophy between members of the Republican Party remains today.

It may seem hard to believe today, but in Massachusetts the Republicans once had been the dominant party for more than eighty years prior. As a strong and vocal anti-slavery state, citizens of the Commonwealth were quick to embrace the principles of the Republican Party and support candidates such as Abraham Lincoln and the Republicans who followed.

Unfortunately, the Republican strength in the Bay State slowly started to decline in the 1920s and 1930s with the success of Democrats' efforts targeting immigrant groups and the expansion of social programs. Also, the Democrats were (and still are) extremely effective at gaining the support from labor unions and their mass of workers with promises of support from union related legislation. The following years of New Deal programs and the popularity of F.D.R. resulted in a further decline of the GOP in Massachusetts as well as across the nation.

In 1938, the GOP appeared to be alive again by winning some important congressional seats as some folks started to recognize the long term anti-business economic effects of the New Deal giveaways and of over-zealous business regulation. Around 1940, the control of the Republican Party was taken over by Wendell Willkie and a new Republican progressivism spirit accepted the need for some government intervention in economic and social policy. Although resisted by the hard-core conservatives of the Republican Party, this more left-leaning tone was generally adopted as being the best chance to return to power.

The decision to move to the left by the Republicans seemed to be more politically motivated than principle based. As usual, these shifts in ideology rarely result in electoral success, as the base of my GOP becomes disenfranchised and the voters in general are distrustful of the message and messenger. One of the mistakes made over and over again by some in my GOP is the ill-advised effort of courting liberal voters. I have observed time and time again Republican candidates having this urge to move to the left in hopes of garnering votes away from their Democrat opponent. This does not work to win elections and has a long term negative impact on the Republican Party.

Willkie's attempt to return a Republican to the White House ended badly with another resounding victory for the Democrats overall in 1940. While Roosevelt was without question an extremely popular President, Willkie and the Republicans did not do themselves any favors by ignoring the core values of the GOP. Most critically needed during this time in history was Republicans fighting against the expansion of government's power and working to end the ever-expanding social engineering and increased taxation trends. Sadly, the Republican Party was in the hands of the progressive wing and never connected with the American voters. Time after time in our history, Republicans seem to periodically forget the consistent lesson that the American voters will only support Republican leaders who clearly articulate the values of their party and who are willing to stand up for smaller government, promotion of individual freedoms and personal responsibility, and those who conduct themselves consistent with the conservative principles. Willkie's left-leaning campaign is yet another example of a RINOfailing to understand that Americans have consistently elected Republicans only when they believe they will promote their own core values and beliefs.

After Japan's surprise attacked on Pearl Harbor on December 7, 1941, President Roosevelt led America into the war and patriotic Republicans loyally followed. This was not a time for political wrangling. It was a time when all political figures needed to support our president to defend America. Very different from the recent conduct of some members of the Democrat Party who got in line and relished criticizing President Bush, and in some cases even our troops serving overseas, Republican members of Congress firmly supported F.D.R.'s war policies and, for the most part, the entire nation supported the military.

While Republicans worked with the Democrat president in a bipartisan spirit on the war front, they continued to press for reforms and reductions to the growing size of the social programs which resulted from the New Deal. In 1942, the GOP made substantial electoral gains by campaigning against government price-fixing, overregulation of business and promising to slow the growth of social welfare programs.

One such Republican victory was Thomas Dewey, who won his election for Governor of New York by leading the fight against organized crime, which at the time was a growing and significant problem in many areas of the country. Dewey's law and order character rapidly elevated him to receive the GOP nomination for president in 1944. Unfortunately, Dewey while tough on crime, did not connect with the voters who had developed an enduring fondness for F.D.R. Furthermore, the GOP was fractured along ideological lines. Conservatives were supporting Ohio Senator Robert Taft, son of the former President. The GOP liberals successfully convinced primary voters that Dewey would capture the ethnic and labor vote and had the best chance to win in November.

On election day, both the immigrant and union voters remained loyal to F.D.R. as he had delivered on his promise of increased union control of business and expanded social benefits. History should have taught Republicans that targeting groups of people who are most likely to vote Democrat is usually a waste of effort and resources. More importantly, a GOP candidate should never sacrifice core beliefs in hopes of gaining a few more votes. During this period, the progressive wing of the GOP was able to retain control of the party's national convention because of its strength in the large delegations of the northeastern states and support from the progressive states of the Pacific coast region. Once again the Republican Party suffered defeats as voters saw no real difference between a liberal progressive Republican and a Democrat.

Although the progressive Republicans consistently won the presidential nomination at their conventions, they consistently failed to win the White House. The Republicans managed to regain control of Congress in 1946 with individual candidates who were able to promote a conservative message in their respective districts. But just two short years later, after the GOP again nominated him to the top of the ticket, Thomas Dewey unexpectedly lost the Presidential election to Harry S. Truman.

It was clear by 1948 Massachusetts was strongly trending to become a Democrat stronghold.   For example, in the race for president, Massachusetts was the only New England state to support Harry Truman. By the late 1940s and in the decades to follow, most of the urban-suburban areas of Massachusetts were almost completely Democrat, leaving just a few pockets of strong Republican rural areas, such as Barnstable County. In the years to follow in the Bay State, the influential Kennedy Family worked its way into the leadership of the Massachusetts Democrat Party. The political control by the labor unions increased in scope and strength, seemingly with each passing election.

In political desperation, after the 1948 election, the Republicans at last discovered several issues they could use effectively against the Truman administration. The GOP finally started to step away from the previous liberally minded agenda of the Dewey power base and head back towards its roots of conservatism.

The Korean War, which began as a civil war, certainly had a significant political impact on the United States. The war began on June 25, 1950, when North Korea moved to forcibly reunite North and South Korea under communist control. The war was greatly expanded when the United Nations, led by the United States, and later the People's Republic of China, entered the conflict on opposing sides. The Korean War was the first armed confrontation of the Cold War and set the standard for many later conflicts and the related political issues. Unlike World War I and II, the Korean War created the concept of a geographically limited war, where the two superpowers would fight their battles in another country. There were many sacrifices made by American service members to stop the spread and threat of communism. The United States lost 36,576 of our brave soldiers, sailors, airmen and marines from 1950 to 1953.

Some of the positives coming from the Korean War included the strengthening of the alliances in the western hemisphere and the splitting of Communist China away from the Soviet bloc nations. The war ended when a ceasefire was finally reached on July 27, 1953. A heavily guarded demilitarized zone (DMZ) was established on the 38th Parallel. This border continues to divide the peninsula today with American soldiers standing watch to ensure the freedom of South Korea and maintaining a vital American military presence in the region.

In 1952, with the World War II Supreme Allied Commander General Dwight Eisenhower at the top of the ticket and with the campaign slogan of "I like Ike," the Republicans once again retook possession of 1600 Pennsylvania Avenue. Ike's election ended twenty years of Democrat occupation and a period of unprecedented growth in the size and scope of the power of the federal government. The GOP also won control of Congress. President Eisenhower was able to make inroads in the largely controlled Democratic south, which would serve the Republican Party well in the decades to follow. Despite Dwight Eisenhower's overwhelming electoral successes, it unfortunately did not translate into long term Republican gains across the board. In fact, the Republicans ended up losing control of Congress just two years later in 1954.

Eisenhower was an extremely well liked, trusted and popular President. He was easily nominated for re-election by the Republicans in San Francisco for the 1956 election. Adlai Stevenson, who lost to Eisenhower four years prior, was again nominated by the Democrats at their convention in Chicago. Stevenson made the usual big government liberal proposals calling for the expansion of government services and along with it, a higher level of taxation. He also called for the end of the military draft and proposed a test ban treaty on all atomic weapons, which was the very thing that was keeping America safe from the growing threats from the Soviet Union. Stevenson's proposals were rejected by the voters who recognized Ike was keeping America safe by our increased military power. Eisenhower won a second term with a landslide victory.

President Eisenhower, knowing the seriousness of the Cold War, and with the strong support of the American people, successfully developed the United States into the premier global superpower. By the time Eisenhower left office in 1961, the United States had military bases on every continent and had enjoyed tremendous gains to our military readiness. Ike was the right man for the job, as he fully appreciated the need to build America's military power as the Soviets were expanding their own military capabilities. Americans expect and deserve Republican leaders to take the tough but necessary stances to protect our interests at home and abroad. President Eisenhower gave America what we expected and what we needed at such a point on our history.

While most of white America was enjoying the "Leave it to Beaver" decade of the 1950's, the civil rights movement was also gaining momentum. The United States Supreme Court handed down one of its most important cases of the century in 1954, in the case of <u>Brown v. Board of Education of Topeka, Kansas</u>. The high court's decision held the education of black children in separate public schools from their white counterparts was unconstitutional. The opinion of the Supreme Court stated that the "segregation of white and colored children in public schools has a detrimental effect upon the colored children." The following year, in the follow-up case known simply as <u>Brown v. Board of Education</u>, the Court ordered segregation to be phased out over time, "with all deliberate speed." This decision began the controversial and difficult process of not only changing the physical location of children in schools, but more importantly changing the racial culture of America.

In 1953, just one year prior to the <u>Brown v. Board of Education</u> decision, Earl Warren was appointed Chief Justice of the Supreme Court by President Eisenhower. Warren, a former Republican Governor of California, was described as a conservative justice with integrity and courage. <u>Brown v. Board of Education</u> is correctly considered to be one of those watershed cases in American history; and the decision was authored by a Republican. While I am certain this court case is in just about every American history text book, I would doubt that Republicans get any of the credit for authoring it. Nor does Eisenhower get the credit he deserves for using the strength of the federal government to enforce equal protection under the laws and to protect civil rights.

The very next year in Montgomery, Alabama, a woman by the name of Rosa Parks refused to get out of her seat on a public city bus to make room for a white passenger. This incident sparked yet another significant event in the quest for equal rights for African American citizens. Parks was arrested, tried and convicted for disorderly conduct and violating a local ordinance. After the rumors of the arrest reached the black community, African-American leaders gathered and organized the Montgomery Bus Boycott to protest the segregation of blacks and whites on public buses. The boycott lasted slightly over a year and ended only when the local ordinance segregating blacks and whites on public buses was repealed.

Just two short years later in Little Rock, Arkansas, another major event in the civil rights movement occurred. Arkansas Governor Orval Faubus, a long serving Democrat, called out his state national guard forces to prevent the nine African American students who had successfully sued for the right to attend an integrated school, from attending Little Rock's

Central High School. The nine students had been chosen to attend Central High because of their excellent grades and outstanding personal character. On the first day of school, only one of the nine students showed up because she did not receive the phone call about the danger of going to school. This black student was harassed by white students and their parents outside the school.

While symbolic of the civil rights movement occurring in practically every state at some level, the dangers and stress that these young people endured was tremendous. In the days that followed, the nine students had to carpool to school and were escorted by military personnel. Governor Faubus's order to prevent the students' admission to the previously all white school received the attention of President Eisenhower, who was determined to enforce the orders of the federal courts and protect the students' safety. Eisenhower federalized the Arkansas National Guard and ordered them to return to their barracks. Eisenhower then deployed elements of the Army's 101st Airborne Division to Little Rock to protect the black students. Once again, it was a Republican President who saw that his leadership was necessary to uphold the underlying guarantees of equal protection provided by the 14th Amendment.

History does not only remember Ike as the Republican President who got it right on military and foreign affairs, but also for his vision of the long term infrastructure needs of America. In 1956, President Eisenhower signed legislation establishing the National System of Interstate and Defense Highways. This program resulted in about 41,000 miles of new highways all across America. While first conceived as the National Defense Highway system designed to move military equipment and personnel more efficiently, Eisenhower's foresight of the critical needs of our growing superpower status resulted in enhancing the stream of commerce and providing recreational opportunities for Americans and visitors to visit and enjoy all corners of the United States by automobile.

Meanwhile, back in the Massachusetts political scene, John F. Kennedy defeated Henry Cabot Lodge Jr., for the United States Senate in 1952, ending the powerful Cabot-Lodge Republican dynasty that had dominated Massachusetts politics since the Revolutionary War days. On the state legislative level, Democrats would enjoy steady gains and ultimately assume strong majorities in both houses of the State Legislature. The Democrats would also dominate the Governorship for twenty-two years out of the thirty-four year period from 1957 to 1990.

On a national level, next came Richard Nixon, who would lose the 1960 Presidential election narrowly to the young and charismatic Massachusetts Democrat and World War II hero, John F. Kennedy. While Kennedy was certainly a strong candidate with a great deal of support from his family and organized labor, as well as the rumored support of some unsavory types, the Republican Party seemed to be suffering from a lack of a consistent message to the voters as to the foundational conservative principles they stood for. Conflicts within the party were significant as the progressive and conservative wings of the party were each vying for power and control and failed to unite on election day.

In the years to follow, the Democrats were once again in control of the White House with the election of J.F.K. A growing conservative base was beginning to emerge and seize key positions within Republican circles. This new Republican "right wing" was building momentum among local Republican groups across the nation. This newly energized conservative base was primarily composed of hard-core conservatives who had been alienated by the more liberal or progressive Republicans' failure to reverse the myriad of social programs enacted during the F.D.R. New Deal period decades earlier.

The newly energized right wing of Republican Party was gaining strength with conservatives, particularly in the southern states. Along with Catholics in the north who identified with the GOP's anticommunist views and on a variety of social issues, a new GOP conservative base was quickly growing. These factions within the GOP were correctly concerned that unless the United States aggressively fought the Cold War, which was the real and present threat of the spread of communism, America would likely face yet another world war. With the growing threat of nuclear weapons, it was likely that no nation would be able to claim victory without suffering a tremendous loss of civilian life. While considered by some at the time as extremists, in retrospect, history has a much more favorable view on the hard-liners as the Cold War ended without the use of any nuclear weapons.

The conservatives successfully took firm control of the Republican Party and defeated the more liberal-leaning eastern Republican establishment in 1964 as they secured the Presidential nomination for Arizona Senator Barry M. Goldwater. Goldwater won a bitterly contested battle for the nomination against New York Governor Nelson A. Rockefeller. Goldwater's nomination was tirelessly opposed by liberal eastern Republicans who argued that Goldwater's hard line foreign policy stances would bring about a deadly face to face confrontation with the Soviet Union and push the United States into a nuclear war.

Due to the bitterness of the primary, Republicans failed to unite to support their nominee and Barry Goldwater lost to Lyndon B. Johnson by one of the largest electoral margins in United States history. The Republican Party also suffered a significant setback nationally by losing seats in both houses of Congress. Many Republicans at the time angrily turned against Goldwater claiming that his defeat had significantly set back the Republican chances in the future. However, in just two short years, the Republican Party recovered from the 1964 election defeats and picked up forty-seven new seats in the House of Representatives in the mid-term election. It was also this time that a new medium was becoming more and more powerful to reach voters with political messages. By 1960, over eighty-five percent of American homes had at least one television set. The expanded access and ever increasing programming transmitted directly into the living rooms of America would change politics forever and in fact is still evolving today.   It was the television set where most people became familiar with future political figures such as Ronald Reagan, who at the time was appearing as a character actor and as the host of the General Electric Theater weekly program.

While serving as the corporate spokesman for General Electric and appearing at countless union halls and functions promoting the television show, Reagan was making his move (whether he realized it or not) into politics and developing his own views of the political issues of the day. The future president and former Democrat, struck a cord with the common folks who heard him speak to issues they cared deeply about. Reagan railed on the anti-big government sentiment which was growing due to the increasing burden of the income tax and expanding government regulation.

With or without television, during this period of time the Republican Party was still split into two ideological segments without a clear single identity, which is always necessary in order to connect with the majority of voters. While Goldwater's defeat allowed the liberals to pass a significant number of their "Great Society" programs, the defeat and subsequent internal shakeup of the GOP leadership cleared the way for a younger generation of American conservatives to mobilize. Goldwater followers mostly rallied behind Ronald Reagan, who became Governor of California in 1966. Reagan was becoming more and more firm in his conservative beliefs as he was also gaining a national following.

The conservative movement toward the right was reflected in a broader shift of economic power and population away from the GOP's old northeastern political base, including Massachusetts, and more toward the south and west where the votes were necessary to win back the White House, and quite frankly, where the people were most closely aligned with the core values of my GOP.

Whether the Republican Party has given up on the blue states of the northeast is not totally clear (I know that I have not!), but the focus has certainly shifted to reach out to voters in other areas of the country who already embrace Republican principles, rather than trying to change the values of the party in an attempt to appease the more liberally minded RINO's of the northeast. For the most part, this fact is still evident today. Many of the Republican office holders from the northeast often seem more worried about appeasing the liberals than standing up for the underlying GOP principles involved. In my view, this has resulted in the GOP failing to connect with many voters who happen to reside in a blue state.

The 1963 assassination of President John F. Kennedy, without question, had a tremendous impact on our country and created a great deal of political uncertainty and social unrest. Just a few years later, and with the controversial Vietnam War raging, America was growing more and more divided on the support of the military mission. The anti-war movement had two key establishment allies. Civil rights leader Reverend Martin Luther King Jr., and Senator Robert F. Kennedy, who campaigned as a presidential candidate to end the war, were in the forefront of both the civil rights and anti-war movements.

The year 1968 has often been described as one of those key political turning points in our nation's history. That year both King and Kennedy were murdered resulting in an even greater sense of instability and uncertainly for America. Reverend King was in Memphis, Tennessee to show support for striking sanitation workers when he was gunned down outside his motel room on April 4th. The gunman was James Earl Ray, a white convicted felon who had escaped from a Missouri state prison. The assassination sparked riots across America which resulted in some forty-six people dead and thousands more injured. Two months after Martin Luther King was killed, and as he celebrated victory in the California presidential primary, Robert Kennedy was killed by Sirhan Sirhan. This Palestinian refugee was angered by Kennedy's pro-Israeli views. Both King and Kennedy were young men at the time of their murders. King was only 39 and Kennedy was 42 years of age.

It was during this time that Richard Nixon seemed to understand the meaning of these tragic events and the emotions that the country was feeling as they watched their nightly evening news. Reports of young people protesting the war and the increasing media reports of drug use shocked most of America. Many families who had established themselves during the stereotypical "Leave it to Beaver" setting of the 1950's were having an increasingly difficult time reconciling the growing trend of liberal hippies protesting our troops, inner city "black power" movements and college students holding signs supporting the Vietcong movement while burning the American flag.

Richard Nixon entered the Republican convention as the clear front runner and easily won the nomination on the first ballot. He promised that he would be the voice of the quiet and hard working Americans, "those who do not break the law, people who pay their taxes and go to work, who send their children to school, who go to their churches...people who love this country and cry out that enough is enough, let's get some new leadership." With all of the turmoil in the country during this period of American history, this was a powerful message.

On the other side of the political aisle, the Democrats went through a grueling and ugly primary campaign. Eugene McCarthy, an early opponent of the war in Vietnam, almost upset the sitting President Lyndon Johnson in the New Hampshire primary. The harshness of the primary battle was later said to have convinced Johnson not to run for re-election, as the negative campaigning had taken a tremendous personal toll. Very similar to today's political climate where the extreme liberals in the Democrat power base attempt to push office seekers as far to the left as possible during the primary season, the liberals pushed McCarthy so far into extremistville, that middle America simply could not support his candidacy at the end of day. It was the long term security of America and the desire for traditional family values that prevailed on election day.

Richard Nixon campaigned against rising crime and claimed he would restore "law and order." Both such issues hit home with conservatives within the Republican power base and with the electorate in general. Nixon was elected president by a strong electoral vote count, but a narrow popular vote margin. During the campaign, Nixon referred to his base of support as the "Silent Majority" and recognized that his political messages were connecting with voters in new areas that traditionally had not supported Republicans. Southern white voters, blue-collar union workers and Catholic voters now recognized the family values of the GOP were their own values and they were willing to vote Republican in order to preserve them. This base of new voters would provide a solid foundation for the GOP for the decades that followed.

While the Republican Party was connecting with middle America during this time period, African Americans rejected the GOP's conservative populist approach and some in the Republican Party fostered the alienation of the minority voters perhaps for political gain elsewhere. Richard Nixon's Vice-Presidential running mate, Sprio Agnew made several statements concerning the plight of the inner cities and the civil rights movement. While this may have helped Nixon with the southern white vote, it sent a message (even if not correct or intended) to African American voters that the Republican Party was no longer interested in their issues. This was very unfortunate as since the founding of the Republican Party, my GOP had been inclusive to all groups and people who shared our political beliefs and principles.

The political damage done during the 1968 election concerning relations between African Americans and the GOP has resulted in a continued decline of support from minority groups for Republican candidates. Just the opposite was occurring in the Democrat Party, as they were doing their very best to encourage African American leaders to become more active in their own party. While the end of this story has not yet been told, my GOP must be aware of this history if we are going to avoid a similar future error.

President Nixon's administration became moderate on many policy decisions both at home and across the globe. This movement to the political middle ground certainly did not meet the expectations of the conservative base of the party who had hoped that Richard Nixon was a true man of character and someone who shared their own conservative values. The

Watergate scandal reflected badly on all elements of the GOP and stopped any progress the Republicans had hoped to make.

Once again, Republicans were reminded of the double standard between Republicans and Democrats when it comes to scandals. The media was relentless calling for Nixon's resignation following the Watergate scandal. In contrast, despite Bill Clinton's perjury conviction and numerous personal errors in judgment, the editorials of the major newspapers suggested the country should simply move on and forget Clinton's mistakes. While not making any excuses for Richard Nixon's involvement in Watergate, I believe he did the right thing by resigning the presidency and allowing America and the GOP to start the long and difficult process of moving on.

While things were difficult for the GOP, the Democrats were organizationally a mess themselves, as they had been torn apart by the Vietnam War, race relations and various divisive social issues. It was during this time that the Democrat Party became more and more influenced by the liberal elites. They opposed the troops fighting in Vietnam, opposed the death penalty, and became even softer on crime. The Democrat Party also began to reject many of the traditional family values, which many conservative members of their own party found disturbing. Conservative Democrats were powerless, as the liberal element had gained full control of the Democrat Party leadership circle.

The GOP had the perfect opportunity to win the hearts and minds of the American people. Many historians agree that Richard Nixon had the intellect, experience and ability to achieve many great things as President, but it was not to be, as Watergate drained all the momentum the Republicans had gained in the 1968 election. It was a sad and disappointing day for the GOP and the nation when Richard Nixon resigned the office of the presidency on August 8, 1974. Nixon's rise to power was like a Shakespearean tragedy. Richard Nixon was the hero who suffered and struggled against all odds to achieve greatness and power, but at the end of the story, he would fall from grace due to his own personal demons and inner personality conflicts.

Richard Nixon will always be remembered for his betrayal of the American people and of the Republican Party. Perhaps in the years to come when history is able to have a clearer picture, maybe he will also be thought of for his many accomplishments and foreign policy foresight. Nixon's trip to China and normalizing relationship with this growing superpower did much to keep the world at peace. Along with his Secretary of State, Henry Kissinger, Nixon's efforts in the Middle East and the Soviet Union, including the treaty to reduce long-range nuclear weapons in 1972, should not be forgotten. We cannot know "what if" Richard Nixon had not been president; but on issues regarding national security, it is likely that the world became a safer place thanks in no small part to the efforts of Richard Nixon.

With Nixon's departure from office and the country holding a strong sense of distrust in government in general, Gerald Ford took possession of 1600 Pennsylvania Avenue. Ford had a unique path to the White House. He had been appointed Vice-President when Agnew was forced from office due to a corruption scandal. Gerald Ford had previously served with great distinction in the House of Representatives for over twenty years. He was generally well respected on both sides of the political aisle.

Just one short month after Richard Nixon had resigned the office of the presidency and in the face of the growing pressure of the Watergate scandal, Gerald Ford announced his decision to grant Nixon a full pardon for any crimes he may have committed while president. The pardon was a decision that would serve to define Ford's presidency and his remaining political life. Gerald Ford will forever go down in political history as the person who gave Richard Nixon his pardon. All other acts or accomplishments will always be in the background. We can never know what was in Gerald Ford's heart when he issued his pardon, but history has treated the pardon as more of an attempt to heal the wounds of Watergate, rather than a political favor granted to Richard Nixon. President Ford's own words say it best:

> "My conscience tells me clearly and certainly that I cannot prolong the bad dreams that continue to reopen a chapter that is closed. My conscience tells me that only I, as President, have the constitutional power to firmly shut and seal this book. My conscience tells me it is my duty, not merely to proclaim domestic tranquility but to use every means that I have to insure it. I do believe that the buck stops here, that I cannot rely upon public opinion polls to tell me what is right. I do believe that right makes might and that if I am wrong, ten angels swearing I was right would make no difference. I do believe, with all my heart and mind and spirit, that I, not as president but as a humble servant of God, will receive justice without mercy if I fail to show mercy."

In 1976, President Gerald Ford only narrowly defeated former California Governor Ronald Reagan in the Republican primaries. Ronald Reagan, who had succeeded Barry Goldwater as the hero of the Republican right wing would have to wait another four years, as the Republican base had an overwhelming sense of loyalty toward Ford for weathering the political storms following Watergate. While most GOP insiders knew that due to the Nixon pardon, Ford was most likely not electable, Ford had done his duty to the nation and to the party and at least deserved a shot at holding the presidency for the GOP.

This loyalty to Gerald Ford was not enough, as a relatively unknown peanut farmer named Jimmy Carter from Georgia would win the general election. It was clear that the American people wanted a change in Washington, D.C. While Gerald Ford had done as much as anyone had expected of him, the majority of voters decided to give an outsider to the Washington, D.C. Beltway scene a chance to govern the country.

Change is what the American people wanted and change is certainly what they got. Jimmy Carter's Presidency is widely considered to be one of the worst in American history. The Carter administration faced major problems in the areas of a deficient energy supply, crippling high interest rates and rising unemployment. Inflation soon became the leading economic problem for the nation. It was soon apparent that Jimmy Carter was ill-prepared to lead America during this time of fiscal crisis. For example, President Carter hoped that by discouraging borrowing (by raising interest rates) and slowing down America's economy that it would lessen the rate and effects of inflation. Of course we now know that Carter made exactly the wrong decisions. Carter's popularity was at an all-time low by July of 1979.

To make matters even worse for the president, in November of 1979, Iranian militants seized the United States Embassy in Tehran, Iran and held American hostages. Just one month later, the Soviet Union invaded Afghanistan. It was evident that America needed to respond, as we were losing respect, both economically at home and militarily across the globe. In an effort to free the hostages in Iran, President Carter ordered military action, which was labeled Operation Eagle Claw. Unfortunately, due to poor planning, the mission resulted in the deaths of five heroic Air Force Airmen and three of our brave Marines. With the failure of this important mission, it was growing more and more clear that America needed a new leader and the Republicans had just the right man for the job. His name was Ronald Wilson Reagan. His time had finally come.

In 1980, Jimmy Carter put up a fight to hold the White House, but with the economy in a tailspin, the hostages still being held in Iran, and an apparent weakened state of military readiness of American forces, Jimmy Carter badly lost the election to the Republican challenger, Ronald Reagan. Reagan even won Massachusetts, a state any Democratic candidate could almost always count as a sure-thing victory.

The "Gipper," as Ronald Reagan was affectionately often called, won 489 electoral votes to Carter's 149. Reagan also won the popular vote by more than ten percent. On January 21, 1981, the day after Jimmy Carter left office, the hostages were freed and Americans started the long awaited process of once again feeling good about themselves and their country. This election not only marked the Republicans return to the White House, but also marked the end of a period where the eastern liberal-leaning GOP establishment, with leaders such as Nelson Rockefeller and others like him, ruled the inner control of the GOP. The Republican conservative base was now in charge and they had their man at 1600 Pennsylvania Avenue.

Ronald Reagan's successes and popularity finally brought together the formerly Democrat southerners, along with the northern, white, middle-class and Catholic voters who were historically most concerned about the social issues. What had been started by conservatives in 1968 had finally been achieved as the "Silent Majority" voted in overwhelming numbers for Reagan. For the first time since the J.F.K. era, such conservative-minded voters now considered themselves to be Republicans. It was not just the social issues that lead to Reagan's tremendous electoral success. Business owners saw the failed polices of Jimmy Carter and other liberals who attempted to manipulate the free enterprise with restrictive price controls and other big government attempts to manipulate economic activity. Ronald Reagan found support from all corners of America.

Further additions to the Republican ranks at this time were many formerly nonpolitical evangelical Christians. The groups had suffered great political and judicial losses with adverse decisions on outlawing prayer in public schools and allowing abortion practically on demand. Prior to the Reagan Revolution, many evangelical types had stayed out of politics. Ronald Reagan's message of hope and optimism inspired a new and soon to be extremely powerful political base for conservative candidates for many years to come.

Ronald Reagan was viewed almost immediately with optimism, hope and patriotism from the American people. After the Vietnam War, Watergate, and the energy and economy problems of the Carter term in office, the American people recognized that Reagan was correct in his free market views and desires to reduce the reliance on government for answers. The Republican Party had been blessed by Reagan's popularity and his unique ability to communicate directly with the American people on a deeply personal level.

On a personal note, it was at this time I became increasingly more interested in politics. As mentioned in the opening chapter, I grew up in the home of my grandparents, who were what I would characterize as old school Democrats or F.D.R. Democrats. It was during the 1980 presidential debates between the incumbent Jimmy Carter and challenger Ronald Reagan when I knew that I was a Republican. While Carter and his liberal friends wanted more government interference, Ronald Reagan was clear with his message that Americans desired less government influence, lower taxes and a renewal of the American dream and a spirit of patriotism. Ronald Reagan reminded us that it was just fine to believe America was the greatest nation on earth!

This was also a key political turning point for my family as well. My grandfather was always eager to engage me in political argument, and I must admit that he usually got the best of me. But even this life-long Democrat could no longer defend the principles and positions of his political party. My family is just one of the hundreds of thousands who realized in 1980 that America needed a new leader and a new direction. At the age of eighty-eight, my grandfather recognized that his party was no longer what it once was and that Ronald Reagan was a lot like him; a former Democrat who had not left his political party, but whose party had left him.

Dealing skillfully with Congress and taking his message directly to the American people when Congress refused to move his important pieces of legislation, Reagan pushed through legislation to stimulate economic growth, curb inflation, increase employment and strengthen our national defense. Most importantly, was a renewal of our national self-confidence and pride. America was in desperate need to feel good about itself after four years of the Carter administration. Ronald Reagan's personal style, political positions and vision for the country was right on target.

All of these factors helped Reagan win a second term with an unprecedented number of electoral votes. "Peace Through Strength" was Ronald Reagan's primary strategy for both ending the Cold War and pursuing his foreign policy agenda in general. Similar to Teddy Roosevelt's mantra of "speak softly and carry a big stick," Ronald Reagan appreciated that the best way to keep America safe was to make her the premier military superpower in the World. President Reagan's confidence and ability to deliver straightforward messages to other world leaders left no doubt that we were prepared to do whatever was necessary to protect America and our interests around the World. Even those who did not share Reagan's political views respected them, as they knew his political positions where grounded in principle and common sense and not a result of the most recent public opinion poll.

This character trait is one that all Republicans should follow. All too often we see our elected leaders not only changing votes on issues, but seemingly shifting their entire personal values system. Obviously, when this happens, voters are no longer able to predict with certainty what position the elected official will take on the next issue. Not only politically devastating to a single political candidate, but when a political party fails to stay true to its core values and beliefs, voters fail to have confidence in what position and actions the party's candidates will take if elected.

The one major scandal that plagued Ronald Reagan's tenure as president was the Iran-Contra affair. The charge against Reagan and his administration was that he approved the illegal sale of arms to Iran in return for the release of American hostages being held by an Islamic terrorist group in Lebanon. The profits realized from the sale of the arms were allegedly diverted to the Contras who were fighting in Nicaragua. Despite the conviction of his national security advisor, Admiral John Poindexter, Ronald Reagan recovered politically. Most Americans believed even if not proper conduct by the administration, the intentions of all were in the best interest of the United States. The issue surrounding Iran-Contra was, at worst, a mistake in personal judgment and an over reliance on staff members, and not an inherent character flaw of the President. I believe this is why the American people quickly moved on after Reagan accepted personal responsibility for any mistakes made.

Reagan also declared war against international terrorism, obviously long before it was politically acceptable to do so. The president sent

American bombers to Libya after clear and convincing evidence was discovered that Libya plus was involved in an attack on American soldiers in a West Berlin nightclub. Ronald Reagan was a man who stood for American power and strength, such as the highly successful Grenada rescue mission. He was exactly the right man for the job, as Americans needed a leader and the Republican Party need a savior.

In Reagan's eight years in office he increased defense spending by thirty-five percent, while improving relations with the Soviet Union. In dramatic and historic meetings with Soviet leader Mikhail Gorbachev, the two super-power leaders negotiated a treaty that would ultimately eliminate intermediate-range nuclear missiles. Reagan's personal relationship with Gorbachev proved to be invaluable to averting a confrontation between these two nuclear powers. Perhaps Ronald Reagan' s most memorable moment as president was at the Brandenburg Gate in West Berlin, Germany on June 12, 1987. In what has become one of the most well know speeches of the Reagan Presidency and perhaps in United States history, he challenged the Soviet President General Secretary Gorbachev with these famous words:

> "…if you seek peace, if you seek prosperity for the Soviet Union and Eastern Europe, if you seek liberalization: Come here to this gate! Mr. Gorbachev, open this gate! Mr. Gorbachev, tear down this wall!"

While this was one of hundreds of such challenges Reagan directed at the Soviet Union, it was perhaps the most symbolic and successful. These words will go down in history as one of the symbols marking the end of the Cold War. Often times, political leaders are remembered for their actions in battle during times of war or crisis, but little credit is given to those who kept our nation safe without actually going to war. Ronald Reagan deserves as much credit as we can give him for keeping America and the world safe from an unwinnable nuclear confrontation.

On the home front, Reagan was equally impressive with sweeping reforms to social entitlements, including reductions in welfare spending. This not only ended the vicious cycle of racial and cultural dependence on government, but it also helped fund the tax cuts Reagan was able to push through Congress. Reagan's economic polices became know as "Reaganomics" or "trickle down economics." History has proven his policies were successful at creating an economic environment which led to much of America's prosperity well after Ronald Reagan departed the White House.

When President Ronald Reagan left office he had successfully reinvigorated the American people and changed the mindset that government was the default answer to many of our problems. Without a doubt, Reagan had fulfilled his campaign pledge of 1980 to restore "the great, confident roar of American progress and growth and optimism." After eight years of Ronald Reagan in the White House, the Republican Party was once again the political party of the common man and the party that motivated Americans to believe in a positive future of our nation. Reagan inspired countless numbers of future Republicans, including yours truly to become politically active. His legacy is one which will live forever in our history by the way he conducted himself as president and the principles for which he stood without any reservations or apologies.

Without Ronald Reagan winning the 1980 election, the Republican Party, and in fact this country, would not be as strong, prosperous or as proud as we are today. History has deservedly been good to Ronald Reagan. In most polls concerning who people believe has been our greatest President, Ronald Wilson Reagan is always first or second.

In 1988, after serving eight years as Vice-President under Reagan, George H.W. Bush won the Republican Presidential nomination. He and his vice-Presidential running mate, Dan Quayle of Indiana, easily defeated the Democrat candidates, Governor Michael Dukakis of Massachusetts and Senator Lloyd Bentsen, Jr., of Texas. Without question, America was still feeling good about Reagan's two terms and Bush rode Reagan's political "coattails" into 1600 Pennsylvania Avenue. Americans saw George H.W. Bush as both the loyal Vice-President of Ronald Reagan, but more than that, they wanted to continue the policies and work of Ronald Reagan. Who was better to do so than his own right- hand man?

One of Bush's first measures as President was to propose legislation to bail out the financially troubled savings and loan institutions and get Americans feeling confident in their financial institutions. Under Bush's lead, Congress passed a $159 million ten-year plan to rescue the ailing banks. Unfortunately, the scope and cost of the problem grew and the large federal budget deficit created from overspending by Congress was a major issue fiscally and politically. In what would turn out to be the greatest political mistake of his presidency and contrary to a campaign pledge of "No New Taxes," George Bush agreed to raise taxes to help pay down the growing budget deficit. This policy shift negatively impacted his popularity, particularly among conservative Republicans who of course felt betrayed that a Republican president would both go back on his word and also increase taxes.

There are many things to learn from a review of political history and without question, Bush's reversal of tax policy provides us with two lessons. First, when a politician makes an unequivocal promise, such as "No New Taxes," voters rarely forgive them when they change course. Secondly, the GOP base fully and rightly expects Republican office holders to hold the line on increasing any tax. When a Republican office holder fails to do so, the GOP faithful are alienated and often discontinue their efforts to promote and support future Republican candidates. Additionally, when a Republican proposes or votes in favor of increased taxation at any level, independent voters become unable to see the difference between voting for a Republican or a Democrat.

In the 1990 elections in Massachusetts, due to the growing unpopularity of Democrat Governor Michael Dukakis, which in part resulted from his failed presidential bid, Republican Bill Weld connected with the voters to retake the governor's office. Weld would be the first Republican to reside in the state's corner office since 1973. Weld's victory translated into wins for Republicans seeking legislative seats as well, reducing the Democrat's super-majorities in the State Senate and House of Representatives. The Massachusetts Republican Party appeared to be back on track. Despite retaining the corner office with Governors Paul Celluci, Jane Swift, and Mitt Romney, the number of Republicans in the legislature continued to slide in the years which followed.

Two years after Bill Weld's victory, the GOP had 16 of the 40 seats in the State Senate. In the years to follow, Republicans would see a slow and steady decline to today's level of only 5 seats. Taking a look at the Massachusetts House of Representatives, we see a very similar pattern of a declining number of elected Republicans. With each passing session, the numbers of GOP members has been on a steady downward trend despite there being a Republican governor from 1990 to 2006. In the House of Representatives, the number of Republican legislators reached a modern day high of 38 in 1991. As I write this Chapter in 2009, we are sitting at a record low of 16.

In global politics, President Bush presided over a period of great political change around the world. The communists of eastern Europe were replaced by representative governments. The long time divided Germany was finally reunited as Gorbachev actually did "tear down that wall" Ronald Reagan challenged him to do and ultimately the Soviet Union broke apart, in effect ending the Cold War period. Also in 1989, Bush sent troops to remove Panama's dictator, General Manuel Noriega, who had been convicted in the United States on drug trafficking charges. The World was becoming more democratic and freedom was spreading to oppressed people across the globe.

The period of relative peace ended in 1990 when Iraq's dictator Saddam Hussein invaded its neighbor to the south, the country of Kuwait. Showing his political experience and masterful diplomatic skills, Bush led an international alliance approved by the United Nations to force a withdrawal by Iraq from Kuwait in 1991. With very few allied military causalities, operations Desert Shield and Desert Storm were considered to be tremendous successes and Bush's favorability rating numbers soared.

Notwithstanding his many successes overseas, Bush's successes in foreign affairs were more than offset by an economic recession hitting back on the home front. Despite serving as Ronald Reagan's Vice-President for eight years and seeing the positive economic impact of Reagan's tax cuts, President Bush failed to appreciate the negative impacts of his approval to the increase in federal income taxes. The economy became a decisive issue in the 1992 election campaign. "It's the economy, stupid," was the slogan used during Bill Clinton's successful 1992 presidential campaign against George H.W. Bush. Governor Bill Clinton of Arkansas won the Democrat's nomination and H. Ross Perot, a Texas businessman ran as an independent candidate. Perot certainly made the race unique and is also credited by many as being a spoiler. On election day many conservatives ended up casting their ballot for Perot as they could not forgive Bush for breaking his no new taxes pledge. This political factor and the overall weakness in the economy resulted in Bill Clinton defeating the sitting President Bush with 370 electoral votes to Bush's 168.

Soon after taking office in 1992, President Clinton called for nearly $500 billion in tax increases. Although Republicans and some conservative Democrats opposed his plan to raise taxes, Congress finally gave the new president much of what he had asked for. Clinton also won congressional approval for the North American Free Trade Agreement (NAFTA) with Canada and Mexico, which for better or worse has changed the face of America's economy forever.

The political tide had shifted and was certainly in favor of the Democrats. While it appeared Bill Clinton had a wealth of political capital to spend, one of his top political priorities, which was being pushed by his wife Hillary Clinton, was health care reform (AKA – universal health care for all). Quickly labeled correctly as a form of socialism, the plan met with stiff opposition. Critics complained that his proposal would cost too much and lead to government interference in the health care system. Ultimately, President Clinton had to abandon the idea. Not only was the failure to enact socialized medicine a significant political defeat for the new president, it also created a negative view of the First Lady. Hillary Clinton's rough demeanor and push for a new form of socialism disappointed many Americans. Both conservatives and moderates were taken aback as she seemed too arrogant and acted in a manner inconsistent with the First Ladies who came before her. Certainly many First Ladies have been involved in political issues before Mrs. Clinton arrived in Washington, D.C., but Hillary Clinton was different as it appeared she was controlling the political agenda, not simply promoting the president's ideas. This did not sit well with many Americans. If Hillary Clinton is ever elected President, one has to wonder what influence Bill Clinton might have. Would we have de facto co-Presidents or would Bill be satisfied managing the White House "affairs?"

Controversy and scandal surrounded the Clintons throughout their eight years in office. The first major scandal was related to investments President Clinton and the First Lady made in the Whitewater Development Corporation, a land development firm back in Arkansas. Other charges would follow, including the infamous sexual harassment claim made by a former Arkansas state government employee, Paula Jones, and the scandal regarding President Clinton's sexual relationship with White House intern Monica Lewinsky. While a seemingly endless number of books have been written about these scandals, the purpose of mentioning them in this historical context is to reflect on the damage done to the office of the presidency itself.

These personal scandals and ethical issues by the Clintons contributed greatly to the Democrat Party's defeat in the 1994 midterm elections and helped the Republicans gain control of Congress for the first time in 40 years. Another significant reason for the Republican sweep of the midterm elections was the "Contract with America." This was a document released by the Republican legislative leadership during the 1994 Congressional election campaign.

The Contract and resulting political strategy was offered by a large team of Republican Representatives; however, Newt Gingrich is primarily credited with the overall movement and its success. The Republican Party's dramatic success in the 1994 Congressional elections was directly attributed to the principles outlined in the Contract with America and the voters desiring the GOP to embrace the conservative principles upon which my

GOP was founded. The movement was successful because it touched the hearts, minds and souls of Americans in all fifty states, including even my home state of Massachusetts. While presented to the media as new ideas, much of the actual text of the Contract with America was from former President Ronald Reagan's 1985 State of the Union Address.

The Contract detailed the actions the Republicans promised to take if they again became the majority party in the United States House of Representatives. Many of the contract's policy ideas also originated at the Heritage Foundation, which has consistently promoted conservative principles, even when some Republican's in office have not. The Contract with America was introduced about six weeks before the 1994 Congressional election and was signed by all but two of the Republican members of the House and all of the Party's non-incumbent Republican Congressional candidates.

A central theme was that it promised to end the budget deficit by cutting wasteful spending and to renew the public's faith in their political leaders. Both such goals were of course directly aimed at President Clinton as well as being wholly consistent with the core philosophy of my GOP. Proponents and supporters said the Contract was revolutionary in its commitment to offering specific legislation for a vote on the floor of Congress and not just an effort to grab headlines during a political campaign.

Often times, the best that one in elective office can do is to force the opposing side to push the voting button and go on record for all the public to see. The promise of forcing matters to the floor for a formal roll call has always been a successful political tactic for Republicans, whether they are in the majority or the minority. Once an elected official is on record for having voted for or against a given bill, the system that our Founding Fathers created takes care of the rest. Of course this is true only if the media and voters ultimately hold the political figure accountable for their votes.

Despite the early success of Newt Gingrich and other Congressional Republicans, Bill Clinton easily won his re-election bid in 1996. Clinton received only forty-nine percent of the popular vote. The Republican nominee was former United States Senator and World War II hero, Bob Dole of Kansas. Dole never seemed to make that necessary personal connection with the voters and many conservatives failed to support the more moderate Dole. Once again Independent candidate H. Ross Perot was in the race, although he probably did not have as great of an impact on the 1996 election as he did in 1992.

While the loss by Bob Dole was disappointing for Republicans, even more distressing for members of the Reagan Revolution was that the so-called Reagan Democrats stopped voting Republican. These were mostly blue-collar workers with conservative social had either voted for Perot or simply gone back to voting Democrat. While Bob Dole was certainly a former distinguished member of the United States Senate and worthy of ascending to the Presidency, he was no Ronald Reagan. Dole's moderate views on many issue failed to connect with those who had previously crossed party lines and who had voted for Ronald Reagan and George H.W. Bush in 1988.

Allegations of misconduct continued to plague President Clinton in his second term. In addition to the ongoing investigation into the Whitewater investments and the Paula Jones case, his re-election brought new charges that he and Vice President Gore had engaged in questionable fund-raising activities during the 1996 election campaign. As mentioned, the most damaging controversy stemmed from charges that President Clinton had an improper relationship with a 21-year-old former White

House intern, Monica Lewinsky. On December 19, 1998, President Clinton was impeached by the House of Representatives on charges of perjury and obstruction of justice related to his testimony concerning his relationship with Ms. Lewinsky.

In United States history, only Democrat Andrew Johnson in 1866 had been impeached. After a trial in the Senate, the President was acquitted on both the impeachment and perjury charges; however, President Clinton continued to face the possibility of a future indictment on criminal charges connected with the Lewinsky scandal. Bill Clinton, while certainly a well liked President by many, will forever be scarred with the personal scandals that surrounded him and the First Lady. The Clinton terms in office began a period of time where politics seem to have taken an increased partisan tone, which unfortunately continues to this day.

When writing about history, it is usually unwise to offer comments about recent happenings. Time has a way of molding events and circumstances to reflect a sense of fairness and clarity which is often not possible in the emotional context of current events. In the interest of completeness and knowing full well that time may change the way President George W. Bush is remembered, I will close this chapter with a few observations concerning President Bush and how the GOP has faired over these last eight years.

In 2000, George W. Bush became the first son of a former president to win the White House since John Quincy Adams, son of John Adams. On the road to winning the presidency, George W. benefited not only from the examples of his father, but also that of his grandfather, Prescott Bush, a widely respected United States Senator. Not to be left out of the family's political tree, is George W's brother, former Florida Governor Jeb Bush. The Bush family has enjoyed a long history of public service to this nation and while modern approval ratings may not be overly favorable to George W., I suspect that with time, the Bush family will be remembered with appreciation and respect for their service to America.

George W. Bush and his 2000 victory over Democrat Al Gore (who we know well had ousted Bush's father only eight years earlier) gave the new President Bush the opportunity to restore his family's political reputation as well as returning a Republican to the White House. The 2000 Presidential race turned out to be one of the closest in American history and only added to the growing partisan tone in America's political climate. When all the votes were counted (a discussion for many other books and one which I choose not to expand on), and following the highly controversial Florida Supreme Court and United States Supreme Court decisions, George Bush's victory in Florida was affirmed. The final electoral vote totals were 271 for Bush to 266 for Gore.

While a win is a win and the Republican Party was happy to be back in the White House, the closeness of the election and subsequent court battles added to the growing division among many Americans. This election greatly added to the "gotcha" style of politics which has taken hold since Bill Clinton's victory in 1992.

September 11, 2001, is without question one of those few dates that will forever live in the minds and souls of all of us and in American history. Just as the bombing of Pearl Harbor and World War II defines a period of time and an entire generation, the 9/11 terrorists attack on America and years of war that have followed defines the Bush Presidency and recent American history.

The war against terrorism continued to dominate virtually all aspects of Bush's Presidency and appropriately so. The threats to our way of life are indeed real and the freedom of those across the globe would forever change if the terrorists were allowed to expand their fear and influence. Whether the liberals wish to acknowledge it or not, there are those Islamic extremists who wish the end of America and will stop at literally nothing to end our way of life. President Bush has unmistakably made it his mission to ensure that we are as safe as possible and that freedom is spread across the globe. While it is indeed unpopular and unpleasant to realize the sacrifices that must be paid to protect our homeland, there is no doubt President Bush will be remembered for his steadfastness on this war against terrorism. While I certainly do not agree with all of President Bush's tactics or beliefs, I do appreciate his conviction and firmness in doing all that is possible to protect our homeland from another attack.

It is far too early to determine how America and our allies will ultimately deal with the ongoing threat of Islamic extremism and the associated dangers to freedom, but it is clear that our safety and security is in the hands of Republicans. This is true whether we are in the majority or minority position in Congress. The Democrat Party does not seem to have the fortitude to or political support from within itself to stay the course necessary to ensure the battles against those who wish to end our way of life are conducted away from American soil. The war on terror is complicated, long and comes with a heavy cost of loss of life and finances. Hopefully, the Republican Party's elected officials will have the foresight and strength to lead the way to ensure this enemy is defeated.

In 2002, Republicans won enough seats in Congress to increase their majority in the House and more importantly to regain control of the United States Senate. The American people knew that the Republican Party was the best choice to protect our country from any future acts of terrorism. One of the first acts of the new Republican Congress was to approve Bush's proposal for a new cabinet level department. The newly created Department of Homeland Security was necessary to focus federal efforts against terrorism and to coordinate the use of intelligence among the various law enforcement and military entities. The remainder of George W.'s first term was for all practical purposes consumed by ensuring America responded to the growing threat of terrorism.

The election of 2004 ended in another victory of President George W. Bush. Once again the Republicans won primarily based on our need and desire to maintain security against the threats of terrorism. George W. Bush won nearly all of the same states as he had in 2000; however, for this election President Bush enjoyed a clear win in the popular vote over Massachusetts Senator John Kerry.

The Republicans were successful during the 2004 election in part by attacking Kerry in his most vulnerable areas, such as portraying him as a "flip-flopper" and as someone who could not be trusted to fight the war on terror. Following the election, the Republicans were in a position of strength and had a tremendous opportunity to promote and enact core Republican pieces of legislation unrelated to the war on terror. Such GOP initiatives included passing permanent income tax reductions, social security reform and strengthening our immigration laws and borders. Students of political history know that with every political opportunity comes a political responsibility. My GOP had a unique opportunity to change the course of the country by passing conservative measures as they had control of the White House, the House and the Senate. If they worked together, Republicans could have changed the face of Washington, D.C. and the nation for a very long time.

To put it bluntly, my GOP in Washington. D.C. wasted the chance to accomplish a great many things, both political and of substance. Having blown the opportunity to address many of the domestic issues that Americans cared deeply about, the 2006 midterm elections were a disaster for Republicans. After the votes were tallied, the Democrat Party celebrated a sweeping victory as they took control of the House, the Senate and a majority of governorships and state legislatures from the Republican Party. In just two years, what appeared to have been a mandate from the American people had been almost completely reversed.

The 2006 campaign season was one of the dirtiest in recent memory as candidates and political parties on both sides of the aisle engaged in very negative styles of campaigning. While scandals dominated the news media with allegations of marital infidelity, and the influence of lobbyists hurt a few specific Republican candidates, the wide scale GOP losses were a result of a much larger cause.

While I have offered my views of the results of the 2006 and 2008 elections in an earlier chapter, it is likely that history will offer a clearer analysis as more years pass. The talking heads on the television talk shows and the editorial writers of the print media provided their own political observations with an endless number of reasons why the voters returned Congress and the White House to the Democrats. While I agree that there is rarely a single reason for any political success or failure, it is my view that the Republican Party and many of our office holders lost touch with the principles of my GOP and the very reason why Americans vote Republican.

While many issues and challenges have faced George W. Bush and his administration these last eight years, history will not likely speak of the lack of personal scandals inside the White House, which were so common in the Clinton White House. I believe as the decades pass, George W. Bush will be viewed as the right man for America following the attacks on

September 11th. A President who recognized what had to be done and who did his best.

The issues discussed in this book are those principles I am referring to when I speak to my GOP's need to stay firm in our principles and values. Issues such as real immigration reform, budgetary spending controls, fighting for tax reductions, welfare reform, honoring the will of the voters, and avoiding personal scandal are just a few things Republicans need to focus on to make America that "shining city upon a hill" Ronald Reagan spoke of in his farewell address.

To be clear, I do not speak as an official of the Republican Party nor do I expect to always agree with its platform or the positions of its leaders, but unless we can get back on track and learn the historical lessons of our successes and failures, the GOP losses in 2006 and 2008 might just continue into the election of 2010 and beyond.

What is evident from our review of the history of the Grand Old Party is that when we have leaders who stay firm and strong to the core beliefs of the Republican Party, the American people are more than willing to embrace them. However, during those times where the elected Republican officer holders are nothing more than "RINO's," with their finger held up to the political wind, the voters fail to see why our party deserves their support and I guess at the end of the day, that is exactly what we deserve.

The future is bright with opportunity for my GOP and those who share our values and beliefs. The key is to learn the lessons from history and always stand firm on our Republican principles!

Chapter Thirteen – Inner Circle Acknowledgments

Since the beginning of my political career, I am blessed to have been surrounded with a group of people who have not only served me well as political advisors, but more importantly, I consider all to be trusted friends. This group of loyal souls has earned the title of my "Inner Circle." Some folks call such groups their "Kitchen Cabinet" which is a term first used by the political opponents of President Andrew Jackson, This term describes the unofficial advisors Jackson consulted and who entered the White House via the side kitchen door. I use the term "Inner Circle," as I seek and obtain advice from a great number of people, but there is an Inner Circle of them whom I rely upon the most for their straightforward, candid and honest guidance.

In fact, my desire to seek elective office was triggered by one of these very individuals. It was Dennis Fonseca who would later become my Campaign Chairman who put the first concrete thought in my head about running for the Legislature. Dennis and his equally politically astute wife Carol had invited my wife Lisa and me to attend a Flag Day dinner in 2001. While enjoying the usual rubber chicken dinner and talking politics, Dennis asked me the point blank question, "Have you ever considered running for elective office?" I must admit this question caught me off guard as the dinner's discussion had not been about me at all. Furthermore, as Dennis is one of the most well-respected leaders in Cape Cod GOP circles, to think he thought I would make a good candidate surprised me.

While I do not recall whether my response was even remotely coherent, from that point on, rather than being one of those people who attended Republican events to support the Party or some other candidate, I was now thinking about becoming a candidate myself. From that day on, my political life began to evolve with a sense of direction and purpose and

Dennis and Carol would remain at my side as great friends and dedicated members of my Inner Circle.

While Dennis and Carol have done more for my political career than I could ever list here, the most beneficial guidance and direction they ever offered was during my first campaign when I was under constant attack from negative- style campaign tactics. As I was trying to stay focused on remaining positive and ignoring all the bad advice to counter attack my opponent, Dennis and Carol delivered to me verses one through six of the Fifty-Seventh Psalm, which reads:

1   Be gracious to me, O God, be gracious to me;

for my soul takes refuge in Thee;

and in the shadow on Thy wings I will take refuge in Thee,

until destruction passes by.

2   I will cry out God most high,

to God, who accomplishes all things for me.

3   He will send from Heaven, to save me;

He reproaches him who tramples upon me.

God will send forth His loving kindness and His truth.

4   My soul is among lions;

I lie among those who breathe forth fire,

even the sons of men whose teeth are spears and arrows,

and their tongue a sharp sword.

5   Be exalted above the heavens, O God

let Your glory be over all the earth.

6   They have prepared a net for my steps;

my soul is bowed down;

they dug a pit before me,

they have fallen into it themselves.

Not only did these words help keep me focused and allow me the energy to go on and win the election with a positive message, they remain beautifully framed and displayed on my living room wall (a gift from Dennis and Carol). This constant reminder serves me well to never yield to the pitfalls of our often negative political system. I also owe Carol Fonseca a big thank you for providing her outstanding feedback on this book.

Initially, as I was going through the process whether or not to challenge a three-term liberal Democrat incumbent, it soon became clear that I needed a trusted political manager to help me avoid the usual mistakes that most first time candidates make, and ultimately end up losing. In addition to Dennis Fonseca, Frank Pannorfi stepped forward and signed up as my Campaign Manager. Frank and I had known each other from being members of the Sandwich Republican Town Committee, but little did I know the friendship that would blossom as we have worked closely together since 2002. Frank can best be described as a stubborn New Jersey transplant who always has your back covered. While retired from a successful career in the corporate world, Frank is anything but corporate. He is one of those few people who can sincerely be trusted with any confidence. While appearing to be tough and unmovable on many issues, I have always found his heart to be in the right place.

With a Campaign Manager and Chairman in place, it was apparent that I also needed someone around me who had the experience of actually winning campaigns. Dennis and Frank would do anything for me, but I also needed someone who knew inside politics. Just as I am blessed to live in a conservative legislative district, I was equally fortunate to have sitting next to me at many of the local Republican meetings one of the most insightful political minds I would ever have the pleasure to meet. His name is Dave Neal. A proud Vietnam veteran, who has served elected officials for decades in Washington, D.C., the State House, and on the local level, Dave is the most loyal Republican I have ever known and one of the few people who really understands what it takes to win an election. Over the years which followed, Dave and his wife Karen, one of the sincerest and sweetest people on this earth, were always faithfully by my side. Karen would literally give you her last dollar if you needed it. She is always positive and encouraging. They both have become so much more than advisors, they are true lifelong friends. While I trust and appreciate the advice and counsel of many, Dave is the one who gets the first call when I have doubts about a political issue. While I have not always taken Dave Neal's advice, at the end of the day, I usually wish that I had.

In future years and campaigns other folks would come forward and join my Inner Circle. Randy and Mary Hunt, a couple who relocated from Texas to Sandwich, would become my Campaign Treasurer team. In addition, they have worked countless hours helping me to produce my cable television show, the "Jeff Perry Report." Randy, who is also my C.P.A., brings a unique combination of deep intelligence and a sarcastic sense of humor to the Inner Circle. His wife Mary is one of the people who apparently does not have the ability to say "no" to any request I make for assistance. Simply put, the Hunts are friends and advisors who are just plain fun to be around.

Sometime around 2005, I realized that I could not attend every political event. The number of GOP elected officials was dwindling and I was receiving more requests to make personal appearances. These factors introduced Gerry Nye into the Inner Circle. Gerry, also a Vietnam Veteran is really a Libertarian at heart. He had been a customer of Sandwich Variety Store, which I owned for several years before running for elective office. Each morning, Gerry and his dog would come to the store around 6:00 a.m.

to purchase the Wall Street Journal and talk politics. Little did I know then, that just a few short years later, Gerry would be my District Outreach Coordinator and serve as my stand-in at events my schedule did not allow me to attend. The best way to describe my friend Gerry is that he is sincerely dedicated and worried about the future of his country. Gerry has an insight into a side of politics that is unique and deeply intellectual. Putting together his deep love for America, his intelligence and his friendship makes him invaluable to my political efforts.

Sometimes political advisors turn into friends and sometimes friends turn into political advisors. The latter is the case with Skip and Nancy Sandborg. Over the years, my wife Lisa and I got to know the Sandborgs both politically and socially and the more time we spent with them, the more our friendship grew. They are a part of the Inner Circle as they provide a sincere and straight-forward perspective which is invaluable when making political judgments. All too often, people who serve in political office for a while lose their connection to opinions and views of people outside of their political circles. Nancy is an organizer and dedicated task master. For example, when I was looking for volunteers to organize my house party schedule in the 2008 election, Nancy was quick to raise her hand and jump right in.

Skip holds back very few of his opinions, whether he agrees or disagrees with me. Along with Dave Neal, Skip is the person I often contact when I am having trouble determining how I will vote on an upcoming question before the legislature. I know they both will give it to me plain and straightforward. More than just talking the talk, Skip is a worker. In fact, he volunteered to organize my early morning campaign standouts; not always an enjoyable task on those cold late October mornings. Nancy and Skip are invaluable to my efforts as I always know they are loyal and faithful to the cause.

The latest addition to the inner circle who I feel compelled to acknowledge is my law partner, Kevin Flannigan. Since organizing the law firm of Flannigan and Perry, P.C. and working with Kevin on a daily basis, it has become readily apparent that, not only is he an extremely skilled attorney, but more importantly, Kevin has a heart of gold and would do anything to help his friends. Words on this page cannot express how much I appreciate Kevin's advice and mentoring in both the political and legal worlds.

Last but certainly not least, is my Chief of Staff Taylor White and his wife, Jenn. While technically not part of my campaign team, Taylor has served as my Legislative Aide and Chief of Staff since I was first elected in 2002. I first met Taylor in 2002 when I was running for the first time. He had just moved to Sandwich and appeared at a local Republican meeting. To make a long story shorter, Lisa and I ended up renting him a room in our home in exchange for campaign work. Soon after my victory in 2002, Taylor moved out and I hired him as my Legislative Aide. Being two young Republican conservatives in Massachusetts, Taylor and Jenn have earned my appreciation for fighting the good fight for our values and beliefs. I would also like to specifically acknowledge Jenn's sacrifices of allowing Taylor the time to work for such a difficult and demanding boss. Taylor has experienced most of the trials and tribulations of being an elected official and served me well in my legislative battles. I am certain that Taylor has a bright future in politics.

While not members of the Inner Circle any longer due to their move to New Hampshire, this chapter would not be complete without a mention of Carol and Paul Hotz. During my first two campaigns, no two people did more hard-core campaigning than the Hotzs. Carol organized envelope stuffing parties which took over her entire house, she made telephone calls, organized events, you name it, Carol did it! Never to be outdone, Paul used his pickup truck to carry around a huge "Perry for State Rep" sign 24-7 and was always the first person to arrive at a sign standout. If you ever wonder how dedicated someone can be to a campaign, I will introduce you to Paul Hotz. I will never forget the day I saw Paul arrive at a sign standout with a stool in one hand and my campaign sign in the other (following his full knee replacement). I was at a loss for words as how to express my appreciation. Paul and Carol were with me at every step during my first two campaigns and because of people like them, I have had the privilege to serve in the Massachusetts Legislature.

While there are many stories from campaigns, the one that I think says it all about my Inner Circle and core group of supporters occurred in April of 2002. It was a bitterly cold and rainy evening outside the Bourne High School as I gathered with my supporters in preparation of the annual Bourne Town Meeting. Our goal for the evening was to hold Perry campaign signs and hand out literature to those arriving at the meeting.

About a dozen of my campaign volunteers had arrived and just as we were getting organized outside the main doors of the high school, the rain and wind picked up, literally making it difficult to stand in one place. Feeling bad that I was asking people to be blown around the parking lot getting soaked, I suggested that we pack it up and head home. To my surprise, no one wanted to leave! There we were, about twelve "fools" getting drenched while attempting to hold campaign signs as the winds were whipping us around. I am not sure what the people attending the meeting thought of us, but from that point forward, I knew I had people who would do anything for me. Now, some six years later, whenever it might be foul weather, people like Skip and Nancy Sandborg remind me of the high standard we set at that Bourne Town Meeting and thus we never cancel a campaign event due to weather.

Perhaps we all take our family members for granted, but I cannot close this chapter without spending a little time expressing how critical my loved ones have been to my political success. First and foremost, my beautiful wife Lisa has been with me every step of the way. She has seen the good, the bad and the ugly side of it all. From endless campaign and political events to countless "rubber chicken" dinners and meetings, whenever and wherever she is needed, she is. I could fill an entire chapter outlining all she has done quietly behind the scenes to support my political efforts. But more than attending the events and doing the work behind the scenes of a campaign, she is my other half. It is unquestioned that without Lisa's love, personal sacrifices and support, I would not be who or where I am today. I am confident that there are not too many spouses who would have shouldered the burdens and made the personal sacrifices she has made for me on personal, educational and political levels. Lisa makes me want to push myself to the next level, but never lets my sense of self-importance get too big. Whether or not one believes in soul mates, I know that I have found mine.

My mother, Millie, and her dear friend, Bud Godfrey, both in their eighties now, have to be my biggest fans! I could not keep them away from a campaign event if I tried. Every fundraiser, sign standout or parade, there they are. In fact, Bud sometimes sets out on his own campaign strategy. It was the 4th of July Parade in 2002 when Bud decided that rather than follow the group, his efforts would be better served by trailing my opponent with a "Perry" sign. We did not know what Bud was up to at the time as we became worried that perhaps the heat of the day had gotten the better of him.

After an exhaustive search of the parade route, we found him still closely following my opponent with my campaign sign prominently displayed. When questioned why he wandered off, Bud told us that he did not want my opponent to be seen without a Perry sign near by.

My son Christopher and his wife Tiffany are also always there to support me. Whether it is stuffing envelopes at the kitchen table, writing letters to the editors of the local newspapers or rounding up their friends to attend one of my fundraisers, I am blessed to have the love and assistance of these two fine young people. As with most of us who have children, my son Christopher has always inspired me to want to be a better person and make him proud of his father. I hope he knows how proud I am of him for the advances he has made in his life. There are few things in this world that bring me more joy than seeing him, Tiffany and Faith, their daughter, enjoying their lives.

My sister Kendra and I are opposites is so many ways, but when it comes to family and supporting each other's plans and efforts, I am so very thankful she is in my life. Far from being politically involved, Kendra is supportive in valuable ways. Aside from being the most talented photographer I have ever met, including sometimes at my political events, just knowing I have her love and acceptance is critical to who I am.

I am also blessed to have a mother-in-law, Elaine Dandrea, who unlike the stereotypes is someone I actually love and respect. I must admit that some twenty-two years ago when I first met her, she intimidated me a bit with her straightforward opinions, but this is one of the things I have come to appreciate the most. Mumé (as she is affectionately called) and I have a system. Living forty-five minutes away, she cannot make every event so we use a rating system. I tell her how important a political event is on a scale from one to ten. Whenever I tell her I need her, she is always there supporting me, including doing a tremendous job of editing this book. Oh by the way, she did a terrific job raising Lisa (as well as sons Dale and Phil).

This chapter would not be complete without a few words on the person that makes my days on Beacon Hill more enjoyable. Representative Donald Humason of Westfield and I have become the best of friends. Don is one of those rare individuals you meet and instantly like. The people of Westfield are fortunate to have such a hard working and competent individual as their legislator. He and I have shared our personal and political thoughts going on seven years as we sit nearby to each other on the House floor. Don and I are also pretty close with our political ideology and work ethic. During the many frustrating days and nights fighting for our conservative beliefs, the friendship I have developed with Don has been invaluable. One that I am sure will last a lifetime.

Certainly, there are many more people whom I consider to be close friends and advisors and who are important to my political success, but space does not allow me to list the positive attributes of each of them. They know who they are and I remain forever grateful for their friendship and support. Included in this list are those people who lend their financial support, stuffed envelopes, made telephone calls, attended events, held campaign signs, wrote letters to the editors, placed a Perry sign in their front yard and hosted "coffees" in their homes.

This list tops some 2,000 different folks over the years. I thank each and every one of them for their loyal support. I could not have won my first election in 2002 without you and you certainly have been my inspiration to continue.

Chapter Fourteen - Final Thoughts

According to recent statistics, the number of registered Republicans continues to decline in Massachusetts. With the disturbing fact that my GOP currently possesses just sixteen of the one-hundred and sixty House of Representatives seats, only five of the forty State Senate positions, has zero members of Congress from Massachusetts and holds none of the state's constitutional offices, either we have reached the bottom for the Republican Party in Massachusetts and better days are ahead or we are just about to become extinct.

The good news is that trends among the Bay State voters show that those not associated with any political party comprise just over half of the state's registered voters. This fact continues to give my GOP a fighting chance when we hold true to our core values and issues. The Democrats account for about thirty-seven percent of the total electorate. Republicans are just around twelve percent. The remaining fifty-one percent are either undeclared or a member of one of the minor political parties.

These statistics may appear next to hopeless for my GOP, but remember that Massachusetts voters supported Ronald Reagan twice and they also recently elected a string of Republican governors for sixteen straight years. While always an uphill and difficult battle for Republicans in the Bay State, I sincerely believe that our future is full of opportunities for great political success.

In this book, I have attempted to demonstrate that there are certain traits and beliefs that voters attach to every political party and by association to its candidates. While these traits and beliefs can certainly change over time, there are basic assumptions that the voting public makes when one calls oneself a Republican. Certainly, ensuring fiscal responsibility, fighting to make government smaller and closer to the people, protecting family values and reducing taxes are beliefs that, if you choose to label yourself as a member of the Republican Party, you had better be prepared to conduct yourself in accordance with such principles. History shows that when a member of the GOP fails to embrace our party's core value system, they face the significant risk that the voters who typically support Republican candidates might just choose to stay home on election day or cast their vote for some third party candidate in protest.

Now, I am not suggesting that every Republican who loses an election does so because they abandoned the party's platform. Such an analysis would be overly simplistic and also downright untrue in some cases. What I am suggesting is that even when the voters have a solid understanding of who a candidate is as a person, when that candidate no longer stands for what the voters expect, there is very little reason for the voter to cast their ballot for such a candidate. Unpredictability by any candidate or elected official of any political party is almost always a recipe for failure on election day.

Today, one of the key reasons why many voters are willing to give Republicans their vote is the increasing size and scope of government itself. The bottom line is that whether it is mandating citizens to purchase a certain insurance product, banning certain foods from our diets or paying state employees to "volunteer," government is growing more intrusive and powerful with each passing generation. While socialism does not occur overnight, unless those who believe in the core principles of my GOP stand up and fight against each and every unnecessary expansion of government, one morning in America we might just wake up and realize we have lost our personal freedoms that we hold so dear. Republicans are the only hope America has to save us from ultimately becoming a socialist nation.

Without a doubt, if my GOP is ever going to reconnect with the people we wish to represent, we need to wholly embrace the principles of our party. Fighting against benefits for illegal immigrants and promoting a culture of law and order are certainly in line with what citizens want and need Republicans to stand for! Having outlined all the problems and costs of illegal immigration, we need to do more than simply fight against the attempts by the liberals who will go on pandering to the illegals. We also need to present a comprehensive plan to address all aspects of the immigration issues.

Elected office-holders from the GOP must make sure that illegal immigrants never gain access to any of our taxpayer funded benefits. It is a betrayal to the platform of our party and it sends the wrong public policy message to citizens and non citizens alike. America is the land of the free (and the brave), but "free" was never intended to mean "free" money from the government for everyone who wanted it. "Free" in America should stand for the principal that along with the freedoms we all enjoy comes a necessary personal responsibility to take care of yourself, your family and your neighbors.

Welfare reform in 1996 was a strong step toward getting back to such principles, but much work remains to truly become both a compassionate nation and one that does not create a generational cycle of dependence on Uncle Sam. The bottom line is that there is absolutely no reason why an able bodied welfare recipient should not be required to put forth an effort to become a productive member of society. Not only can we no longer afford lifetime welfare benefits, but philosophically my GOP should never foster a culture of dependence on government.

Hopefully, one day in the very near future, the general electorate will realize the many abuses occurring in our political system are a lot more than political games. They are seriously eroding all of our rights and privileges we hold so dear. The media has an important role in maintaining an open and honest political system. During my four terms serving in the House of Representatives, myself and a few others have been complaining about the legislature's failing to honor the will of the voters, back room deals, consolidation of budget amendments and other abuses of the legislative process, but so few in the media seem to care. It seems as if the media does not report on such things as they accept it as part of Massachusetts politics.

Every abuse of the legislative process should be front page news; as each time this happens, democracy and the role of our elected legislators is diminished. The abuses of the process occur at least in part because the media in general fails to hold political leaders responsible for their individual actions and also because of one-party control of the process. If the media would more closely monitor the legislative sessions and report all of the abuses, it is likely there would be less of them occurring, and when they do, perhaps the voters would ultimately have the necessary information to hold elected officials accountable.

I am extremely and sincerely concerned that the citizens' right to speak at the ballot box appears to be in serious jeopardy. The legislature has a disappointing record of ignoring the vote of the citizens and manipulating the process to serve the majority party's liberal-leaning agenda. For our part, I am confident that my GOP will continue to offer bills and amendments to, at the very least, force the majority party to be accountable for their failures. Whether or not the collective general public will ever be engaged and care enough to remove elected officials who betray their own constituency is yet to be determined. But one thing for sure, if there is no political consequence to pay for dishonoring the voters, the status quo will likely continue.

Taxation is another one of those core issues which my GOP needs to remain firm on. While much progress had been made during the Reagan years to stabilize and lower the marginal federal income tax brackets, the business community now appears under attack with higher taxes clearly on the horizon.

While my GOP is often labeled as the political party of big business, my opposition to increased business taxes has nothing to do with my desire to protect corporations. Republicans need to remind people that supply-side economic theory does work when all of its components are honored, including the most important element of reductions to unnecessary and wasteful spending programs. When implemented completely, history tells us that people and businesses will pay fewer taxes as a percentage of their income and government overall will have a greater amount of revenue to provide necessary services.

The Republican platform and those who run for elective office under it should support pro-growth style tax cuts, which clearly boost economic performance and expand individual opportunities to provide for their family. While the issue of corporate tax loopholes is a slightly different question than the appropriate effective tax rate for all businesses, the same principles apply. Targeted tax breaks to a certain business group offer real incentives to create additional economic activity by said business. The primary problem as I see it in Massachusetts is that there is little certainty as to what the tax policy will be in the future.

While some liberal politicians argue that taxes should be higher in order for government to provide more services, if these same folks would bother to seriously study sound economic policy, they should join my GOP and support more tax cuts like the ones adopted on the federal level by the Republican Congress and President Bush in 2003. The problem continuing in Washington, D.C. and on Beacon Hill is that despite record high levels of revenue collections, the spending remains unchecked.

Republicans need to remind themselves of the principles of Ronald Reagan and the successes of supply-side economic theory. The problem is not getting my GOP to acknowledge that such theories really do work or that they are matters of sound public policy; the real problem is apparently getting my GOP to stand firm against the attractions of pork barrel spending and legislative earmarking. Elected officials from both political parties are in an extremely tough position on this issue. If a legislator gets in the budget line too often for their special local or pet projects, they are often correctly criticized for wasting taxpayer money. On the other hand, if a legislator decides to stand a principled position and say no to "bringing home the bacon," it is entirely possible that a future political opponent will accuse them of being an ineffective elected official.

While certainly a difficult question for some as to what the proper approach for an elected legislator should be, and one that has gone on in Washington, D.C. and state houses from sea to shining sea for a very long time, it is my view that Republicans need to get off the gravy train of excessive spending and return to what the people expect us to be; the political party of fiscal restraint and responsible government spending. For if my GOP simply continues to get in line with the Democrats for our share of the pork and earmarks, we are giving the American people yet another reason not to support our candidates. Even more importantly, we will be guilty of passing along an unsustainable pattern of spending to future generations to pick up our expense tab.

If our nation is going to remain one of law and order, the actual text of the constitution and the Founding Fathers' intentions must always be honored. My GOP must never allow the constitution to be tampered with for political sake. Whether it benefits the conservatives or liberals, our first allegiance must always remain to the constitution itself! For example, the interpretation of the Second Amendment or any other constitutional provision must be done so with an honest and strict construction of the actual text. When judges usurp our Framers' intention and read their own personal meaning into the text, it most often has led to disastrous results throughout United States history. The theory of the living and breathing constitution or a broad interpretation theory of the constitution has also been responsible for many of this nation's worst Supreme Court rulings.

While I have offered my views of the results of past elections in earlier chapters, it is likely that history will offer a clearer analysis as more years pass. The talking heads on the television talk shows and the editorial writers of the print media provided their own political observation with an endless number of reasons why the voters returned Congress and the White House to the Democrats. While I agree there is rarely a single reason for any political success or failure; it is my view that the Republican Party and many of our office holders and candidates have lost touch with the principles of my GOP and the very reason why Americans vote Republican in the first place.

The issues discussed in this book are those principles I am referring to when I speak to my GOP's need to stay firm in our principles and values. Issues such as real immigration reform, budgetary spending controls, fighting for tax reductions, true welfare reform, honoring the will of the voters, and avoiding personal scandal are just a few of such things Republicans need to focus on to make America that "shining city upon a hill" which Ronald Reagan spoke of in his farewell address.

From our review of the history of the Grand Old Party we know that leaders who stay firm and strong to the core beliefs of the Republican Party, the American people are more than eager to embrace them; however, during those times when the elected Republican officer holders are nothing more than "RINO's," with their finger held up to the political wind, the voters fail to see why our party deserves their support and I guess at the end of the day, that is exactly what we deserve.

The Republican Party has a long and proud tradition of protecting and expanding the rights of our citizens. Despite the fact that modern-day Democrats would have the voters believe otherwise, it was their party that fought against freedom for slaves and against the rights of women to vote. An honest view of history shows it has been the Republicans who have stood for the underlying principles of the Declaration of Independence and the Constitution.

Far from a scientific study, I conducted a review of six United States history textbooks used at the college level. Unfortunately, and not really to my surprise, I was unable to locate any reference or credit given to the GOP for our efforts promoting the rights of minorities or women. While certain politicians of their time are appropriately given kudos for their individual efforts, the Republican Party as an entity is not. Perhaps a liberal media bias or maybe too many people, including historians, fail to appreciate the efforts of my GOP. Whichever you believe true, members of my party need to speak out more often about our history and proudly educate our fellow citizens. While we often refer to Ronald Reagan and Abraham Lincoln, we would do our party a better service if we reflected on our other tremendous successes throughout the history of the United States. The future is bright with opportunities for my GOP and those who share our values and beliefs. The key is to learn the lessons from history and always stand firm on our Republican principles!

I cannot think of a more fitting end to our time together than to quote Ronald Reagan one last time, as nothing more need be said:

> *"I believe our Republican Party is the true party of the future because our vision, ideas, and proposals seek to bring out the best in America by challenging the best in our people. The Great Opportunity Party believes in challenging people to do better. The Democratic leadership still insists on challenging government to grow bigger."*

-The End-